# CALIFORNIA
# STYLE MANUAL

A Handbook of Legal Style
for California Courts
and Lawyers

**THIRD EDITION**

By

ROBERT E. FORMICHI

Reporter of Decisions, Supreme Court of California, 1969–
Assistant Reporter, 1963–1969

i

**CITE AS:**
**California Style Manual (3d ed. 1986) section . . . ,**
or, within parentheses,
**Cal. Style Manual (3d ed. 1986) § . . .**



**Library of Congress Catalog Card No: 85-63636**



**ISBN 0-936629-00-2**

# TABLE OF CONTENTS

# FOREWORD

In November of 1984, the people of California gave their strong approval to Proposition 32. This historic measure marks the first reform of California Supreme Court procedures in this century.

Rules of Court were promptly adopted to implement Proposition 32. These rules, in turn, affect various aspects of the style in which opinions are cited and published in the Official Reports.

The third edition of the California Style Manual constitutes the first revision in the past decade. This new volume reflects the advent of Proposition 32 and also incorporates changes in usage and refinements that have occurred during the last 10 years.

The California Style Manual is intended to enhance both the clarity and the precision of the Official Reports. It is hoped that this latest edition will be of assistance to the California bench and bar.

Rose Elizabeth Bird
Chief Justice of California

**APPROVED**
**BY**
**THE SUPREME COURT OF CALIFORNIA**

To the Reporter of Decisions:

Pursuant to the authority conferred on the Supreme Court of California by Government Code section 68902, the California Style Manual, Third Edition, as submitted to this court for review, is approved and adopted as the official organ for the styles to be used in the publication of the Official Reports.

Dated January 2, 1986.

Rose Elizabeth Bird
Chief Justice of California

# PREFACE TO THIRD EDITION

The passage of time since the 1976 revision of this manual has brought with it major changes in California's appellate review and opinion publication practices. Rules of court authorizing the partial publication of Court of Appeal and appellate department of the superior court opinions have been adopted. Procedures of the Supreme Court governing the review of decisions of the Courts of Appeal have been significantly modified and the court's disposition options following the grant of review have been importantly expanded. An elaborate array of court rules to implement these major changes has become operative. During this 10-year period the variety of materials being cited has broadened and new legislation bearing on the contents of this manual has been enacted. As always, experience has taught new and better ways.

The foregoing evolutionary developments have called for the publication of this third edition to continue the manual as the comprehensive, convenient, and current standard reference for California appellate court style practices. It is expected that this edition will be kept current with occasional pocket supplements.

Context permitting, use of the masculine gender in the manual, as in past editions, should be deemed to include the feminine; and vice versa.

I am grateful to Kingsley B. Eaton, Chief Deputy Reporter of Decisions, and Jackie Kuhn, Assistant Reporter of Decisions, for taking on many of the tasks that I normally perform so that this edition could be published as early as practical after the adoption effective May 6, 1985, of the rules of court providing for the new Supreme Court review practices. I am especially indebted to Senior Deputy Reporter of Decisions John Millar for his major assistance in all phases of the preparation and production of this manual. For the first time, camera-ready proof for the manual was prepared in-house by the Judicial Council's typographical staff all of whom deserve accolades for rapidly preparing this complex manuscript.

Robert E. Formichi

January 2, 1986.

# PREFACE TO SECOND REVISED EDITION

Since its first appearance some 34 years ago this manual has been accepted and relied upon by both bench and bar as the standard for legal appellate style in the State of California.

This extensively expanded and completely revised edition is designed to update the materials previously presented and to make those changes warranted by new legislation, accepted new style practices and experience. New topics and subject matter have been incorporated where practice has indicated a need. A resolute effort has been made to enhance the usefulness of the materials by amplifying tables, expanding rule explanations and employing, by way of illustration, a greater variety of rule applications. Necessarily there will be some repetition in order to minimize the inconvenience of cross-reference.

This edition will also differ from its predecessors in that specialized materials of interest primarily to the publishers of the Official Reports have been omitted. Believing that ready access to materials in a reference work such as this is of prime importance, the index has been expanded and completely reframed. A table of abbreviations used has been added.

I am indebted to Kingsley B. Eaton, Chief Assistant Reporter of Decisions, to Floy J. Kuhn, Assistant Reporter of Decisions, to Julie G. Pasteur, former Assistant Reporter of Decisions, and to Rita Klingen of the Reporter's office, for their valuable comments, suggestions and assistance.

Robert E. Formichi

April 19, 1976.

# PREFACE TO REVISED EDITION

This manual has been out of print for a long time, and the frequent calls for copies have indicated a need for a new edition. Many practices have developed or have been adopted during the lapse of almost two decades, and a number of changes have been made with a view toward simplification. While the general form of the first edition has been followed to some extent, there has been considerable revision throughout the book. A wholly new index, greatly enlarged, should be more helpful to the reader in locating the desired point.

Wm. Nankervis, Jr.

September 1961.

# PREFACE TO FIRST EDITION

This manual represents an attempt to state the chief rules and practices which govern the preparation, form and publication of opinions of the appellate courts of California. It is designed primarily as a guide for the courts, the Reporter of Decisions and the publishers of the official California Reports and advance sheets. It is believed, however, that law offices and law publishers and printers may find it useful in their work.

The sources of the material herein are numerous and varied. On matters of English style, we acknowledge our indebtedness to the following standard reference manuals: United States Government Printing Office Style Manual, 1939 ed.; A Manual of Style, University of Chicago Press (10th ed.); Mawson and Robson, Complete Desk Book (1939); Opdycke, Get it Right! (1939); Woolley, Mechanics of Writing; Woolley, Handbook of Composition; and Ives, Text, Type, and Style, Atlantic Monthly Press. The following dictionaries have been consulted: Merriam-Webster International Dictionary (2d ed.); Bouvier's Law Dictionary; Black's Law Dictionary; and Ballentine's Law Dictionary. We have also made use of the following manuals dealing particularly with law writing and printing: A Uniform System of Citation, published by the Harvard Law Review Association (6th ed.); and California Law Review Style Book, University of California School of Jurisprudence. A considerable part of this work, however, sets forth the standardized practices of the Reporter.

The major portion of the research was done by my colleague, Wm. Nankervis, Jr., and his long experience as Assistant Reporter of Decisions has also made possible the detailed statement of the unwritten practices of this office.

Among those who contributed advice and suggestion were J. Oliver Tucker, Managing Editor of McKinney's California Digest; H. B. Clark, Managing Editor, Bancroft-Whitney Co.; Elizabeth Ent, of the editorial staff of Bancroft-Whitney Co.; Darwin A. Allen, of the staff of the Recorder Printing & Publishing Co.; and Alice A. Williams, Secretary to the Reporter of Decisions.

A few observations on the form and arrangement may be helpful. The chapters are internally arranged in a logical sequence, but with consecutive section numbers to facilitate citation. The index does not attempt to give all possible cross-references. Instead, the material has been listed under general topics such as Capitalization, Title of Case, etc. The index references are to sections, not pages. Because of the necessity of covering separately the rules for printed and for typewritten opinions, and for advance sheets and official reports, some slight repetition is unavoidably present.

This is a first edition, and it was produced as speedily as possible in order to meet the imperative need for standardization of these practices. Necessarily there will be some defects and some points upon which further experience will indicate a need for change. It is our hope that those who use the work will express themselves freely on all controversial matters and that from time to time the work may be revised and improved.

B.E. Witkin

February 10, 1942.

# TABLE OF FREQUENTLY USED ABBREVIATIONS

It is noted that the abbreviation table lists the predominant usage in the manual. There will be some deviation where practice has established differing styles under specific circumstances, e.g., the manual has adopted the abbreviation "opn." for "opinion." However, practice has established a reference to the Opinions of the Attorney General of California as "Ops.Cal.Atty.Gen." Likewise capitalization of abbreviated forms will sometimes depend upon where and how the form is used.

## A

Administrative Office of the Courts ... .............................. AOC
Administration, administrative .. admin.
Advance ...................... adv.
Affirmed ...................... affd.
Affirmed by memorandum opinion ... ...................... affd. mem.
Affirmed *per curiam* .. affd. *per curiam*
Affirmed under the name of ........ ................... affd. *sub nom.*
Affirming ...................... affg.
Agricultural Code (now Food & Agr. Code) ............. Agr. Code
Alabama ....................... Ala.
Alaska ...................... Alaska
Amendment ................. amend.
American Annotated Cases ......... ...................... Ann. Cas.
American and English Annotated Cases ....... Am. & Eng. Ann. Cas.
American Bar Association ....... ABA
American Decisions ........ Am.Dec.
American Jurisprudence ...... Am.Jur.
American Jurisprudence Second ..... ...................... Am.Jur.2d
American Law Institute ........... ALI
American Law Reports ....... A.L.R.
American Law Reports Digest, Second Series ............... A.L.R.2d Dig.
American Law Reports, Federal Series ...................... A.L.R.Fed.
American Law Reports, Second Series ........................ A.L.R.2d
American Law Reports, Third Series .. ........................ A.L.R.3d
American Reports ............. Am.R.
American State Reports ...... Am.St.R.
And others ................... et al.
And the following ........... et seq.
Annotated, annotation ..... ann., annot.

Annual ........................ ann.
Ante meridian ................. a.m.
Appeal dismissed ......... app. dism.
Appeal pending ........ app. pending
Appellate .................... App.
Appendix .................... appen.
April ........................ Apr.
Arizona ...................... Ariz.
Arkansas ..................... Ark.
Article, articles ............ art., arts.
Assembly .................. Assem.
Assembly Bill Number ............. ................. Assem. Bill No.
Assembly Concurrent Resolution Number ...... Assem. Con. Res. No.
Assembly Constitutional Amendment Number .. Assem. Const. Amend. No.
Assembly Joint Resolution Number ... .............. Assem. Joint Res. No.
Assembly Journal ......... Assem. J.
Assembly Resolution Number ........ ................. Assem. Res. No.
Assistant .................... Asst.
Association .................. Assn.
Atlantic Reporter ................ A.
Atlantic Reporter, Second Series ..... .............................. A.2d
At that place ................. *op. cit.*
At the same place ........... *loc. cit.*
Attorney ...................... Atty.
Attorney General ......... Atty. Gen.
Attorney General Opinions ......... ................. Ops.Cal.Atty.Gen.
August ....................... Aug.
Avenue ...................... Ave.

## B

Ballot Pamphlet ......... Ballot Pamp.
Banking Code ........... Bank. Code
Basic Approved Jury Instructions .. BAJI
Beverly Hills Bar Journal ............. ................. Bev. Hills Bar J.

Board . . . . . . . . . . . . . . . . . . . . . . . . Bd.
Boulevard . . . . . . . . . . . . . . . . . . . . Blvd.
Building . . . . . . . . . . . . . . . . . . . . . . bldg.
Bulletin . . . . . . . . . . . . . . . . . . . . . . Bull.
Bureau . . . . . . . . . . . . . . . . . . . . . . . Bur.
Business and Professions Code . . . . . .
 . . . . . . . . . . . . . . . . Bus. & Prof. Code

## C

California . . . . . . . . . . . . . . . . . . . . . Cal.
California Administrative Code . . . . . . .
 . . . . . . . . . . . . . . . . Cal. Admin. Code
California Administrative Register . . . .
 . . . . . . . . . . . . . . Cal. Admin. Register
California Appellate Reports . . Cal.App.
California Appellate Reports,
 Second Series . . . . . . . . . . Cal.App.2d
California Appellate Reports,
 Third Series . . . . . . . . . . . . Cal.App.3d
California Appellate Reports
 Supplement . . . . . . . . . Cal.App.Supp.
California Appellate Reports
 Supplement, Second Series . . . . . . . .
 . . . . . . . . . . . . . . . . Cal.App.2d Supp.
California Appellate Reports
 Supplement, Third Series . . . . . . . . . .
 . . . . . . . . . . . . . . . . Cal.App.3d Supp.
California Attorney General Opinions . .
 . . . . . . . . . . . . . . . . Ops.Cal.Atty.Gen.
California Center for Judicial
 Education and Research . . . . . . CJER
California Compensation Cases . . . . . .
 . . . . . . . . . . . . . . . . Cal.Comp.Cases
California Digest Official Reports,
 Third Series . . . . . . . . . . . . . . . . . . . .
 . . . . . . . . . . . . Cal.Dig.Off.Rep.3d Ser.
California Jurisprudence . . . . . . Cal.Jur.
California Jurisprudence Second . . . . .
 . . . . . . . . . . . . . . . . . . . . . . . Cal.Jur.2d
California Jurisprudence Third . . . . . . .
 . . . . . . . . . . . . . . . . . . . . . . . Cal.Jur.3d
California Jury Instructions, Civil . . BAJI
California Jury Instructions, Criminal . .
 . . . . . . . . . . . . . . . . . . . . . . . . . . CALJIC
California Law Review . . . . . . Cal.L.Rev.
California Law Revision Commission
 Report . . . . . . . . . . . . . . . . . . . . . . . .
 . . . . . . . Cal. Law Revision Com. Rep.
California Lawyer . . . . . . . . . . Cal.Law.
California Office of State Printing
 Style and Procedure Manual . . . . . . .
 . . . . . . . . . . . . . . . . . . . . . SPO Manual
California Public Utilities Commission . .
 . . . . . . . . . . . . . . . . . . . . . . . Cal.P.U.C.

California Railroad Commission . . C.R.C.
California Reporter . . . . . . . . . . Cal.Rptr.
California Reports . . . . . . . . . . . . . . Cal.
California Reports, Second Series . . . .
 . . . . . . . . . . . . . . . . . . . . . . . . . . Cal.2d
California Reports, Third Series . . Cal.3d
California Rules of Court . . . . . . . . . . . .
 . . . . . . . . . . . . . . . . Cal. Rules of Court
California State Bar . . . . . . . . . . State Bar
 [for abbreviations of various State
 Bar rules see *post,* § 66]
California State Bar Journal . . State Bar J.
California Uniform Commercial Code .
 . . . . . . . . . . . . . . . . Cal. U. Com. Code
California Unreported Cases . . . . . . . . .
 . . . . . . . . . . . . . . . . . . . . . . . Cal.Unrep.
California Western Law Review . . . . . .
 . . . . . . . . . . . . . . . . Cal.Western L.Rev.
Certiorari . . . . . . . . . . . . . . . . . . . . . cert.
Certiorari denied . . . . . . . . . . cert. den.
Certiorari granted . . . . . . cert. granted
Chapter, chapters . . . . . . . . . . . ch., chs.
Chief Justice . . . . . . . . . . . . . . . . . C. J.
Circuit . . . . . . . . . . . . . . . . . . . . . . . . Cir.
Civil Code . . . . . . . . . . . . . . . Civ. Code
Clause . . . . . . . . . . . . . . . . . . . . . . . . . cl.
Clerk's Transcript . . . . . . . . . . . . . . . C.T.
Code of Civil Procedure . . . . . . . . . . . .
 . . . . . . . . . . . . . . . . . . Code Civ. Proc.
Code of Federal Regulations . . . . C.F.R.
Colorado . . . . . . . . . . . . . . . . . . . . Colo.
Column . . . . . . . . . . . . . . . . . . . . . . . col.
Comment, comments . . . . . com., coms.
 [except where there is a potential
 for confusion]
Commercial Code . . . . . . . Com. Code
Commission . . . . . . . . . . . . . . . . . Com.
 [except where there is a potential
 for confusion]
Commission on Judicial Performance . .
 . . . . . . . . . . . . . . . . Com.Jud.Perform.
Commissioners . . . . . . . . . . . . . . Comrs.
Committee . . . . . . . . . . . . . . . . . . Com.
 [except where there is a potential
 for confusion]
Company . . . . . . . . . . . . . . . . . . . . . Co.
Compare . . . . . . . . . . . . . . . . . . . . . . cf.
Compensation . . . . . . . . . . . . . . . Comp.
Concurring, concurrent . . . . . . . . conc.
Conference . . . . . . . . . . . . . . . . . . Conf.
Congress . . . . . . . . . . . . . . . . . . . . Cong.
Congressional Record . . . . . Cong. Rec.
Connecticut . . . . . . . . . . . . . . . . . Conn.

House of Representatives ........ H.R.
House of Representative Journal .. H.R.J.
House Resolution Number..H.Res. No.
Housing Authority ..... Housing Auth.

**I**

Idaho........................Idaho
Illinois...........................Ill.
Illustration .................... illus.
Improvidently ................ improv.
Incorporated................... Inc.
Indiana........................Ind.
Industrial Accident Commission of
    California (decisions cite).....I.A.C.
In propria persona........in pro. per.
Institute, institutions ....... Inst., Insts.
Instructions...................Instns.
Insurance Code ........... Ins. Code
Internal Revenue Code..Int.Rev. Code
International ................ Internat.
In the same place .............. *ibid.*
In the work quoted ........... *op. cit.*
In the work quoted above ...........
.................... *op. cit. supra*
Iowa..........................Iowa

**J**

January........................Jan.
John F. Kennedy Law Record ........
...........J. F. Kennedy L. Record
Joint............................J.
Journal .........................J.
Judge ..........................J.
Judgment.....................judg.
Judicial........................Jud.
Judicial Council of California ........
...........Judicial Council of Cal.
Judicial Panel on Multidistrict
    Litigation..................J.P.M.L.
Junior..........................Jr.
Jurisdiction.....................jur.
Jurisdiction noted .......... jur. noted
Justice...........................J.

**K**

Kansas ...................... Kan.
Kentucky ...................... Ky.

**L**

Labor Code.............. Lab. Code
Law Revision Commission Reports....
.......Cal. Law Revision Com. Rep.
Lawyer........................Law.
Lawyers' Edition .............. L.Ed.
Lawyers' Edition, Second Series ......
....................L.Ed.2d

Lawyers' Reports Annotated .... L.R.A.
Lawyers' Reports Annotated Digest ...
.......................L.R.A. Dig.
Lawyers' Reports Annotated (New
    Series) .................. L.R.A.N.S.
Legislative .................. Legis.
Legislature .................... Leg.
Lincoln Law Review .... Lincoln L.Rev.
Long Beach Bar Bulletin .............
............. Long Beach Bar Bull.
Los Angeles .................... L.A.
Los Angeles Bar Bulletin ...........
..................... L.A. Bar Bull.
Los Angeles Bar Journal .... L.A.Bar J.
Los Angeles Lawyer ........ L.A. Law.
Louisiana ......................La.
Loyola Consumer Protection Journal ..
.......... Loyola Consumer Prot.J.
Loyola University of Los Angeles
    Law Review.......Loyola L.A. L.Rev.

**M**

Maine.........................Me.
March ........................ Mar.
Maryland ...................... Md.
Massachusetts ................ Mass.
McKinney's Digest..........McK.Dig.
Memorandum ................. mem.
Michigan .................... Mich.
Military and Veterans Code ..........
.................. Mil. & Vet. Code
Mimeograph................. mimeo.
Minimum......................min.
    [except where there is a potential
    for confusion]
Minnesota....................Minn.
Minute, Minutes...........min., mins.
    [except where there is a potential
    for confusion]
Mississippi ................... Miss.
Missouri ...................... Mo.
Modified ..................... mod.
Montana ..................... Mont.
Municipal Court ........... Mun. Ct.

**N**

Namely ....................... viz.
National ...................... Nat.
Nebraska ..................... Neb.
Nevada ...................... Nev.
New Hampshire ................ N.H.
New Jersey....................N.J.
New Mexico .................. N.M.
New York ..................... N.Y.

New York Supplement . . . . . . . . . . N.Y.S.
New York Supplement, Second
Series . . . . . . . . . . . . . . . . . . . . . N.Y.S.2d
Nonpublished . . . . . . . . . . . . . . . nonpub.
North Carolina . . . . . . . . . . . . . . . . . N.C.
North Dakota . . . . . . . . . . . . . . . . . . N.D.
North Eastern Reporter . . . . . . . . . . N.E.
North Eastern Reporter, Second
Series . . . . . . . . . . . . . . . . . . . . . . N.E.2d
North Western Reporter . . . . . . . . . N.W.
North Western Reporter, Second
Series . . . . . . . . . . . . . . . . . . . . . N.W.2d
November . . . . . . . . . . . . . . . . . . . . Nov.
Number, numbers . . . . . . . . . No., Nos.

**O**

October . . . . . . . . . . . . . . . . . . . . . . Oct.
Office . . . . . . . . . . . . . . . . . . . . . . . . off.
Official . . . . . . . . . . . . . . . . . . . . . . . Off.
Ohio . . . . . . . . . . . . . . . . . . . . . . . . Ohio
Oklahoma . . . . . . . . . . . . . . . . . . . Okla.
Opinion, opinions . . . . . . . . . opn., opns.
Opinions of Legislative Counsel . . . . . .
. . . . . . . . . . . . Ops.Cal.Legis.Counsel
Opinions of the Attorney General . . . .
. . . . . . . . . . . . . . . . . Ops.Cal.Atty.Gen.
Oregon . . . . . . . . . . . . . . . . . . . . . . Ore.
Ordinance . . . . . . . . . . . . . . . . . . . . Ord.

**P**

Pacific Law Journal . . . . . . . . Pacific L.J.
Pacific Reporter . . . . . . . . . . . . . . . . . P.
Pacific Reporter, Second Series . . . P.2d
Page, pages . . . . . . . . . . . . . . . . . p., pp.
Pamphlet . . . . . . . . . . . . . . . . . . . pamp.
Paragraph . . . . . . . . . . . . . . . . ¶ or par.
Part, parts . . . . . . . . . . . . . . . . . pt., pts.
Partially published . . . . . . . . . par. pub.
Penal Code . . . . . . . . . . . . . . Pen. Code
Pennsylvania . . . . . . . . . . . . . . . . . . . Pa.
Pepperdine Law Review . . . . . . . . . . . . .
. . . . . . . . . . . . . . . . Pepperdine L.Rev.
Petition . . . . . . . . . . . . . . . . . . . . . . petn.
Plurality . . . . . . . . . . . . . . . . . . . . . plur.
Political Code . . . . . . . . . . . . . Pol. Code
Post meridian . . . . . . . . . . . . . . . . . p.m.
Practice . . . . . . . . . . . . . . . . . . . . . Prac.
President . . . . . . . . . . . . . . . . . . . . . Pres.
Presidential Proclamation . . . Pres.Proc.
Presiding Justice . . . . . . . . . . . . . . P. J.
Probable jurisdiction noted . . . . . . . . . .
. . . . . . . . . . . . . . . . . . . prob. jur. noted
Probate Code . . . . . . . . . . . . Prob. Code
Professional . . . . . . . . . . . . . . . . . . Prof.

Proposition . . . . . . . . . . . . . . . . . . . Prop.
Propria persona . . . . . . . . . . . . . pro. per.
Public Contract Code . . . . . . . . . . . . . .
. . . . . . . . . . . . . . Pub. Contract Code
Procedure . . . . . . . . . . . . . . . . . . . . Proc.
Public Law . . . . . . . . . . . . . . . . . . Pub.L.
Public Resources Code . . . . . . . . . . . .
. . . . . . . . . . . . . Pub. Resources Code
Public Utilities Code . . Pub. Util. Code
Public Utilities Commission . . . . . P.U.C.
Published . . . . . . . . . . . . . . . . . . . . . pub.
Puerto Rico . . . . . . . . . . . . . . . . . . . P.R.

**Q**

Quarterly . . . . . . . . . . . . . . . . . . . . . . Q.

**R**

Railway . . . . . . . . . . . . . . . . . . . . . . . Ry.
Railroad . . . . . . . . . . . . . . . . . . . . . R.R.
Regular Session . . . . . . . . . . Reg. Sess.
Regulation, Regulations . . . Reg., Regs.
Rehearing . . . . . . . . . . . . . . . . . . . rehg.
Rehearing denied . . . . . . . . . rehg. den.
Rehearing granted . . . . . rehg. granted
Report . . . . . . . . . . . . . . . . . . . . . . . Rep.
Reporter . . . . . . . . . . . . . . . . . . . . . Rptr.
Reporter's Transcript . . . . . . . . . . . . R.T.
Resolution . . . . . . . . . . . . . . . . . . . . Res.
Restatement . . . . . . . . . . . . . . . . . . Rest.
Retransferred . . . . . . . . . . . . . . . retrans.
Revenue and Taxation Code . . . . . . . . .
. . . . . . . . . . . . . . . . Rev. & Tax.Code
Reversed . . . . . . . . . . . . . . . . . . . . revd.
Reversed *per curiam* . . revd. *per curiam*
Reversing . . . . . . . . . . . . . . . . . . . . revg.
Review [law reviews] . . . . . . . . . . . . Rev.
Review denied . . . . . . . . . . review den.
Review granted . . . . . . . review granted
Revised . . . . . . . . . . . . . . . . . . . . . . . rev.
Revised edition . . . . . . . . . . . . . rev. ed.
Rhode Island . . . . . . . . . . . . . . . . . . R.I.
Rules . . . . . . [see applicable section for
specific rules]
Ruling Case Law . . . . . . . . . . . . . . R.C.L.

**S**

Sacramento . . . . . . . . . . . . . . . . . . . Sac.
Same . . . . . . . . . . . . . . . . . . . . . . . . . *id.*
San Diego Law Review . . . . . . . . . . . . .
. . . . . . . . . . . . . . . . San Diego L.Rev.
San Francisco . . . . . . . . . . . . . . . . . . S.F.
Santa Clara Law Review . . . . . . . . . . . .
. . . . . . . . . . . . . . . Santa Clara L.Rev.
Santa Clara Lawyer . . . Santa Clara Law.
School Code . . . . . . . . . . . . . Sch. Code

United States Statutes at Large . . . . Stat.
United States Supreme Court . . . . . . . . .
. . . . . . . . . . . . . . . . . U.S. Supreme Ct.
United States Supreme Court
Reports . . . . . . . . . . . . . . . . . . . . . . U.S.
United States Supreme Court
Reports, Lawyers' Edition . . . . . . L.Ed.
United States Supreme Court
Reports, Lawyers' Edition,
Second Series . . . . . . . . . . . . . . L.Ed.2d
United States Treaties and Other
International Agreements . . . . . . U.S.T.
University . . . . . . . . . . . . . . . . U. or Univ.
University of California, Davis Law
Review . . . . . . . . . . . . U.C. Davis L.Rev.
University of California at Los Angeles
. . . . . . . . . . . . . . . . . . . . . . . . . . UCLA
University of San Fernando Valley Law
Review . . U. San Fernando Val. L.Rev.
University of San Francisco Law
Review . . . . . . . . . . . . . . . . U.S.F. L.Rev.
University of Southern California Tax
Institute . . . . . U.So.Cal. 1983 Tax Inst.
University of West Los Angeles
Law Review . . . . . . U. West L.A. L.Rev.
Unpublished . . . . . . . . . . . . . . . . unpub.
Unreported . . . . . . . . . . . . . . . . . unrep.
U.S. Code Congressional and
Administrative News . . . . . . . . . . . . . .
. . . U.S. Code Cong. & Admin. News

Utah . . . . . . . . . . . . . . . . . . . . . . . . . Utah

## V

Vacated . . . . . . . . . . . . . . . . . . . . vacated
Vehicle Code . . . . . . . . . . . . . Veh. Code
Vermont . . . . . . . . . . . . . . . . . . . . . . Vt.
Versus . . . . . . . . . . . . . . . . . . . . . . . . . v.
Virginia . . . . . . . . . . . . . . . . . . . . . . Va.
Volume . . . . . . . . . . . . . . . . . . . . . . vol.

## W

Washington . . . . . . . . . . . . Wash. & Wn.
  [see *post*, § 77]
Water Code . . . . . . . . . . . . . . Wat. Code
Welfare and Institutions Code . . . . . . .
. . . . . . . . . . . . . . . Welf. & Inst. Code
West Virginia . . . . . . . . . . . . . . . W. Va.
Western State University Law
  Review . . . . . . . . Western St.U. L.Rev.
West's California Digest . . . . . . . . . . . .
. . . . . . . . . . . . . . . . . . West's Cal.Dig.
West's California Legislative Service . .
. . . . . . . . . . West's Cal. Legis. Service
West's California Reports . . . . Cal.Rptr.
Whittier Law Review . . . Whittier L.Rev.
Wisconsin . . . . . . . . . . . . . . . . . . . . Wis.
Work cited above . . . . . . . *op. cit. supra*
Wyoming . . . . . . . . . . . . . . . . . . . . Wyo.

# AUTHOR'S PROOFREADING RULES

Those who read proof of opinions will greatly assist the Reporter of Decisions office, publishers and printers, and contribute to the accuracy and prompt publication of opinions, if they will observe the following rules:

(a) Use printer's marks and symbols. (See *post,* pp. xix–xx.) It is not only shorter but avoids misunderstandings.

(b) Answer queries directly and categorically. Do not write merely "O.K." beside a query, because the printer will not know whether you mean "O.K. as printed" or "O.K. to change." If the change is authorized indicate approval by the words "make change." If the suggested change is rejected use the word "stet."

(c) Copy going to opinion authors will be marked with black lead pencil. To avoid questions as to the origination of a correction or query, proofreaders should mark copy with a colored pencil, preferably red.

(d) Type or print all corrections and notations if there is any question of the legibility of the proofreader's longhand.

(e) Answer all queries. Questions are asked only in those instances where satisfactory information is not available from sources at the Reporter of Decisions office. Because of the tightness of publication schedules unanswered queries often require costly and time-consuming long distance phone calls.

(f) Return opinion proof promptly. In order to ensure that the Supreme Court's policy of early publication of the bound volumes of the Official Reports is carried out it is essential that opinion copy be promptly read, corrected and returned to the Reporter of Decisions office *with all queries answered* by the date marked on the title page of the judge's proofs for the opinion. (See *post,* §§ 264, 265.)

# PRINTER'S MARKS FOR USE IN CORRECTING PROOF

⊙ Period

⌃ Comma

⊢⊣ Hyphen

⌃ Colon

⌃ Semicolon

? Question mark

! Exclamation mark

⌄ Apostrophe

❝ ❞ Quotation marks

⟙ₘ One-em dash

²ₘ Two-em dash

⊃ Close up

# Space

eq# Equalize spacing

less # Less space

ld. > Insert lead

⋀ Caret—denotes place where material is to be added

↻ Turn to proper position

[ or ] Move to left or right

⎤ or ⎣ Move up or down

‖ Align vertically

⚌ Align horizontally

∿ Transpose—used in text

tr Transpose—used in margin

stet Let it stand

δ Delete

∂ Delete and close up

(|) Parentheses

[|] Brackets

¶ Paragraph

no ¶ No paragraph—run on

sp Spell out

rom Roman type

___ Italics—underscore words to be italicized in text

ital Italics—used in margin with letter or word in text circled

∿ Boldface—wavy line beneath words to be boldfaced

bf Boldface—use in margin with word or words in text circled

wf Wrong font

= Small capitals— underscore letter or letters

sc Small capitals— used in margin with letter or letters in text circled

≡ Capitals—underscore letter or letters

caps Capitals—used in margin with letter or letters in text circled

≡ Underscoring used to note capitals and small capitals

*cap+sc* Capitals and small capitals—used in margin with word or words in text circled

/ Lowercase—slash through capitals

*lc* Lowercase—used in margin with letter or letters in text circled

Ⓧ Broken letter—correct or reprint

*run on* Carry over to next line

δ/? Question to author to delete or not

a/∧ Superior or inferior

# CAPITALIZATION

**§ 1. In General.**—No attempt has been made to state styles covering all types of capitalization usage. The purpose of this chapter is to provide a variety of rules and examples fitting situations that experience has shown most frequently occur in the drafting of appellate court opinions and briefs. Most capitalization questions not covered usually can be resolved by referring to the United States Government Printing Office Style Manual (rev. ed. 1984) (hereafter GPO Manual) or the California Office of State Printing Style and Procedure Manual (1980 ed.) (hereafter SPO Manual). In case of variance in the names of California places, bodies, entities, officers, etc., the SPO Manual is to be preferred. The consistent use of the capitalization guides noted herein for appellate court work and in the publication of the Official Reports will greatly assist in achieving a uniform Official Report style and more importantly in overcoming the highly undersirable effect of varying and conflicting practices within the same publication.

## A. Governmental Bodies

**§ 2. Cities and Towns.**—Capitalize "city" or "town" only when part of a proper name. (See *post,* § 6 for exception.)

| | |
|---|---|
| Redwood City; City of Redwood City | defendant city |
| | respondent city |
| City of Los Angeles | |
| Sacramento City Council | the council; the city council |
| Town of Los Gatos | the town |
| City Manager and City Clerk of Long Beach | the city manager and city clerk; Smith, city manager, *but,* City Manager Smith |

(See also SPO Manual, pp. 13–14 and *post,* § 53.)

## § 3. Counties.—Capitalize "county" or "counties" only when part of a proper name. (See *post,* § 6 for exception.)

| | |
|---|---|
| Solano County | the county |
| County of Solano | appellant county |
| Superior Court of Butte County | the superior court |
| Los Angeles and Riverside Counties | defendant counties |
| City and County of San Francisco | respondent city and county |

## § 4. States.—Capitalize "state" or "states" only when part of a proper name. (See *post,* § 6 for exception.)

| | |
|---|---|
| State of California | the state |
| New York State | a state |
| States of Nevada and California | respondent states |
| | several western states |
| State Lands Commission | the state commission |
| State Personnel Board | the state board; the board |

## § 5. Districts.—Capitalize "district" or "districts" only when part of a proper name. (See *post,* § 6 for exception.)

| | |
|---|---|
| Tulare Irrigation District | the district |
| East Bay Municipal Utility District | respondent district |
| Palo Verde Unified School | a school district in |
| District of Riverside County | Riverside County |

## § 6. Exception to Sections 2–5.—An author may capitalize words such as "city," "town," "county," "state," "district," "board," "council," etc. when standing alone if he or she has first formally adopted the use of such words as abbreviated expressions to designate the more lengthy proper titles. The use of this technique in appellate work avoids unnecessary repetition of lengthy titles and permits the reader to identify parties and follow the flow of the material presented without distracting and repetitive phraseology.

"He rendered services in various departments of the City of Los Angeles (hereafter the City), . . ." (*Benguiat* v. *City of Los Angeles* (1971) 15 Cal.App.3d 621, 622.)

"Plaintiff . . . appeals from a judgment denying a writ of mandate to compel defendant Board of Education of the City of Modesto (Board) . . . ." (*Bekiaris* v. *Board of Education* (1972) 6 Cal.3d 575, 580.)

(See also *post,* § 25.)

# B. Legislative Bodies and Officers

## § 7. Local Bodies.

| | |
|---|---|
| the Board of Supervisors of Marin County | respondent board |
| the Mendocino County Board of Supervisors | the board |
| the City Council of Berkeley | the city council |
| the Berkeley City Council | the council |

3

## § 8. State Bodies.

the California Legislature*
the Legislature*
the Assembly (Assem.)
the Senate (Sen.)

the legislative branch
a legislative department
state legislators
senatorial districts
the house

* Capitalize the word "legislature" when standing alone only when referring to the Legislature of California. However, the word "legislature" is always capitalized when used as a part of a proper name; e.g., "the Legislature of Nevada" and "the Nevada Legislature."

## § 9. National Bodies.

United States Congress
Congress
Senate
House of Representatives
Sixty-third Congress
89th Congress

congressional

the upper house
the lower house
the legislative branch
the national lawmakers

## § 10. Legislative Committees.—Capitalize only when proper or established titles are used.

Senate Committee on the Judiciary
Assembly Constitutional
  Amendment Committee
Joint Budget Committee; the
  Joint Committee
the Rules Committee
Committee on Revenue and
  Taxation

the committee
the amendment committee


a joint committee
a rules committee
the Jones committee

(See *post,* § 58, for capitalization of legislative committee and interim committee reports.)

## § 11. Legislative Officers.

**(a) State and National Officers.**—Capitalize words denoting office when they immediately precede the officer's name.

Senator Dawn Smith; Member of the Assembly Brown; Congressman Cuthbert B. Twille.

Capitalize words or groups of words denoting high legislative office after the officer's name or, if standing alone, when used as a substitute for the name of the party referred to.

Wilbur Lanka, Chairman of the House Ways and Means Committee, will speak at Hoover University this Friday.
I understand, Senator, that you are in favor of this bill.
*But:* Whenever a senator resigns from office, the resignation must be in writing and submitted to the presiding officer of the house.

**(b) Local Officers.**—Capitalize words denoting office when they immediately precede the officer's name, not when standing alone or when used as a substitute for the name of the party referred to.

> It is certain Supervisor Green will attend the meeting.
> The supervisor will be present.
> I am informed, supervisor, that your vote was not counted.

Capitalize words denoting office directly following a local legislative officer's name only when full and formal descriptions are given.

> John Smith, chairman of the city's civil service board, will speak at the luncheon.
> *But:* Supervisor John Rohne, Chairman of the Encino Civil Service Commission, will speak at the luncheon.

## C. Courts and Judicial Officers

**§ 12. Federal Courts.**—Capitalize when full or accepted formal titles are used, not when a partial title or name is given or the reference is to a court or courts generally. Note the exception where the abbreviated reference is to the Supreme Court of the United States.

| | |
|---|---|
| United States Supreme Court | the court |
| Supreme Court of the United States | the high court |
| Supreme Court (**Capitalize even when standing alone.**) | the high federal court |
| United States Court of Appeals, Ninth Circuit | the circuit court |
| Ninth Circuit Court of Appeals | the circuit court of appeals |
| the Ninth Circuit | the court of appeals |
| Circuit Court of the United States for the Ninth Circuit | |
| United States District Court | the district court |
| United States District Court for the Eastern District of Arkansas | the federal district court |
| District Court of the United States for the District of Columbia | |
| United States Claims Court | the claims court |
| United States Court of International Trade | the court of international trade |
| United States Customs Court | the customs court |
| Tax Court of the United States | the tax court |
| United States Court of Military Appeals | the military appeals court |

Note: Use lowercase for court martial or courts martial. (See also *post,* § 81.)

5

## § 13. State Courts.

§ 13. **State Courts.**—Capitalize when full or accepted formal titles are used, not when a partial title or name is given or the reference is to a court or courts generally. Note exceptions where the abbreviated reference is to the Supreme Court of California or one of the California Courts of Appeal.

| | |
|---|---|
| Supreme Court of California | the court |
| California Supreme Court | the court stated |
| Supreme Court (Capitalize even when standing alone.) | the state's highest court |
| Court of Appeal, Fourth Appellate District, Division One | the court |
| Division One of the Court of Appeal, Fourth Appellate District | the appellate courts |
| Court of Appeal (Capitalize even when standing alone.) | (See *post,* § 14 for capitalization of divisions.) |
| Fourth Appellate District | |
| Superior Court of San Bernardino County* | the superior court |
| | the court |
| Superior Court of the State of California for the County of San Bernardino | the probate department of the superior court |
| San Bernardino Superior Court | |
| San Bernardino County Superior Court | |
| Appellate Department of the Superior Court of Los Angeles County | the appellate department |
| Juvenile Court of Los Angeles County | the juvenile court |
| the Tehama County Juvenile Court | |
| Municipal Court for the Los Angeles Judicial District of Los Angeles County | the court |
| | the municipal court |
| Municipal Court for the Los Angeles Judicial District | |
| Riverside Municipal Court | |

While technically all municipal courts are in judicial districts, custom has sanctioned opinion references without designation of the district where confusion will not result.

| | |
|---|---|
| Justice Court for the Biggs Judicial District of Butte County | respondent justice court |
| | the court |

---

*See 2 Witkin, California Procedure (3d ed. 1985) Courts, section 161, pages 188, 189, for a discussion of whether there is a single statewide superior court or 58 superior courts, 1 in each county.

Justice Court for the First Judicial
District of Tuolumne County

plaintiff justice court

Small Claims Court for the
Alameda Judicial District of
Alameda County
Small Claims Division of
the Municipal Court for
the Glendale Judicial District
of Los Angeles County
the Amador County Small Claims
Court [after identification in full]

the small claims court
the court

Technically, a small claims court is part of a justice or municipal court, and not a separate court, but it is often referred to as a court. (See Code Civ. Proc., §§ 116.1, 116.7, 116.8, subd. (b).)

§ 14. Divisions of Courts.—In referring to superior, municipal or justice courts, capitalize "department," "law and motion department," etc., only when used as a part of a formal title, as when it appears in the caption of a pleading. Otherwise use lower case, as, "The matter was transferred to the law and motion department."

In referring to a Court of Appeal, capitalize the word "division" when used to designate a specific part of a specific court; e.g., "Court of Appeal, First Appellate District, Division One"; "When Division Two met in a special session on July 1 . . . ."; *but,* "the Supreme Court may transfer cases from one division of a Court of Appeal to another."

§ 15. Judges, Court Commissioners, Referees, and Temporary Judges.—Other than the exception noted below, do not capitalize the following titles unless used with a person's name: justice, associate justice, assigned justice, presiding judge, acting presiding judge, judge, temporary judge, court commissioner, and referee.

Always capitalize "Chief Justice" and "Acting Chief Justice."

Capitalize presiding justice and acting presiding justice when the court on which they serve is specified; e.g., the Presiding Justice of the Court of Appeal, Third Appellate District, the Presiding Justice of the Court of Appeal, First Appellate District, Division Two; *but,* a justice of the Supreme Court, a judge of the Superior Court of Orange County, the referee of the Los Angeles Municipal Court's traffic division.

(See *post,* §§ 285-294 for styles of noting editorial information.)

§ 16. Judicial Officers.—Appellate court usage has established the following capitalization styles.

ATTORNEY GENERAL:
the Attorney General of California
the California Attorney General
the Attorney General

7

**ATTORNEY GENERAL (Continued)**

Chief Deputy Attorney General Smith — the chief deputy attorney general

Chief Assistant Attorney General Roberts — the chief assistant attorney general

Assistant Attorney General Green — an assistant attorney general

Deputy Attorney General Jones — a deputy attorney general

Deputy Attorneys General Janet Smith and Timothy Jones — Nancy Moon, a deputy attorney general, stated

**ATTORNEYS:**

Attorney Smith — the trial attorney
the state's attorney
plaintiff's attorney
Smith, the attorney for plaintiff

**BAILIFFS:**

Bailiff Smith — a bailiff of the Superior Court of Los Angeles County
the bailiff

**CLERKS:**

Clerk of the Supreme Court — the clerk

Clerk of the Court of Appeal of the Fourth Appellate District — a Court of Appeal clerk

Clerk Jones — the clerk

County Clerk Jones — Jack Jones, the county clerk

the County Clerk of Fresno County — the county clerk

**CONSTABLES:**

Constable Smith — a Humboldt County constable

**CORONERS:**

Coroner Green — the coroner

County Coroner Smith — the coroner's report

the San Joaquin County Coroner — Paul Pound, the county coroner

the Coroner of Siskiyou County

**COURT ADMINISTRATORS:**

the Administrative Director of the Courts — the administrative director

Superior Court Administrator Jones — the superior court administrator

the Executive Officer of the Los Angeles County Superior Court — the executive officer

Municipal Court Coordinator, San Bernardino County Municipal Court District — the court coordinator

**COURT REPORTERS:**

Court Reporter Jones — a court reporter of the Superior Court of Orange County

Reporter Jones — the Orange County court reporter

**DISTRICT ATTORNEYS:**

District Attorney Roth — the district attorney

the District Attorney of Butte County — a district attorney

the Sutter County District Attorney

Assistant District Attorney Brown — an assistant district attorney

Deputy District Attorney White — a deputy district attorney

**JURORS:**
Juror Smith
Jurors Smith and Jones
Foreman Green

James Smith, a juror

Mr. Green, foreman

**MARSHALS:**
Marshal Dillon
the Marshal of the Municipal Court
of Riverside County for the
Riverside Judicial District
Deputy Marshal Festus

the marshal
a deputy marshal

**PUBLIC DEFENDERS:**
[See State Public Defender]

**REPORTER OF DECISIONS:**
Reporter of Decisions of the
Supreme Court

the reporter

**SHERIFFS:**
Sheriff Green
the Sheriff of Los Angeles County
the Sierra Sheriff
Deputy Sheriff Green

the sheriff

a deputy sheriff of Los Angeles
County

**STATE PUBLIC DEFENDER:**
the State Public Defender
Deputy State Public Defender Howe
Deputy State Public Defenders
James Eli and Mary Moore

the public defender
a deputy state public defender

Jane Drew, a deputy state
public defender, stated

# D. Administrative Bodies

**§ 17. State Agencies, Departments, Commissions, Boards and Their Subdivisions.**—Capitalize designations of governmental administrative units when complete formal titles are used or when usage has established formal but abbreviated titles. Do not capitalize words such as "commission," "department," or "board" when standing alone even when referring to a specific governmental unit. (See, however, *ante*, § 6.)

the Judicial Council of California
Judicial Council
Public Utilities Commission
State Lands Commission
Department of Industrial Relations
Employment Development
Department
Division of Highways and Programming
Division of Driver Safety and Licensing
Board of Prison Terms
State Board of Equalization
State Department of Health Services
Board of Medical Quality Assurance
California Law Revision Commission
Law Revision Commission

the council

the commission
respondent commission
the department
respondent department

plaintiff division
the division
the board
the state board
respondent department
defendant state board
the commission
the commission's report

**§ 18.   Local Bodies.**—Same capitalization style as noted in section 17, *ante.*

| | |
|---|---|
| San Francisco Fire Department | the fire department |
| Stockton Civil Service Commission | the civil service commission |
| Oakland Police Department | the police department |
| Grand Jury of Los Angeles County | the grand jury |

*But note:*
Los Angeles County jail
Los Angeles police station

**§ 19.   The State Bar.**—In order to achieve uniformity, the following capitalization styles have been adopted:

| | |
|---|---|
| State Bar of California | the bar (also: the bench and bar) |
| California State Bar | respondent bar |
| the State Bar | petitioner bar |
| the Board of Governors | the board |
| the State Bar Court | the court |
| State Bar Court, Hearing Department, District No. 2, Eastern Division | the State Bar Court<br>a hearing department of the court |
| State Bar Court, Review Department | the review department |
| State Bar Office of Trial Counsel | the office wrote petitioner |
| the Committee of Bar Examiners of the State Bar | the committee |
| California Board of Legal Specialization | the board |

(See also *post,* §§ 33, 66.)

# E.   Executive Officers

**§ 20.   In General.**—Capitalize adjectives and common nouns denoting executive office when they immediately precede the officer's name. Capitalize common nouns denoting executive preeminence or distinction standing alone when used as a substitute for the officer's name. (See *post,* § 21 for illustrations.)

**§ 21.   Specific Officers.**

**(a) The President and Cabinet Officers:**

| | |
|---|---|
| President Reagan | the president of John Doe Company |
| the President | |
| the Commander-in-Chief | the president of the fraternity |
| former President Carter | |
| ex-President Johnson | the president of the board of supervisors |
| President-elect | |
| Donald Hodel, Secretary of the Interior | |
| the Secretary of State | |

**(b) The Governor:**

Governor Smith                              the governor of each state
Fred Smith, Governor of California
the Governor

**(c) Lieutenant Governor, Attorney General, Controller, Secretary of State, Treasurer and Superintendent of Public Instruction:** Same as Governor.

**(d) Heads of Major Departments and Commissions of State Government.**—Capitalize when full titles are given. Do not capitalize titles of subordinates unless used in an adjective form preceding the officeholder's name:

Director of the Department          the director
  of Alcoholic Beverage Control     respondent director
Director of the Employment          the chief deputy director of the
  Development Department              Department of Agriculture
Commissioner of the Department      defendant commissioner
  of Corporations
Commissioner of the Department
  of Insurance
Chairwoman of the State Water       the chairwoman
  Resources Control Board
Chairman of the Air Resources Board  plaintiff chairman
Assistant Executive Officer         the assistant executive officer
  Fred Green; *but,* Fred Green,      of the Franchise Tax Board
  assistant executive officer
  of the Franchise Tax Board
Chief of Staff of the               the business service officer of
  California National Guard           the Air Resources Board
Director of the California          director of the CRD
  Rehabilitation Department

**(e) City, County and Other Local Officers.**—Capitalize titles of local officials only when used in an adjective form preceding the officeholder's name or with the name of the political subdivision:

Mayor Green                         the mayor
City Manager Green                  the city manager
Chief of Police Smith               the chief of police
the Santa Barbara Chief of Police
Los Angeles Police Officer Jones    Jones, a Los Angeles police
Police Officer Jones                  officer
Water Commissioner Brown            the water commissioner
the Fire Chief of Orinda            the fire chief
                                    city tax collector, assessor,
                                      controller, sheriff, constable,
                                      superintendent of schools, etc.

## F. Miscellaneous Rules

**§ 22. Words Part of Proper Name.**—Capitalize otherwise common nouns and adjectives when part of a proper name. Plurals under this usage are also capitalized.

| | |
|---|---|
| Market Street | Seventh and Market Streets |
| Sunset Boulevard | Sacramento and San Joaquin Rivers |
| Roosevelt Dam | |
| Lower California | Lakes Tahoe and Arrowhead |
| Ingleside Station | San Lorenzo Creek |
| Folsom Prison | Southern California |
|   *But:* state prison | |

See SPO Manual pages 13 and 14 for a list of geographical titles.

**§ 23. Words Not Part of Proper Name.**—The addition of a number, letter or date to a common noun to indicate sequence or time or for the author's convenience in referring to material does not form a proper name and capitalization is therefore not used. Lowercase the word "count" even though it may be capitalized in the clerk's transcript, and, as to spelling out the count number or using roman or arabic numerals, follow the style used in the complaint.

| | | |
|---|---|---|
| count one | page two | section 12 |
| count II | exhibit A | title VI |
| article I | paragraph 17 | volume 9 |
| schedule A | appendix two | July 9th order |
| chapter 6 | division 3 | part 2 |

(See also *post,* § 35.)

**§ 24. "People."**—When the People of the State of California is a party litigant the word "People" is capitalized when standing alone. However, when the reference is to the people as a group and not as a party to the litigation do not capitalize.

Evidence was introduced by the People.
The people have not voted on that issue.

**§ 25. Parties—Substitute Designation.**—Ordinarily the position occupied by a party (plaintiff, defendant, appellant, respondent, executor, etc.) is shown without capitalization, whether the designation is used alone or in conjunction with a party's name; e.g.,

He pointed to plaintiff Jones.

Where a case involves several parties, or the acts of third persons, and the author, for convenience, adopts a short form of reference in order to avoid the repetition of lengthy names, the substitute designation should be capitalized; for example, the opinion might recite:

"Bridge and Construction Company, hereafter referred to as Bridge, made an agreement with American British Commercial Bank and Trust Company, hereafter called the Bank, regarding certain work on land adjoining plaintiff's residence."

When the parties are subsequently referred to as "Bridge" and "Bank" those terms should be capitalized. (See also *ante,* § 6.)

Where a reference is editorial, rather than textual, party designations are normally capitalized, see for example, *post,* Chapter V, Title of Case and Chapter VI, Editorial Information. (See also *ante,* § 6.)

**§ 26.  Proper Names With Definite Article.**—Often a company, newspaper, periodical, etc., will use the definite article as a part of its official name. In order to facilitate legal references and to avoid repetitious indexing, "the" is disregarded in case titles and running heads and for that reason is not capitalized where used in opinion texts.

 the Blue Bird Insurance Company
 the Los Angeles Times
 the Readers Digest
 the Page Investment Co.

(See also *post,* §§ 27, 212, 219, 259.)

**§ 27.  Organizations.**—Capitalize the names of political parties and their members, associations, clubs, societies, schools, fraternities, religious bodies, companies, and firms.

| | |
|---|---|
| the Democratic Party | the party |
| a Republican | republican form of government |
| Communist Party | communist propaganda |
| California Nurses Association | plaintiff association |
| Society of California Pioneers | the society |
| the Olympic Club | defendant club |
| Stanford University | the university |
| the Smith Realty Corporation | |
| Northern California Council of Churches | |
| the Ajax Paper Company | |

(See also *ante,* § 26 and *post,* §§ 212, 219, 259, for noncapitalization of the article "the" in titles.)

**§ 28.  Opinion Headings and Subheadings.**—Irrespective of the style adopted it is essential that all headings be treated alike throughout the opinion. Subheadings likewise are treated alike although they may differ in style from the headings.

**(a) Short Headings and Subheadings.**—Where the majority of headings or subheadings are short (normally not more than two typewritten lines) it is preferable to use caps and small caps. The use of italics is at the author's choice. Capitalize all words except articles, conjunctions and short prepositions (three or less letters). Capitalize the first and last words regardless of what part of speech they are, e.g., Was the Evidence All In?; An Option Was Not Exercised. Capitalize the first word following a colon, dash or similar break; e.g., Comparative Negligence: A New Theory.

**(b) Extended Headings or Subheadings.**—Normally these are more in the nature of complete sentences and are discussional as distinguished from the customary abbreviated topic titles, and the preferred style is to use italics but without caps and small caps. (See, e.g., *San Clemente Ranch, Ltd.* v. *Agricultural Labor Relations Board* (1981) 29 Cal.3d 874, 883.)

## § 29.    Constitutions, Amendments and Subdivisions Thereof.

**(a)** Capitalize the word "Constitution" when referring to a specific constitution but not when referring to constitutions generally.

> Prosecution by information, authorized by the state Constitution, is not in contravention of the federal Constitution. Several state constitutions have similar language.

**(b)** Do not capitalize derivatives.

> A person has a constitutional right to be free from unreasonable searches and seizures. The statute is clearly unconstitutional.

**(c)** The words "federal" and "state" preceding the word "Constitution" are not capitalized.

> the federal Constitution, the state Constitution, the state and federal Constitutions

**(d)** Capitalization styles for references to constitutions, amendments, and subdivisions thereof are:

> United States Constitution, the California Constitution, the Constitution of the United States
> article VI, clause 2 of the United States Constitution
> Fourteenth Amendment of the United States Constitution
> Fifth, Sixth and Fourteenth Amendments
> 14th Amendment
> Amendment XIV (Note: never use "th" with roman numerals.)
> Bill of Rights
> equal protection clause
> supremacy clause
> commerce clause of the United States Constitution
> due process clause
> section 8, article I of the California Constitution
> article I, section 8 of the California Constitution
> section 2¾ of article II of the California Constitution

(See *post*, §§ 38–40 for additional citation styles.)

## § 30.    Statute Titles.—Capitalize all official short titles of statutes, all popular titles, and uniform laws, for example:

| | |
|---|---|
| Penal Code | Uniform Commercial Code |
| State Civil Service Act | California Uniform Commercial Code |
| State Bar Act | Broughton Act |
| Blue Sky Law | Indeterminate Sentence Law |
| Negotiable Instruments Act | Determinate Sentencing Act |

Do not capitalize unofficial or generic names of statutes, such as "statute of frauds" or "statute of limitations." In referring to a particular statute previously cited with full title, do not capitalize "act," "statute," or "code" when standing alone, for example, "The act provides . . . ." (See also *post,* § 32.)

**§ 31. Charters.**—Capitalize "charter" when used as part of the title of a formal document or when preceded or followed by a geographic adjective but not when standing alone.

| | |
|---|---|
| the Charter of Stockton | the charter |
| the Stockton Charter | the city's charter |
| the Stockton City Charter | |

(See also *post,* § 53.)

**§ 32. Miscellaneous Usage and Familiar Doctrines.**—Capitalize: Afro-American, Asiatic, Black (synonym for Negro), Caucasian, Hispanic, Negro, Oriental, and White (synonym for Caucasian).

Do not capitalize the names of familiar doctrines such as last clear chance and res ipsa loquitur. (See also *ante,* § 30.)

**§ 33. Rules.**—Capitalize "Rule" when part of a title, not when preceding a number: "The California Rules of Court," but: "Under rule 5-104 of the Rules of Professional Conduct . . . ."

However, capitalize "Rule" when it starts a citation enclosed in parentheses and the parentheses do not fall in the middle of a sentence, since its use then is analogous to the first word of a sentence; e.g., This is prohibited. (Rule 5(c), Cal. Rules of Court.) But: This is prohibited (rule 5(c), Cal. Rules of Court) under either alternative.

(See also *ante,* § 19 and *post,* §§ 64, 66.)

**§ 34. Time.**—Use lowercase for "o'clock" and abbreviations "a.m." and "p.m."

(See also *post,* § 190(c).)

**§ 35. Article, Section, Part, Chapter, etc.**—Capitalize these words only when used as a title. Do not capitalize the words or their abbreviations when used as part of a citation, e.g. (Const., art. VI, § 4). When such a word starts a citation enclosed in parentheses, and the parentheses do not fall in the middle of a sentence, it is treated as starting a sentence, and it should then be capitalized; e.g., The Constitution limits the power to grant pardons. (Art. V, § 8.)

(See also *post,* §§ 46 and 40 for abbreviation styles and *ante,* § 23.)

**§ 36. Letter Compounds.**—Whether the term is hyphenated or not, the descriptive letter should be capitalized in such expressions as:

| | | |
|---|---|---|
| A-bomb | I-beam | T-square |
| D-Day | S-curve | X-ray |

# CHAPTER I
## —Notes—

# CHAPTER II

# CITATIONS

## E. Case Reports

## F. General Rules of Citation

## G.  Secondary Materials

## H.  Federal Materials

**§ 37. In General.**—The following sections are designed to provide citation styles for those sources most often relied upon in the preparation of opinions and briefs. It is anticipated, however, that the variety of materials covered and the examples noted are sufficiently broad to be of assistance in the citation of most other sources. The paramount objective of any citation style must always be to clearly identify the source relied upon and to provide that information which will facilitate the reader's location of the cited material. Generally, it should be noted that where a source cited is not commonly known or its availability limited, more detailed information is needed and less abbreviation desirable.

## A. Constitutions

**§ 38. Distinguishing California's Constitution From Others.**—In referring to the California Constitution the descriptive words "California" and "state" are frequently omitted when no confusion will result, e.g., "The Constitution provides . . . ." Hence, references to other constitutions should contain the name of the state or "federal," "United States," or some similar designation except where the context makes such descriptive words superfluous. Within parentheses the abbreviation "Cal." *always* precedes the abbreviation "Const.," e.g., (Cal. Const., art. VI, § 10).

> The due process clause of the United States Constitution forbids enforcement. Compare section 1 of article III of the federal Constitution.
> (U.S. Const., 6th Amend.; Cal. Const., art. I, § 7.)

**§ 39. Repealed, New, Recently Amended or Transferred Sections.**—Generally, the fact that a cited section of the California Constitution is new, repealed or has recently been amended or transferred should be noted. If this cannot be readily accomplished within the body of the text, footnotes as illustrated below are appropriate.

> Article XI, section 7½,[1] provided . . . .
> Article II, section 10,[2] provides . . . .
> (Cal. Const., art. I, § 28, added by initiative, Primary Elec. (June 8, 1982) commonly known as the Victims' Bill of Rights.)
> Under the authority of amended article XVI, section 17,[3] respondents theorize . . . .
> Pursuant to article I, section 16 of the California Constitution [4] . . . .
> (See Cal. Const., art. XIII, § 1, as adopted Nov. 5, 1974.)[5]

---

[1] Repealed June 2, 1970.

[2] New section adopted June 8, 1976. The provisions of this section were transferred from article IV, former section 24.

[3] Amendment adopted June 5, 1984.

[4] At the time this case was argued the appropriate constitutional provision was article I, section 7. Its number was changed by vote of the people on November 5, 1974.

[5] Former article XIII, section 1, was substantially consistent in the parts pertinent to this appeal.

(See *post,* § 40 for additional illustrations.)

**§ 40. Abbreviations.**—Do not abbreviate the words constitution, article, section, subdivision or clause, etc., when used in the body of a sentence outside parentheses; when a constitution or division thereof is cited within parentheses, the abbreviation forms noted below are appropriate.

(U.S. Const., art. V.)
(U.S. Const., art. VI, cl. 2.)
(U.S. Const., art. I, § 5, cl.3.)
(U.S. Const., 6th & 14th Amends.)
(U.S. Const., Amend. VI; Cal. Const., art. I, § 7.)
(U.S. Const., 8th Amend.; Cal. Const., art. I, § 6.)
(Cal. Const., art. II, § 15.)
(Cal. Const., arts. IV, V, & VI.)
(Cal. Const., art. VI, § 1, & art. III, § 1.)
(Cal. Const., art. XIII, § 28, subd. (f), par. (3).)
(Cal. Const., art. VI, § 10, formerly Cal. Const., art. VI, § 5.)
. . . (art. IV, § 21, subd. (b)) . . . .
. . . (art. IX, 2d par. of § 9, subd. (b)) . . . .
. . . former article XX, section 22 (now art. XV, § 1) . . . .
(See former art. XXIV, § 4, now renumbered as art. VII, § 4.)
Section 17, subdivision a of article XVI (formerly art. XIII, § 42) . . . .
The Constitution (art. XX, § 22) . . . .
(Cal. Const. of 1849, art. IV, § 37.)
(. . . former art. VI, § 4, Cal. Const. of 1879, repealed in 1966.)
(Cal. Const. Revision Com., Proposed Revision (1966) p. 63.)
(Debates & Proceedings, Cal. Const. Convention 1878–1879, pp. 1038–1039, 1478–1481.)

(See also *ante,* §§ 29 and 35 for capitalization styles and § 39 for where there have been recent changes.)

## B. California Statutes and Codes

**§ 41. Statutes.**—Normally statutes are cited to the session laws of the Legislature as located in "Statutes and Amendments to the Codes" (1850 to date) by reference to year, chapter, section and page; e.g.,

(Stats. 1949, ch. 456, § 1, p. 799.)

In those years in which the Legislature held extra sessions it is common to find the laws enacted during the extra sessions published in the volume of "Statutes and Amendments to the Codes" for the following year. Where this is the situation the correct citation is,

(Stats. 1957, First Ex. Sess. 1956, ch. 10, § 1, p. 298.)

If the citation to the statute is in the body of the opinion, as distinguished from a reference within parentheses, abbreviations are not used, e.g.,

Section 1042 is based on Statutes 1919, chapter 178, section 7, pages 267–268.

Within parentheses references to different statutes are separated by semicolons, not commas.

(Stats. 1949, ch. 456, § 2, p. 799; Stats. 1969, ch. 515, § 1, p. 1125.)

(See *post,* § 42 for the citation of recently enacted statutes.)

**§ 42.  Recently Enacted Statutes.**—By the November 7, 1972, constitutional amendment of article IV, section 3, of the California Constitution the previously annual regular sessions of the Legislature were lengthened to two years. The Legislature now convenes in regular session on the first Monday in December of each even-numbered year and adjourns on November 30 of the following even-numbered year. The Governor may by proclamation cause the Legislature to assemble in special session.

Pursuant to Government Code section 9600, for legislation enacted in 1973 and subsequent years, the effective date of all nonurgency bills which become statutes is January 1 following the year designation for the chapter laws, e.g., a nonurgency bill which becomes "Chapter _____, Statutes of 1975" is effective on January 1, 1976. Urgency measures are effective upon enactment. The effective or operative dates of some bills are delayed. When a bill is enacted it becomes a chapter and is assigned a chapter number by the Secretary of State. (See Gov. Code, § 9510.) While a regular legislative session now covers two years, each year's *enacted* bills are independently numbered. Enacted bills deposited with the Secretary of State "from the beginning of the two-year session through December 31 of the odd-numbered year shall be designated 'Statutes of [odd-numbered year], Chapter _____.' Bills deposited with the Secretary of State after December 31 of the odd-numbered year shall be designated 'Statutes of [even-numbered year], Chapter _____.' " (Gov. Code, § 9510.5.)

As an illustration, an enacted nonurgency bill deposited with the Secretary of State on March 1, 1986, might be assigned chapter 100 and would be immediately cited as (Stats. 1986, ch. 100).

Recently enacted statutes are published by chapter number at an early date in publications such as Deering's California Advance Legislative Service and West's California Legislative Service, and parallel references to such publications are encouraged until the appearance of the statute cited (in code form) in Statutes and Amendments to the Codes, e.g.,

(Stats. 1985, ch. 870, No. 4 Deering's Adv. Legis. Service, p. 1220.)
(Stats. 1985, ch. 870, No. 8 West's Cal. Legis. Service, p. 924.)

(See §§ 44 & 47 for additional illustrations and § 55 for legislative bill citation styles.)

**§ 43.  Uncodified Statutes.**—Some statutes for a variety of reasons were never codified but remain "statutes in force" outside the codes. A number of these statutes have been collected and appear in such works as Deering's Water—Uncodified Acts and Deering's Uncodified Initiative Measures and Statutes and have been assigned "Act" numbers or other sequential designations by the publishers.

In quoting or referring to these uncodified statutes the appropriate citation style includes a reference to both the session laws and the independent collection, e.g.,

(Stats. 1961, ch. 1942, § 1, p. 4092, Deering's Wat.—Uncod. Acts (1970 ed.) Act 206, p. 46.)

(Stats. 1970, ch. 947, § 1, p. 1705, Deering's Wat.—Uncod. Acts (1973 Supp.), Act 206, p. 10.)

(See *post,* § 52 for the citation of initiative measures.)

## § 44. Codes.

**(a) Citation Outside Parentheses.**—Codes are cited by their full titles when not within parentheses. Abbreviations are not used. The code name is given, followed by "section" spelled out and the number; no comma is necessary between the code designated and the word "section," e.g.,

Code of Civil Procedure section 410
Section 844 of the Penal Code
Probate Code section 236, subdivision (b)
Government Code section 66801, article VII, subdivision (a)
Elections Code, division 8, chapter 1 (§ 11500 et seq.) . . . .

**(b) Citation Within Parentheses.**—Code citations are abbreviated within parentheses. The code abbreviations are followed by a comma, the section symbol (§) and the number, e.g.,

(Gov. Code, § 3752.)
(Prob. Code, § 1651, subd. (a).)
(Pen. Code, §§ 118, 118a, 126.)
(Code Civ. Proc., §§ 537–561, 690–690.52.)

Use a double section symbol when citing more than one section:

(Pen. Code, §§ 118, 126.)
(Prob. Code, §§ 250–256.)
(Civ. Code, §§ 1808.4, 1810.2–1812.52.)

However, only one section symbol is used if the reference is to a single section and those following:

(Bus. & Prof. Code, § 16700 et seq.)

In typewritten copy, if the typewriter does not have a key for the section symbol (§), use the abbreviation "sec."

**(c) Repealed Code Sections.**—Where the author is comparing or contrasting existing code sections with repealed sections the citational information required as to the repealed sections is generally dependent upon usage. If the author wishes to note that the repealed section's provisions are carried over into a new enactment, the following styles are available:

> In 1970 subdivision (d) of section 11580.1 of the Insurance Code was repealed, but similar language was added to section 11580.1 as subdivision (b) (4).

> The applicable dismissal statutes were repealed and reenacted as Code of Civil Procedure section 583.310 et seq. in 1984 without substantive change. (Stats. 1984, ch. 1705, § 4, p. 925 [repealed]; Stats. 1984, ch. 1705, § 5, pp. 927-928 [reenacted].)

> (Former Ins. Code, § 11580.1, subd. (d), repealed 1970, now § 11580.1, subd. (b)(4).)

Where the author paraphrases the contents of the repealed enactment he need note only the prior section number:

> (Former Ed. Code, § 13129, subds. (e) and (h), now § 13174, subds. (e) and (h).)

However, where the author *refers* the reader to the earlier enactment it is best to cite to the "Statutes and Amendments to the Codes" containing the applicable language followed by the repealing citation and, where material, the effective date, e.g.,

> (Civ. Code, § 2975, added by Stats. 1959, ch. 528, § 2, p. 249 and repealed by Stats. 1963, ch. 819, § 2, p. 1997, eff. Jan. 1, 1965.)

"A section of a statute may not be amended unless the section is reenacted as amended." (Cal. Const., art. IV, § 9.) Accordingly, California's code sections are reprinted in full upon amendment, and, unless the effect of a modification or repeal is at issue, it is not necessary to refer to the initial enactment and later amendments as is sometimes required when citing sources that publish only the portion of the material that *is* amended.

## § 45. Code Sections With Subdivisions.

—Since the Legislature has employed a variety of techniques in numbering and lettering code sections and their subdivisions, care must be exercised to ensure accurate references. To illustrate, section 227 of the Civil Code has several subdivisions designated (a) through (d). The Civil Code also contains separate sections designated 227a, 227b, 227c and 227d. If an author wishes to direct the reader to subdivision (a) of section 227 the proper citation is: Civil Code section 227, subdivision (a), or, within parentheses, (Civ. Code, § 227, subd. (a)). Never use 227a, or 227(a), since the reader will not know if the reference is to section 227a, an entirely different section of the code, or to section 227, subdivision (a), the intended section and subdivision.

To preserve uniformity and avoid confusion *all* references to subdivisions of code sections should use the word "subdivision" or within parentheses "subd."

> (Code Civ. Proc., § 409.1, subd. (b).)
> (Pen. Code, §§ 987, 1181, subd. 6.)
> (Elec. Code, § 11503, subds. (d), (e), (f) & (g).)
> (Gov. Code, § 66801, art. V, subd. (b).)
> Probate Code section 1951, subdivision 6

In citing sections containing more than one set of enumerations, if the section or rule distinguishes leading propositions by numbers or letters, "subdivision" or within parentheses "subd." will precede the first cited number or letter, e.g.,

Subdivision (b) (2) of section 2019 of the Code of Civil Procedure
Civil Code section 1782, subdivision (a) (1)
(Code Civ. Proc., § 1193.1, subd. (d) (3).)

If the code as enacted identifies its parts by words, numbers or letters follow the code's designations exactly, e.g., (Pen. Code, § 26, subd. Five.) *not* (Pen. Code, § 26, subd. 5.).

If the section does not designate leading propositions distinguish between them by inserting the word "first" or "second" etc., e.g., section 526, second subdivision 4 of the Code of Civil Procedure, or, within parentheses, (Code Civ. Proc., § 526, 2d subd. 4).

If the code section has several unnumbered or unlettered paragraphs and the author wishes to direct the reader to a specific paragraph use "second paragraph" (outside parentheses) or "2d par." within parentheses, e.g., "section 597f of the Penal Code, second paragraph, provides:" or (Pen. Code, § 597f, 2d par.).

Follow the Legislature's enactment as to the use of parentheses or brackets. For example, if the statute as enacted uses parentheses to enclose a subdivision numeral or letter do not delete the parentheses or change them to brackets. If the statute uses neither parentheses nor brackets, do not add them.

(Prob. Code, § 1043, subd. (4).) *not* (Prob. Code, § 1043, subd. 4.)
(Pen. Code. § 496, subd. 2.) *not* (Pen. Code, § 496, subd. (2).)

**§ 46. Code Abbreviations.**—The following are the abbreviations for the California codes:

| | |
|---|---|
| Agricultural Code [1] | Agr. Code |
| Banking Code [2] | Bank. Code |
| Business and Professions Code | Bus. & Prof. Code |
| California Administrative Code[3] | Cal. Admin. Code |
| California Uniform Commercial Code[4] | Cal. U. Com. Code |
| Civil Code | Civ. Code (not C.C.) |
| Code of Civil Procedure | Code Civ. Proc. (not C.C.P.) |

[1] Superseded by Food and Agricultural Code.
[2] Superseded by Financial Code.
[3] See *post,* section 51.
[4] While section 1101 of California's Uniform Commercial Code provides that the code may be cited as the Uniform Commercial Code, good citational practice requires the addition of the prefix "California" to distinguish the California code from the Uniform Commercial Code, prepared and sponsored nationally, which uses somewhat similar numbering. (See *Goldie v. Bauchet Properties* (1975) 15 Cal. 3d 307, 314–315.)

| | |
|---|---|
| Commercial Code[5] | Com. Code |
| Corporations Code | Corp. Code |
| Education Code | Ed. Code |
| Elections Code | Elec. Code |
| Evidence Code | Evid. Code |
| Financial Code | Fin. Code |
| Fish and Game Code | Fish & G. Code |
| Food and Agricultural Code | Food & Agr. Code |
| Government Code | Gov. Code |
| Harbors and Navigation Code | Harb. & Nav. Code |
| Health and Safety Code | Health & Saf. Code |
| Insurance Code | Ins. Code |
| Labor Code | Lab. Code |
| Military and Veterans Code | Mil. & Vet. Code |
| Penal Code | Pen. Code (not P.C.) |
| Political Code[6] | Pol. Code |
| Probate Code | Prob. Code |
| Public Contract Code | Pub. Contract Code |
| Public Resources Code | Pub. Resources Code |
| Public Utilities Code | Pub. Util. Code |
| Revenue and Taxation Code | Rev. & Tax. Code |
| School Code[7] | Sch. Code |
| Streets and Highways Code | Sts. & Hy. Code |
| Unemployment Insurance Code | Unemp. Ins. Code |
| Uniform Commercial Code[8] | Cal. U. Com. Code |
| Vehicle Code | Veh. Code |
| Water Code | Wat. Code |
| Welfare and Institutions Code | Welf. & Inst. Code |

Abbreviations frequently used in the parenthetical citation of the codes are:

| | | | |
|---|---|---|---|
| and following | et seq. | paragraph | par. |
| article | art. | part | pt. |
| chapter | ch. | parts | pts. |
| clause | cl. | section | § |
| division | div. | sections | §§ |
| following | foll. | subdivision | subd. |
| page | p. | subdivisions | subds. |
| pages | pp. | title | tit. |

(See also *ante,* § 35 re capitalization.)

**§ 47.  Recently Enacted and Amended Codes.**—When citing recently enacted code sections or code amendments which are not available in pocket part form through the popular publications sources as of the filing date of an opinion, the author should provide the reader with the session and chapter numbers effecting the addition or change. (See *ante,* § 42.) Parallel references to publications such as Deering's California Advance Legislative Service or West's California Legislative Service are encouraged since normally they are the most readily

---

[5] Superseded by California Uniform Commercial Code.
[6] Superseded by Government Code.
[7] Superseded by Education Code.
[8] See *ante,* page 25, footnote 4.

available advance sources. It is advisable to notify the reader of recent code changes, even where an earlier enactment is controlling, to minimize the confusion potential.

> Health and Safety Code section 439.3, added by Statutes 1984, chapter 1745, section 12 (No. 8 Deering's Adv. Legis. Service, p. 1124) provides in pertinent part: . . .
> (Bus. & Prof. Code, § 2473, as amended by Stats. 1984, ch. 695, § 2, No. 5 Deering's Adv. Legis. Service, p. 279.)
> Labor Code section 3702, as amended by Statutes 1984, chapter 2, section 1, No. 13 West's California Legislative Service, page 1521, provides: . . .
> (Pub. Resources Code, § 14003, added by Stats. 1984, ch. 1710, § 3, No. 14 West's Cal. Legis. Service, p. 472.)

If the statute was enacted during an extraordinary session of the Legislature that fact should be noted:

> (Ed. Code, § 72247, as amended by Stats. 1984, 2d Ex. Sess., ch. 1, § 5, No. 1 Deering's Adv. Legis. Service, p. 5.)

## § 48. Legislative Schemes.—A comprehensive legislative scheme encompassing numerous consecutive code sections may be cited as illustrated:

> Agricultural Labor Relations Act of 1975 (Lab. Code, div. 2, pt. 3.5, ch. 1, § 1140 et seq.).
> State Aeronautics Act (Pub. Util. Code, div. 9, pt. 1, §§ 21001–21416) . . . .
> The Cartwright Act, contained in division 7 of the Business and Professions Code (§§ 16700–16758), limits . . . .

If the comprehensive legislative scheme involves several codes, or numerous nonconsecutive sections within a single code, then the scheme may be cited by the title of the act and by the relevant statute or statutes:

> The Determinate Sentencing Act (Stats. 1976, ch. 1139; Stats. 1977, ch. 165) requires . . . .

## § 49. Statutory and Editorial Headings.—Headings that introduce code sections, articles, chapters, divisions, etc., which are part of a statute or statutory scheme when enacted by the Legislature are often relied upon as expressions or indications of legislative intent. Complicating the use and significance of these headings is the fact that some of the codes have statutorily stated that these headings are to be disregarded. (See, e.g., Prob. Code, § 4.) Additionally, care must be taken in determining whether the headings were provided by the Legislature or were merely volunteered editorially by the private publisher of the particular code compilation. Where the headings are provided by the publisher authors should omit them or expressly advise the reader of their source. Some publishers will adopt a style to indicate to the reader

that they, and not the Legislature, have inserted the headings. For example, the Bancroft-Whitney Company normally places headings it authors between brackets in its Deering's Codes. A reading of the "foreword" to the publication cited from will usually prove helpful in determining the origin of the headings used.

**§ 50. Annotated Codes.**—In citing code sections from annotated publications do not note the publisher or that the author is citing from an annotated edition. If, however, the author wishes to call the reader's attention to editorial materials following code sections in annotated editions, it is then necessary to describe the material and note publisher, edition, and page, e.g.,

> The intent of the Legislature is evident from an examination of the selected language. (See legis. committee com., Deering's Ann. Corp. Code (1977 ed.) § 110, p. 24.)
>
> (See cases collected in Deering's Ann. Code Civ. Proc. (1981 ed.) foll. § 1263.320 under heading Comparable Sales, pp. 281–283.)
>
> (See legis. committee com., Deering's Ann. Code Civ. Proc., § 1710.45 (1985 pocket supp.) p. 42.)
>
> (See Historical Note, 26B West's Ann. Ed. Code (1978 ed.) § 24600, p. 419.)
>
> (See Cal. Law Revision Com. com., 32 West's Ann. Gov. Code (1980 ed.) § 845, p. 410.)
>
> (See generally, prior law annot., Deering's Ann. Prob. Code (1974 ed.) preceding § 201, pp. 415–416.)

Where editorial materials such as code commissioner comments are reproduced in both Deering's and West's annotated codes it is preferable to cite to both works, e.g.,

> The official code comment on section 9207, prepared by the American Law Institute and National Conference of Commissioners on Uniform State Laws, is in agreement. (See Deering's Ann. Cal. U. Com. Code, § 9207 (1970 ed.) p. 296; 23C West's Ann. Cal. U. Com. Code (1964 ed.) p. 426.)

Occasionally a situation will arise requiring specification of the author instead of the publisher:

> (See code comrs. note foll. 1 Ann. Civ. Code, § 49 (1st ed. 1872, Haymond & Burch, comrs.—annotators) p. 25.)

**§ 51. Administrative Code.**—The California Administrative Code published by the state contains regulations of various state agencies filed with the Secretary of State as provided by the California Administrative Procedure Act. (See Gov. Code, §§ 11370, 11340 et seq.) Courts are required to take judicial notice of "the contents of each regulation or notice of the repeal of a regulation printed in the California Administrative Code or California Administrative Notice Register" (Gov. Code, § 11343.7). Currently, the code contains 25 titles organized in looseleaf binders or microfiches. It is augmented periodically by the

California Administrative Code Supplement which contains integrated material. It is essential in citing these sources to give the title involved as well as the number of the rule or section, e.g.,

Title 17, California Administrative Code, section 14 . . . .
California Administrative Code, title 17, section 7829 . . . .
(Cal. Admin. Code, tit. 22, § 1085–2, subd. (a) (2) (A).)
(Cal. Admin. Code, tit. 8, §§ 10580, 10610, 10904.)
(Cal. Admin. Code, tit. 20, § 1553, Cal. Admin. Code Supp., Register 82, No. 44.)
(Cal. Admin. Notice Register, tit. 18, Register 82, No. 51–Z, Informative Dig., p. A–15.)

**§ 52. Initiative Acts.**—The texts of all initiative measures adopted by the electors within the previous year are required to be published at the beginning of each volume of "Statutes and Amendments to the Codes." (See Gov. Code, § 9766, subds. (d) and (e).) Unfortunately, there have been periods when this provision has not been followed.

Where there have been subsequent modifications and the intent is to cite to the text of the original enactment, it is customary to cite to "Statutes" if that is where the initiative measure was reproduced, e.g., section 2 of the Usury Law as first enacted would be cited as (Stats. 1919, p. lxxxiii, § 2).

Where the act to be cited has been amended and the intent is to cite a section as amended the citation should name the particular act and section and designate one or more of the private legal publications that keep this material current. It is noted that some publications have incorporated these measures into their code compilations and have erroneously assigned code section numbers to them, e.g., the Chiropractic Act, as amended, is published in West's Annotated Business and Professions Code and sections of the act are preceded by the number 1000. Since a citation to an editorial numbering system will erroneously imply codification, authors should cite to the proper publication page and ignore the editorially assigned section numbers, e.g.,

Defendant argues that under section 3 of the Usury Law he is not so restricted. (Deering's Ann. Uncod. Measures 1919–1 (1973 ed.) p. 78.) [or] (10 West's Ann. Civ. Code (1985 ed.) foll. § 1916.12 at p. 178.)
Section 10, subdivision (b) of the Chiropractic Act (3 West's Ann. Bus. & Prof. Code (1974 ed.) p. 147.) [or] (Deering's Ann. Bus. & Prof. Code (1976 ed., 1983 pocket supp.) foll. § 25761 at p. 27) provides . . . .

Since initiative measures such as the Chiropractic Act and the Usury Law are sometimes difficult to locate and identify, an explanatory footnote is often useful, see, e.g., *Cartwright* v. *Board of Chiropractic Examiners* (1976) 16 Cal.3d 762, 764, footnote 1; *Cleveland Chiropractic College* v. *State Bd. of Chiropractic Examiners* (1970) 11 Cal.App.3d 25, 32, footnote 2.

## § 53. Local Ordinances, Codes and Charters.

### (a) Ordinances.

City of Redlands Ordinance No. 1680 provides . . . .
(Tiburon Zoning Ord., §§ 17-20.)
The City of San Juan Capistrano (City) appeals, relying on its earlier enactment. City Ordinance No. 412, enacted November 5, 1980, as amended by City Ordinance No. 423 on May 5, 1981, prohibits . . . .
(L.A. Res. No. 1234.)

### (b) Codes.

Los Angeles Municipal Code sections 21.108 and 21.166[1] . . . .
Section 21.108 (a) preempts . . . .

---

[1]All references hereafter to "section" alone followed by a number and its subdivisions but without a code designation are to the Los Angeles Municipal Code.

(Santa Monica Mun. Code, § 9123D.)
(Torrance Mun. Code, §§ 97.3.1 & 97.3.2(b).)
(S.F. City Planning Code, § 303(b).)
Subdivision (b) of section 303 of the San Francisco City Planning Code defines an "Owner" as . . . .
(Sac. County Code, ch. 9.87, § 9.89.020.)

### (c) Charters.

San Diego City Charter, article IX, section 143 . . . .
(S.F. Charter, §§ 8.341, 8.343.)
Section 5.101 of the Charter of the City and County of San Francisco (hereafter Charter section 5.101) . . . . Charter section 5.101 has preempted . . . .
Santa Monica City Charter (hereafter Charter) . . . . Charter section 1903 (b) provides . . . .

(See *ante,* § 31 for capitalization style.)

Where the enactment cited is not in force at the time of citation it then becomes necessary to specify pertinent dates. (See *ante,* § 39 and *post,* § 122.)

# C. California Legislative and Governmental Materials

§ 54. **In General.**—Appellate courts presented with statutory interpretation issues increasingly are citing to a wide variety of legislative and governmental materials.* Unfortunately comprehensive collections

---

*For a detailed description of these sources, where they can be located and examples of appellate court reliance on them, see Henke, California Law Guide (2d ed. 1976 & ann. cum. supp.) chapter 4, California Legislative Analysis & Intent. See also White, *Sources of Legislative Intent in California* (1972) 3 Pacific L.J. 63; Snyder, *Legislative Source Materials in the California State Archives* (Spring 1971) 66 Notes of California Libraries 363; Kenyon, Locating Legislative Intent by Extrinsic Aids (1966) California State Library, Law Library Paper No. 13; and Note, *California Legislative Materials* (1952) 4 Stan.L.Rev. 367.

of these materials are scarce and in many instances the available documents are not well organized in the publications containing them. It is necessary, at a minimum, to provide an accurate description of the material cited, the body or person responsible for it and pertinent dates. It is desirable to cite to popular secondary publications in addition to the primary source.

**§ 55. Legislative Bills.**—Designate the house of introduction, number assigned, year and session.

**(a) Pre-January 8, 1973, Bills.**—Until the legislative session which commenced on January 8, 1973, a regular legislative session was for a single year. Bills were numbered consecutively through the session. Bills introduced during extraordinary sessions were numbered independently of the regular session. Citation forms are:

Section 1 of Senate Bill No. 176, 1972 Regular Session, provides, . . .
(Sen. Bill No. 176 (1972 Reg. Sess.) § 1.)
Section 4 of Assembly Bill No. 20, 1971 First Extraordinary Session, contains . . . .
(Assem. Bill No. 20 (1971 First Ex. Sess.) § 4.)

**(b) Bills Introduced January 8, 1973, and After.**—Regular legislative sessions formerly held annually are now two-year sessions. (See *ante,* § 42.) The first regular session under the new two-year term was for the slightly shortened period of January 8, 1973, to November 30, 1974. Thereafter each session convenes on the first Monday in December of even-numbered years and adjourns on November 30 of the following even-numbered year. Bills introduced into the Legislature have a life through the end of the session and are numbered consecutively for the two-year period. The citation should note the two-year session span, e.g.,

(Sen. Bill No. 123 (1973–1974 Reg. Sess.) § 1.)
(Assem. Bill No. 123 (1985–1986 Reg. Sess.) § 1.)

**(c) Subsequent History of Bill.**—References to legislative action following a bill's introduction should specify (in addition to the bill's house of introduction, number assigned, year and session) the action taken, its source and date, e.g.,

Senate Bill No. 18, 1972 Regular Session, was amended by the Assembly on May 25, 1972, to include . . . .
(Assem. Amend. to Sen. Bill No. 18 (1972 Reg. Sess.) May 25, 1972.)
(Sen. Amend. to Assem. Bill No. 1 (1985–1986 Reg. Sess.) June 12, 1985.)
(Assem. Office of Research, 3d reading analysis of Assem. Bill No. 20 (1983–1984 Reg. Sess.).)
(Sen. Com. on Judiciary, Analysis of Sen. Bill No. 1827 (1983–1984 Reg. Sess.) as amended Mar. 26, 1984.)
(Sen. Bill No. 958 approved by Governor, Sept. 30, 1981, Sen. Final Hist. (1981–1982 Reg. Sess.) p. 598.)
(Assem. Bill No. 3644, 1st reading Feb. 17, 1984, 2 Assem. Final Hist. (1983–1984 Reg. Sess.) p. 2220.)

## § 56. Constitutional Amendments Proposed by Legislature.—

Citational style is analogous to that of bills. (See *ante,* §§ 55,42.)

Where the proposed constitutional amendment is *not adopted* by the Legislature, designate the house of introduction, number assigned, and session, e.g.,

> (Sen. Const. Amend. No. 1 (1972 Reg. Sess.).)
> (Assem. Const. Amend. No. 1 (1985–1986 Reg. Sess.).)*

Constitutional amendments *adopted* by the Legislature are assigned consecutive chapter numbers and will appear in "Statutes and Amendments to the Codes." In addition to noting the house of introduction, number assigned, and session, specify the assigned resolution chapter and page numbers in "Stats.," e.g.,

> Senate Constitutional Amendment No. 20 (Stats. 1972 (Reg. Sess.) res. ch. 110, pp. 3392–3393) provides: . . .
> (Assem. Const. Amend. No. 14, Stats. 1982 (1981–1982 Reg. Sess.) res. ch. 6, pp. 6691–6692.)

(See *ante,* § 39 for citation of repealed, new, recently amended or transferred sections of the California Constitution.)

## § 57. Legislative Resolutions.—

Citational treatment is analogous to that of bills. (See *ante,* § 55.) Designate house of introduction, number assigned, year and session, e.g.,

> (Sen. Res. No. 1 (1972 Reg. Sess.).)
> (Assem. Res. No. 1 (1985–1986 Reg. Sess.).)*

Adopted concurrent and joint resolutions are assigned resolution chapter numbers and are published in "Statutes and Amendments to the Codes" and should be cited to that source, e.g.,

> (Sen. Joint Res. No. 1, Stats. 1974 (1973–1974 Reg. Sess.) res. ch. 1, pp. 1–2.)
> Senate Concurrent Resolution No. 1 (Stats. 1970 (Reg. Sess.) res. ch. 1, p. 3465) provides . . . .
> (Assem. Conc. Res. No. 8, Stats. 1970 (Reg. Sess.) res. ch. 3, pp. 3475–3476.)
> (Assem. Joint Res. No. 66, Stats. 1982 (1981–1982 Reg. Sess.) res. ch. 1, pp. 6687–6688.)

## § 58. Legislative Committee and Interim Committee Reports.

> See Senate Permanent Factfinding Committee Report on Natural Resources, Geothermal Resources, section 1, page 9, Appendix to Senate Journal (1967 Reg. Sess.).
> (See Sen. Permanent Factfinding Com. Rep. on Natural Resources, Geothermal Resources, § 1, p. 9, Appen. to Sen. J. (1967 Reg. Sess.).)
> See volume 27, number 2 of the Reports of the Assembly Interim Committee (1961–1963) Constitutional Amendments, part ii (Jan. 7, 1963) page 26, 2 Appendix to Journal of the Assembly (1963 Reg. Sess.).

---

*By reason of California Constitution, article IV, section 3, legislative sessions after the 1972 session are for two-year periods. (See *ante,* §§ 42, 55 (b).)

(27 Assem. Interim Com. Rep. (1961–1963) No. 2, Const. Amends., part ii (Jan. 7, 1963) p. 26, 2 Appen. to Assem. J. (1963 Reg. Sess.).)

(See 22 Assem. Interim Com. Rep. (1961–1963) No. 3, Crim. Procedure, p. 157, 2 Appen. to Assem. J. (1963 Reg. Sess.) hereafter cited as Assem. Com. Rep.)

(26 Assem. Interim Com. Rep. No. 1, Economic and Financial Policies for State Water Projects (Feb. 1, 1960) pp. 5, 30.)

(See Sen. Com. Rep. on Governmental Efficiency, Welfare in Cal. (1970) pp. 98–99.)

See Hearings on Senate Bill No. 1, before the California Senate Committee on the Judiciary (1960) page 9 (1 Sen. J. Appen. (1961)).

Note that where the report is published in the Senate or Assembly Journals that source is cited.

## § 59. Legislative Journals; Governor's Messages.

### (a) Legislative Journals.

(4 Assem. J. (1959 Reg. Sess.) pp. 5922–5923.)

(1 Sen. J. (1967 Reg. Sess.) p. 863.)

(1 Assem. J. (1983–1984 Reg. Sess.) p. 1.)

See the opinion of the Legislative Counsel relative to retirement, June 15, 1959, 4 Assembly Journal, 1959 Regular Session, pages 5922–5923.

(Select Committee on Campus Disturbances, Rep. (1969) Appen. to Assem. J. (1969 Reg. Sess.) p. 2.)

(See *ante,* § 58 for additional illustrations.)

### (b) Governor's Messages, Executive Orders.

(Governor's Budget Message to Leg. (Feb. 3, 1970) 1 Assem. J. (1970 Reg. Sess.) p. 423.)

(Governor's Budget Message to Leg. (Jan. 10, 1981) 1 Assem. J. (1981–1982 Reg. Sess.) p. 213.)

(Governor's Veto Message to Assem. on Assem. Bill No. 1941 (Sept. 4, 1969) 4 Assem. J. (1969 Reg. Sess.) p. 8362.)

(Governor's Recommendation to Assem. and Sen. that Assem. Bill No. 18 be favorably considered (Mar. 9, 1970) 1 Assem. J. (1970 Reg. Sess.) p. 1512.)

See Governor's Executive Order No. D–44–85 (extension of state employee early retirement program) March 22, 1985.

(Governor's Exec. Order No. D–45–85 [investment restrictions, S. Africa] Sept. 17, 1985.)

(See also addresses *post,* §§ 117 (e), 118, 124.)

## § 60. Reports of Governmental Departments, Agencies, etc.

(Cal. Dept. Ed., Cal. Pub. Schs., Selected Statistics 1968–1969 (1970) table IV-11, pp. 90–91.)

(Cal. Dept. Ed., Recommendations on Pub. Sch. Support (1967) p. 69.)

(Rep. to Leg. Pursuant to Lab. Code, § 4753, by Stanley Mosk, Atty. Gen. (Jan. 1959) p. 24.)

(See Cal. Water Plan, Dept. Wat. Resources Bull. No. 3 (May 1957) p. 37.)

(Cal. Dept. Justice, Follow-up Study of 1960 Adult Drug Offenders (1968) p. 2.)

(Cal. Controller, Ann. Rep. of Fin. Transactions Concerning Cal. Cities (1966–1967) p. XI.)

(Health & Welf. Agency, Dept. Social Services, Manual of Policy & Proc., Eligibility & Assistance Standards, std. 40–181.22 [hereafter E. & A. Standards].)

(Accord, Final Rep., Cal. Sexual Deviation Research (Dept. Mental Hygiene, 1954) p. 91.)

(See also *ante,* § 59, and *post,* §§ 61, 62, 118, 126.)

## § 61. Legislative Counsel—Opinions and Digests.

### (a) Opinions.

> The opinion of the Legislative Counsel of California No. 15193 filed July 21, 1969, entitled Reapportionment, at page 3, notes . . . .
> (Ops. Cal. Legis. Counsel, No. 15193 (July 21, 1969) Reapportionment, p. 3.)

If the opinion is published in a legislative journal the author should additionally cite to that source. The style then is:

> (See Ops. Cal. Legis. Counsel, No. 15616 (June 30, 1982) Mobilehome Residency Law (Assem. Bill No. 2429) 10 Assem. J. (1981–1982 Reg. Sess.) pp. 17855–17856.)

**(b) Digests.**—Identify document that is digested and note legislative session, e.g.,

> The Legislative Counsel's Digest of Senate Bill No. 176 (1972 Reg. Sess.) states . . . .
> (Legis. Counsel's Dig., Sen. Conc. Res. No. 4 (1985–1986 First Ex. Sess.).)

If the digest cited appears in the Summary Digest section of "Statutes and Amendments to the Codes" and the author wishes to note this source the following styles are appropriate:

> The Legislative Counsel's Digest of Assembly Bill No. 307 (3 Stats. 1971 (Reg. Sess.) Summary Dig., p. 11), notes . . . .
> (See Legis. Counsel's Dig., Sen. Bill No. 1870, 6 Stats. 1982 (Reg. Sess.) Summary Dig., p. 430.)
> (See Legis. Counsel's Dig., Assem. Bill No. 1074, 4 Stats. 1981 (Reg. Sess.) Summary Dig., p. 361.)

## § 62. Law Revision Commission Reports, Comments and Miscellaneous Papers.

> (Recommendations Relating to Sovereign Immunity, No. 1, Tort Liability of Public Entities and Public Employers (Jan. 1963) 4 Cal. Law Revision Com. Rep. (1963) p. 817.)
> (17 Cal. Law Revision Com. Rep. (Sept. 1983) pp. 711–714.)
> (Tent. Recommendation and Study Relating to the Uniform Rules of Evidence, art. VIII, Hearsay Evidence (Aug. 1962) 6 Cal. Law Revision Com. Rep. (1964) appen. pp. 495–496.)
> (See Recommendations Relating to Statutory Forms of Durable Powers of Attorney (Sept. 1983) 17 Cal. Law Revision Com. Rep. (1984) p. 710 et seq.)
> See California Law Revision Commission Comment, Deering's Annotated Code of Civil Procedure section 704.995 (1985 pocket supp.) page 38.
> (See Cal. Law Revision Com. com., Deering's Ann. Code Civ. Proc., § 704. 995 (1985 pocket supp.) p. 38.)

(See also *ante,* § 50.)

## § 63. Ballot Pamphlets—Measures and Arguments to the Voters.

> (Ballot Pamp., Proposed Amends. to Cal. Const. with arguments to voters, Gen. Elec. (Nov. 8, 1966) p. 8.)

(Ballot Pamp., Proposed Amends. to Cal. Const. with arguments to voters, Gen.
Elec. (Nov. 8, 1966), argument in favor of Prop. 1, p. 10.)
See ballot pamphlet containing proposed amendments to the California Constitu-
tion and arguments to the electors for the General Election, November 8, 1966,
at page 8. . . .
(Ballot Pamp., argument in favor of Sen. Const. Amend. No. 3 as presented to
the voters, Gen. Elec. (Nov. 12, 1968).)
(See Legislative Counsel's Cost Analysis, Ballot Pamp., Proposed Amend. to Cal.
Const., Tax and Expenditure Limitations, Special Statewide Elec. (Nov. 6,
1973) pp. 3–5.)
See the Ballot Pamphlet analysis of Proposition 32 by the Legislative Analyst as
presented to the voters for the General Election of November 6, 1984.

# D. Rules of Court; Bar, Judiciary and Judicial Council Sources

## § 64. California Rules of Court

California Rules of Court, rule 224
(Cal. Rules of Court, rule 976.)
(Cal. Rules of Court, rules 106, 976 (c) & 107 (b).)
See Advisory Committee Comment, California Rules of Court, rule 28 (e)(2) . . . .
(See Advisory Com. Comment, Cal. Rules of Court, rule 28 (e)(2).)
(See Draftsman's note, Cal. Rules of Court, rule 27(a).)

Use of "subdivision" in the text or "subd." in parentheses should be
avoided.

## § 64.1. Special Rules, Policies and Practices Originating From Specific Appellate Courts.

—Designate the court of origin, divi-
sion if applicable, the sequential letter or number assigned and an identifying description of the rule, policy or practice cited. These sources
are normally available in publications such as Deering's and West's Annotated Codes (Rules), Deering's California Civil Practice Codes (desk
top ed.) and West's California Rules of Court (desk copy), and a parallel
citation to one of them is recommended.

(Ct. App., First App. Dist., Policy Statement A [Deering's Cal. Civ. Practice
Codes (1985 desk top ed.) p. 1143].)
(Ct. App., Third App. Dist., Settlement Conference Proc. Rules, rule 10 [West's
Cal. Rules of Court (1985 desk copy) p. 469.])
(Cal. Supreme Ct., Internal Operating Practices & Proc., XI A, Disqualification
of Justices.)
(Ct. App., Second App. Dist., Div. 4, Internal Practices, IV, Oral Argument.)

## § 64.2. Standards of Judicial Administration

(Cal. Standards Jud. Admin., § 4.5 [Deering's Cal. Ann. Codes, Rules (Appen.)
(1980 ed.) pp. 495-496].)
Section 4.5, California Standards of Judicial Administration provides . . . .
(See §§ 6.5 & 9, Cal. Standards Jud. Admin.)

(See also *ante,* § 64.1 for use of parallel citations.)

## § 64.3.  California Code of Judicial Conduct.

(Cal. Code Jud. Conduct, canon 2B [Deering's Cal. Ann. Codes, Rules (Appen.) (1980 ed.) p. 532; 23 West's Cal. Codes Ann. Rules, pt. 2 (1981 ed.) p. 459].)

. . . canon 3 of the California Code of Judicial Conduct effective January 1, 1975, . . .

(Cal. Code Jud. Conduct, canon 7A(1)(c).)

(Former Cal. Canons of Jud. Ethics, canon 24.)

(See also *ante,* § 64.1 for use of parallel citation.)

## § 65.  Judicial Council Reports and Studies.

(Judicial Council of Cal., Ann. Rep. (1984) Judicial Statistics, Supreme Court, Summary of Filings and Business Transacted, table T-5, p. 97.)

(Judicial Council of Cal., Ann. Rep. (1984) p. 234.)

(Judicial Council of Cal., 19th Biennial Rep. (1963) Fees in Appellate Courts, pt. I, ch. 10, p. 45.)

The Judicial Council of California, in its Proceedings of the First Sentencing Institute for Superior Court Judges (1965) pages 105–106 (45 Cal. Rptr. appen.), advises . . . .

(Rep. Judicial Council of Cal. Special Com. on Jurisdiction (Nov. 2, 1968) pp. 35–36.)

(Advisory Committee Rep. for Judicial Council of Cal., Comparative Analysis of ABA Min. Stds. for Crim. Justice with Cal. Law (1974), at pp. 73–74.)

(See Judicial Council of Cal., Study of the Role of Arbitration in the Jud. Process (1973) pp. 71–73.)

The Judicial Council of California, in its Report and Recommendation on the Effectiveness of Judicial Arbitration (1983), at page 6, comments . . . .

(See Judicial Council of Cal., Rep. and Recommendation on Effectiveness of Judicial Arbitration (1983) pp. 1–3.)

(See Judicial Council of Cal., Rep. and Recommendation of the Advisory Com. to Implement Prop. 32 (1985) p. 34.)

## § 66.  State Bar Rules, Standards and Opinions.—If the context does not apprise the reader of the origin of the rule cited, i.e., California State Bar, American Bar Association, etc., such designation must be provided in the citation. Where, however, the source is obvious, a shortened reference is sufficient.*

### (a)  Rules of Professional Conduct.

(Former rule 9, Rules Prof. Conduct.)

(Rules Prof. Conduct, rule 2-104 (D)(2) (a).)

---

* It is suggested that the first citation of a State Bar rule provide parallel citations to Deering's California Codes Annotated or West's Annotated California Codes, which are convenient sources of some of these otherwise not commonly available rules, e.g.:

(Rules Regulating Admission to Practice Law, rules XI, XII [Deering's Cal. Codes Ann. Rules (State Bar) (1980 ed., 1985 cum. supp.) pp. 340–341].) [or] [23 West's Cal. Codes Ann. Rules, pt. 2 (1981 ed., 1985 cum. supp.) pp. 202–204].)

State Bar materials that are not published as "Rules" in the annotated code series of private publishers, but appear in the State Bar's voluminous looseleaf California Compendium on Professional Responsibility, may be cited to the latter, e.g.:

(See Cal. Compendium on Prof. Responsibility, pt. II, State Bar Formal Opn. No. 1981–63, p. 4.)

(Rule 5-104, Rules Prof. Conduct of State Bar.)
(Rule 2-111 (A) (4) (a), Rules Prof. Conduct of State Bar.)
. . . rule 6-101 of the Rules of Professional Conduct . . . .
. . . rule 7-106 (A) of the State Bar Rules of Professional Conduct . . . .
Former rule 2-104 (E) (2) (a) (ii) of the Rules of Professional Conduct of the State Bar, repealed 1979 . . . .

**(b) Rules of Procedure of the State Bar.**
(Rules Proc. of State Bar, rule 106.)
. . . rule 644 of the Rules of Procedure of the State Bar . . . .
(Rule 113 (e), Rules Proc. of State Bar.)
Rule 670 et seq. of the Rules of Procedure of the State Bar (adopted pursuant to Bus. & Prof. Code, § 6140.5) require . . . .

**(c) Rules of Practice of the State Bar Court.**
(State Bar Court Rules, rule 1110 (a).)

**(d) Rules Regulating Admission to Practice Law.**
Rule IV, section 41 (3) (b) (i) of the Rules of the State Bar Regulating Admission to Practice Law . . . .
(Rules Regulating Admission to Practice Law, rules II, § 22 & X, § 101.)
(See rule IV, § 41, Rules Regulating Admission to Practice Law.)
Under rule X, section 102 (a), Rules Regulating Admission to Practice Law . . . .

**(e) Law Corporation Rules of the State Bar.**
(State Bar Law Corp. Rules, rule IV A (5).)

**(f) Rules and Regulations of the California Board of Legal Specialization.**
(Rules & Regs. of the Cal. Bd. of Legal Specialization, § 3a (2).)

**(g) Guidelines and Minimum Standards for the Operation of Mandatory Fee Arbitration Programs.**
(Guidelines & Min. Standards for Oper. of Mand. Fee Arbitration Programs, III 5.)

**(h) Rules and Regulations of the State Bar of California.**
(Rules and Regs. of State Bar, art. VI, § 3 A.)

**(i) Rules for Practical Training of Law Students.**
(State Bar Rules for Pract. Training of Law Students, rule V F (1).)

**(j) Minimum Standards for a Lawyer Referral Service in California.**
(Min. Standards for Lawyer Referral Service in Cal., std. 5.2.)

(See also *ante,* §§ 19, 33.)

## § 67. American Bar Association Codes, Standards and Opinions.

(ABA Model Code Prof. Responsibility, EC 6–3, 6–4.)
The American Bar Association's Model Code of Professional Responsibility, Preamble and Preliminary Statement and Ethical Considerations EC 1–5, EC 9–1 and EC 9–6 recommend . . . .
American Bar Association, Model Code of Professional Responsibility (hereafter ABA Code) . . . . [or] (hereafter the CPR) . . . . The CPR concerns itself . . . .
(ABA Model Code Prof. Responsibility, DR 6–101 (A) (2).)
(ABA Model Code Prof. Responsibility, EC 2–2, note 5.)
(ABA Model Code Prof. Responsibility, DR 7–102 (A) (1),(2).)
(ABA Model Code Prof. Responsibility, canon 7.)

(ABA Model Rules Prof. Conduct, rule 8.3.)
Rule 8.3 of the American Bar Association, Model Rules of Professional Conduct (hereinafter the RPC) . . . . The RPC embraces . . . .
(ABA Project on Standards for Criminal Justice, Stds. Relating to Probation (Approved Draft 1970) std. 2.2.)
(3 ABA Standards for Criminal Justice, std. 18–22 (2d ed.1980) p. 18.57.)
Former Canons of Ethics of the American Bar Association . . . . (Canon 29.)
The American Bar Association's Committee on Professional Ethics in its informal opinion No. 528 (1962) notes . . . .
(ABA Committee on Prof. Ethics, opn. No. 105 (1934).)

## E. Case Reports

§ **68. California Official Reports.**—Opinions of the Supreme Court are published in California Reports, now in its third series, and are cited as Cal.3d, Cal.2d, or Cal.

*People* v. *Noab* (1971) 5 Cal.3d 469
*Linsk* v. *Linsk* (1969) 70 Cal.2d 272
*Arnold* v. *Hopkins* (1928) 203 Cal. 553

Opinions of the Courts of Appeal are published in the California Appellate Reports, now in its third series, and are cited as Cal.App.3d, Cal.App.2d, or Cal.App.

*Carlisle* v. *Kanaywer* (1972) 24 Cal.App.3d 587
*Redsted* v. *Weiss* (1945) 71 Cal.App.2d 660
*People* v. *Barbera* (1926) 78 Cal.App. 277

Opinions of the appellate departments of the superior courts likewise appear in the California Appellate Reports and are reported in a separate section or supplement following the Court of Appeal opinions, and a citation to them carries the additional abbreviation "Supp."

*People* v. *Foretich* (1970) 14 Cal.App.3d Supp. 6, 10
*Helgeson* v. *Farmers Ins. Exchange* (1953) 116 Cal.App.2d Supp. 925
*People* v. *Cardas* (1933) 137 Cal.App.Supp. 788

(See *post,* § 71 for advance sheet citation of appellate department decisions.)

**Uniform Pagination**—Under a system of uniform pagination adopted for the third series of the Official Reports, the advance sheets carry the identical pagination used in the later-published bound volumes. However, since some of the opinions appearing in the advance sheets are superseded, modified, qualified by later Supreme Court review, republished at another page or in another volume, ordered by the Supreme Court not to be published in the bound volume, etc., authors should consult the Cumulative Subsequent History Table at the back of the *most recent* advance pamphlet prior to citing an advance sheet opinion. In some situations a call to the clerk will be necessary.

(See *post,* § 69 for citation of preadvance sheet opinions, §§ 88–88.5 for styles of noting subsequent history and § 90 for parallel citation styles.)

## § 69. Preadvance Sheet Citations.

**§ 69. Preadvance Sheet Citations.**—Where an advance sheet citation is not available (normally the first 20 to 25 days following the filing of an opinion), note the date of filing and the docket number, and use blanks to permit later insertion of volume and page, e.g.,

*(A* v. *B* (May 19, 1987, S012345) _____ Cal.3d _____ .)*
*(C* v. *D* (June 10, 1985, B012345) _____ Cal.App.3d _____ .)*
*(E* v. *F* (July 10, 1988, Civ.A. No. 12345, L.A. County) _____ Cal.App.3d Supp. _____ .)*

When volume and page are thereafter available, the publisher will automatically adjust the citation to normal style, i.e., *(A* v. *B* (1986) 200 Cal.3d 100).

**Point Page References.**—Where the citation involves a point page reference in addition to the inception page, a referral to the point page or pages in the typed opinion is necessary to assist the reader and the publisher in accurately identifying the material cited.

**(a) Reference in brackets:**

*(A* v. *B* (May 19, 1987, S012345) _____ Cal.3d _____ , _____ - _____ [typed opn. pp. 8–12].)

**(b) Reference by footnote:**

*(C* v. *D* (June 30, 1985, C011234) _____ Cal.App.3d _____ , _____ - _____ .)*

_____
* Typed opinion pages 12–14.

When the volume and pages are available the citation will be adjusted to normal style.

## § 70. California Unreported Cases.

**§ 70. California Unreported Cases.**—The abbreviation Cal. Unrep. is used in citing the collection of early opinions that were omitted from the Official Reports but subsequently published as the California Unreported Cases.

*Hughes* v. *Mendocino County* (1884) 2 Cal.Unrep. 333
*(Hughes* v. *Mendocino County* (1884) 2 Cal.Unrep. 333.)

(See also *post,* § 75.)

## § 71. Appellate Department Opinions—Advance Sheets.

**§ 71. Appellate Department Opinions—Advance Sheets.**—Opinions of the appellate departments of the superior court are paged independently from the Court of Appeal opinions and pagination for

_____
* New docket-number prefixes introduced, or to be introduced, for the appellate court computer information systems are as follows: Substituting for the Supreme Court prefixes Crim., S.F., L.A., and Sac. is the single prefix S (operative Feb. 1987). Substituting for the prefixes for Court of Appeal docket numbers (1 Crim., 2 Civ., etc.) are the following prefixes, making no distinction between civil and criminal cases: A for the First District; B for the Second District; C for the Third District; D for the Fourth District, Division One, San Diego; E for the Fourth District, Division Two, San Bernardino; G for the Fourth District, Division Three, Santa Ana; F for the Fifth District; and H for the Sixth District. In all cases, the prefixes are followed by six digits, starting at 000001. (See also *post,* §§ 83.3–88.5, 95.)

them is not noted on the spine of advance pamphlets. Therefore, prior to publication of the bound volume, a citation to an opinion of an appellate department should indicate the pamphlet number in which the opinion appears as well as the volume and page numbers so that the reader will be saved a time-consuming search through all the pamphlets of the cited volume, e.g.,

*People* v. *Terry* (1971) 14 Cal.App.3d Supp. 1, pamphlet No. 4.
(*People* v. *Terry* (1971) 14 Cal.App.3d Supp. 1, pamp. No. 4.)

The publisher will automatically adjust the citation for bound volume publication, i.e., *People* v. *Terry* (1971) 14 Cal.App.3d Supp. 1.

(See also latest advance sheet's Multivolume Cumulative Table of Cases and *ante,* § 68.)

### § 72. Public Utilities Commission and California Railroad Commission Decisions.

—The California Railroad Commission by the constitutional amendment of November 5, 1946, was continued in existence as the Public Utilities Commission. Volumes 1 through 46 of the decisions of this commission are cited as "C.R.C." Volume 47 and following, being decisions of the Public Utilities Commission, are cited as "Cal.P.U.C." Advance sheets carry the same pagination as the bound volume.

*Matter of Truck Owners' Association* (1938) 41 C.R.C. 184
*Packard* v. *P.T. & T. Co.* (1970) 71 Cal.P.U.C. 469, 471
*CAUSE* v. *P.T. & T. Co.* (1981) 5 Cal.P.U.C.2d 745, 748

Preadvance sheet opinions are cited as:

(*Pacific Telephone & Telegraph Co.* (1985) _____ Cal.P.U.C.2d _____ , _____ (Dec. No. 83162, p. 6).)

When the volume and page are thereafter available the citation is adjusted to normal style by the publisher.

Unpublished opinions are cited as:

(*Smith Truck Service* (June 10, 1980) Dec. No. 12345, p. 8.)

### § 72.1. Agricultural Labor Relations Board Decisions.

—These decisions are numbered sequentially and are cited as:

(*O.P. Murphy* (Mar. 17, 1977) 3 ALRB No. 26, p. 2.)

### § 72.2. Public Employment Relations Board Decisions.

—Decisions of the Public Employment Relations Board are distributed, on filing, in typescript. Thereafter, they are annotated and appear in the unofficial Public Employee Reporter (Cal. ed.), which, because of its wider distribution, should be used as a parallel citation:

(*Wilson* v. *University of California* (Oct. 18, 1984) PERB Dec. No. 420–H, at p. 21 [8 PERC ¶ 15196, at p. 910].)

### § 73. Attorney General Opinions.

—Opinions of the California Attorney General are cited by volume, page and year. The year is placed in parentheses and follows the page reference. Advance sheets carry the same pagination as the bound volume.

> These arguments are advanced in *Arrest,* 43 Ops.Cal.Atty.Gen. 288 (1964).
> (See also 32 Ops.Cal.Atty.Gen. 75, 76 (1958).)
> (*Revocation of Parole,* 66 Ops.Cal.Atty.Gen. 239, 240 (1983).)
> *Open Meeting Requirements,* 66 Ops.Cal.Atty.Gen. 252, 253 (1983) influences our holding.

**Preadvance pamphlet opinions** are cited as:

> (_____ Ops.Cal.Atty.Gen. _____ (Sept. 4, 1986).)
> (*Issuing of Bench Warrant,* _____ Ops.Cal.Atty.Gen. _____ , _____ (Sept. 4, 1986) [filed opn. p. 4].)

When the volume and page are thereafter available the citation is adjusted to normal style by the publisher.

**Indexed Letters:**

These letters of advice to the Attorney General's clients are occasionally cited. After 1980 the "indexed letter" classification system used by the Attorney General for identification of these documents was discontinued. Many of the documents prepared after 1980 that are available to the public are now published as Attorney General opinions and are so cited. The style for citation of pre-1980 letters is:

> (Cal. Atty. Gen., Indexed Letter, No. IL 76–133 (July 21, 1976).)

## § 74.  California Compensation Decisions.

—Opinions of the California Workers' Compensation Appeals Board[1] and its predecessor the Industrial Accident Commission of California and some of the decisions of a few other state tribunals are reported in "Decisions of the Industrial Accident Commission of California" and its successor publication "California Compensation Cases." Decisions from 1911 through 1935 are cited to the former while opinions following 1935 are cited to the latter.

> *Rabin* v. *Metzger* (1934) 20 I.A.C. 20
> *Pennington* v. *Workmen's Comp. Appeals Bd.* (1971) 36 Cal.Comp.Cases 559

In citing summaries of workers' compensation cases (such as panel decisions denying reconsideration) that do not appear in California Compensation Cases but are published in the unofficial California Workers' Compensation Reporter, the relevant docket number should be included:

> (*Mosqueda* v. *Lear Siegler, Inc.* (1983) 81 L.A. 863–871, 11 Cal. Workers' Comp. Rptr. 252.)

## § 75.  Miscellaneous California Reports.

—Cite as illustrated.

Coffey's Probate Decisions:

> *Estate of Emeric* (1890) 5 Coffey's Prob. Dec. 286

---

[1] As a result of the passage of Proposition 11 at the General Election of November 5, 1974, section 21 of article XX of the California Constitution was amended to recast the terms of that section to use "workers" or "workers'" where the terms "workmen" and "workmen's" had been previously used.

Labatt's District Court Reports:

*People* v. *Whithurst* (1858) 2 Labatt 178

Myrick's Probate Court Reports:

*Estate of Hite* (1879) Myrick's Prob. Rep. 232

(See also *ante,* § 70.)

**§ 76.  Reports of Other States.**—The preferred citational style includes a reference to the official state report and a parallel citation to the National Reporter System. This preference is applicable to the initial and subsequent citation of the decision. Since many private and public California law libraries do not subscribe to the official reports of all 50 states but do contain West's National Reporter System, point page references to this system's regional reporter are recommended.

(*Englund* v. *Buske* (1971) 160 Conn. 327, 328 [278 A.2d 815, 816].)
*Zidek* v. *West Penn Power Co.* (1941) 145 Pa.Super. 103, 104 [20 A.2d 810, 811] assists our analysis.
(*People* v. *Brittain* (1972) 52 Ill.2d 91, 92 [284 N.E.2d 632, 633].)
(See *People* v. *Brittain, supra,* 52 Ill.2d at p. 92 [284 N.E.2d at p. 633].)

Where a state's official reports have been discontinued or where the National Reporter series has become the state's official reports, cite to the appropriate regional reporter noting within parentheses the state, and the authoring state court if not one of last resort.

(*State Department of Highways* v. *Johns* (Alaska 1967) 422 P.2d 855.)
(*Mutual Finance Co.* v. *Martin* (Fla. 1953) 63 So.2d 649.)
(*English* v. *State* (Okla.App. 1969) 462 P.2d 275.)
(*Lotspeich* v. *Chance Vought Aircraft* (Tex.Civ.App. 1963) 369 S.W.2d 705.)

Opinion authors (but not authors of briefs) may omit parallel citations since by contract they are provided by the publisher of the Official Reports. If an opinion author elects to cite only to the National Reporter System he must indicate the state, and the court if not one of last resort. A list of common abbreviations for lower appellate courts is found in A Uniform System of Citation (popularly known as the Harvard Style Manual) (14th ed. 1986) at pages 45–47. The publisher of California's Official Reports will automatically add the official state report citation and adjust the citation to normal style for advance sheet publication.

(See also *ante,* § 69 for the style of citing preadvance sheet decisions, *post,* § 88 for the notation of subsequent history, § 95 for pending case citations and § 90 for the style of noting parallel citations.)

**§ 77.  Abbreviations—State and Regional Reports.**

(a) **State Reports.**—In citations abbreviate all states and territories except Alaska, Hawaii, Idaho, Iowa, Ohio and Utah.

| | | | | | |
|---|---|---|---|---|---|
| Ala. | Colo. | Fla. | Kan. | Md. | Miss. |
| Ariz. | Conn. | Ga. | Ky. | Mass. | Mo. |
| Ark. | Del. | Ill. | La. | Mich. | Mont. |
| Cal. | DC. | Ind. | Me. | Minn. | Neb. |

| Nev. | N.Y. | Ore. | S.C. | Vt. | Wn.App.* |
|------|------|------|------|-----|----------|
| N.H. | N.C. | Pa. | S.D. | Va. | W.Va. |
| N.J. | N.D. | P.R. | Tenn. | Wash. | Wis. |
| N.M. | Okla. | R.I. | Tex. | Wn.2d* | Wyo. |

## (b) National Reporter System.

| | |
|---|---|
| Atlantic Reporter | A. |
| Atlantic Reporter, Second Series | A.2d |
| California Reporter | Cal.Rptr. |
| Federal Reporter | Fed. |
| Federal Reporter, Second Series | F.2d |
| Federal Rules Decisions | F.R.D. |
| Federal Supplement | F.Supp. |
| New York Supplement | N.Y.S. |
| New York Supplement, Second Series | N.Y.S.2d |
| North Eastern Reporter | N.E. |
| North Eastern Reporter, Second Series | N.E.2d |
| North Western Reporter | N.W. |
| North Western Reporter, Second Series | N.W.2d |
| Pacific Reporter | P. |
| Pacific Reporter, Second Series | P.2d |
| South Eastern Reporter | S.E. |
| South Eastern Reporter, Second Series | S.E.2d |
| Southern Reporter | So. |
| Southern Reporter, Second Series | So.2d |
| South Western Reporter | S.W. |
| South Western Reporter, Second Series | S.W.2d |
| Supreme Court Reporter | S.Ct. |

See also A Uniform System of Citation (14th ed. 1986) page 177 et seq. for a comprehensive list of American case reports and their abbreviations. (See also *post,* § 78.)

## § 78.  Early, Renumbered and Reprinted State Reports.—Many

of the early American state reports were initially identified by the name of the reporter of the series with each new reporter renaming and renumbering the volumes he reported. Most jurisdictions have renumbered their reports consecutively or reprinted them sequentially, and citation to the renumbered or reprinted reports alone is sufficient since the designation of a fragmented reporter series is today of little practical benefit.

Where early reports are not renumbered or reprinted, give the reporter designation, year, jurisdiction and page. If the court cited is not of last resort note the authoring court within parentheses. (See also *ante,* § 76. and last par. of § 77.)

> (*Dale* v. *M'Evers* (1823 N.Y.) 2 Cowen 118.)
> (*Hawkins* v. *Johnson* (1832 Ind.) 3 Blackford 46.)

(See *post,* § 80 for the style of citing early United States Supreme Court decisions.)

---

*  By order of the Supreme Court of Washington, March 25, 1940, "Wn.2d" is used for the second series of Washington Reports. Likewise Washington Appellate Reports are cited as "Wn.App." However, the first series of the Washington Reports continues to be cited as "Wash."

**§ 79. Annotated Reports.**—Most annotated reports are cited by volume and page, with the volume number preceding the name of the report, e.g., *Naylor* v. *Conroy* (1957) 67 A.L.R.2d 689. A few, however, are cited by year and letter following the report's name, e.g., *Mastellar* v. *Atkinson* (1915) Ann.Cas. 1917B 502. (For a list of the more frequently cited annotated reports and their abbreviations see *post,* § 110.)

If the intention is to cite only the annotation and not the case see *post,* section 110.

**§ 80. United States Supreme Court Decisions.**

**(a) Opinion Authors.**—An opinion author need cite only to the official reports, i.e., the United States Supreme Court Reports, since by agreement with the California Official Reports publisher parallel citations to the Lawyers' Edition and to the Supreme Court Reporter are furnished for advance sheet and bound volume publication. If an opinion author cites to either the Lawyers' Edition or the Supreme Court Reporter the publisher will automatically substitute the United States Supreme Court Reports citation followed by the unofficial parallel citations in brackets. The contract publisher of the California Official Reports is not required to provide parallel citations for subsequent references to the same decision. However, the present publisher normally cites to the Lawyers' Edition as a parallel for succeeding citations. In some instances the running head title of a United States Supreme Court opinion will differ as between the various reports. The approved style is to use the "official" United States Supreme Court Reports running head and opinion publication copy will be adjusted accordingly.

First citation of Supreme Court decision:

(*Northern Pac. R. Co.* v. *United States* (1958) 356 U.S. 1 [2 L.Ed.2d 545, 78 S.Ct. 514].)

Second citation of decision–different paragraph:

(*Northern Pac. R. Co.* v. *United States, supra,* 356 U.S. 1, 3.)

Second citation—same paragraph with intervening citation:

(*Northern Pac. R. Co.* v. *United States, supra,* at p. 3.)
(*Northern Pac. R. Co., supra,* at p. 3.)

Second citation of decision—same paragraph with no intervening citation: (*Ibid.*) is used when the intent is to repeat the parent citation. (P. 3.), or (At p. 3.), or (*Id.,* at p. 3.) is used, at the author's election, where there is a change of any kind from the parent citation.

(See also *post,* § 92 et seq.)

**(b) Briefs.**

**(1) Bound Volume Citations.**—Lawyers submitting briefs to appellate courts should cite to the official United States Supreme Court

Reports giving parallel citations for the first reference. Subsequent references to the cited opinion need only be to the United States Supreme Court Reports since justices and their staffs can readily locate point page references in the unofficial parallel reports from the official pagination.

(2) **Advance Sheet Citations.**—Lawyers should note all available parallel references to advance sheet citations throughout since the Lawyers' Edition and the Supreme Court Reporter do not provide parallel page references to the official United States Supreme Court Reports for their advance sheet services. (All three services use a uniform pagination system between their advance sheet and bound volume publications.)

(c) **Preadvance Sheet Citations.**—Where advance sheet citations are not available, but the opinion cited has been published in the United States Law Week or some other preadvance sheet publication service, the body of the author's opinion should note the date of filing with blank spaces for the later inclusion of volume and page for the "U.S." reports. A reference in brackets or by footnote cites to the United States Law Week or other publication, e.g.,

(*Liparota* v. *U.S.* (May 13, 1985) _____ U.S. _____ , _____ [53 U.S.L. Week 4530, 4533].)

(*Liparota* v. *U.S.* (May 13, 1985) _____ U.S. _____ , _____ )*

---

*Advance Citation: 53 U.S.L. Week 4530, 4533.

When volume and page are thereafter available the publisher will automatically adjust the citation to normal style for the bound volume edition and delete the footnote or bracketed reference.

Preadvance sheet citations in briefs need note only opinion title, date and the volume and page of the early publication service, e.g.,

(*Walters* v. *National Assn. of Radiation Survivors* (June 28, 1985) 53 U.S.L. Week 4541.)

(*Caldwell* v. *Mississippi* (June 11, 1985) 37 Crim. L. Rptr. 3089.)

(d) **Old Reports.**—Reporters' names are used in the citation of the United States Supreme Court Reports for volumes 1 through 90 U.S. The current form is to carry a parenthetical reference to the reporter and the volume number, e.g.,

(*Buchanan* v. *Alexander* (1846) 45 U.S. (4 How.) 20 [11 L.Ed. 857].)

## § 81. Federal Reports.

(a) **Federal Reporter.**—The Federal Courts Improvement Act of 1982 (Pub. L. No. 97-164 (Apr. 2, 1982) 96 Stat. 25, amended 28 U.S.C. § 1295) established the United States Court of Appeals for the Federal Circuit. The act resulted in the change of some court nomenclature. Commencing with volume 693 F.2d the Federal Reporter has contained cases determined in the United States Courts of Appeals and the Temporary

Emergency Court of Appeals. For a number of years, through volume 692 F.2d, this publication also contained the decisions of the United States Court of Claims and of the United States Court of Customs and Patent Appeals. The equivalent of many of those decisions, e.g., those on appeal from the various boards of contract appeals and the United States Court of International Trade, continue to be reported in the Federal Reporter, but are indexed under and cited to the new United States Court of Appeals, Federal Circuit.

**(1) United States Courts of Appeals:**

(*Alomar* v. *Dwyer* (2d Cir. 1971) 447 F.2d 482.)
(*Baginsky* v. *United States* (Fed. Cir. 1983) 697 F.2d 1970.)
(*McLaughlin* v. *Cheshire* (D.C. Cir. 1982) 676 F.2d 855.)

[1st through 11th, D.C., and Fed. circuits.]

All citations to the Federal Reporter prior to 1912 use the abbreviation Fed., not F.

(*Stewart* v. *Wright* (8th Cir. 1906) 147 Fed. 321.)

**(2) Temporary Emergency Court of Appeals:**

(*Pacific Coast Meat Job. Ass'n, Inc.* v. *Cost of Living Coun.* (T.E.C.A. 1973) 481 F.2d 1388.)

**(3) United States Court of Claims:**

(*Tibbals* v. *United States* (Ct. Cl. 1966) 362 F.2d 266, 269.)

**(4) United States Court of Customs and Patent Appeals:**

(*Application of Winslow* (C.C.P.A. 1966) 365 F.2d 1017.)

**Early Circuit Court Decisions:** Decisions from the old circuit courts, abolished January 1, 1912, use "C.C.," representing circuit court, and the appropriate district and state. States with but one district use "D." after "C.C." with the state, e.g.,

(*Barthet* v. *City of New Orleans* (C.C.E.D.La. 1885) 24 Fed. 563.)
(*United States* v. *Iron Silver Mine Co.* (C.C.D.Colo. 1885) 24 Fed. 568.)

**(b) Federal Supplement.**—(Presently, cases determined in the United States District Courts; Special Court, Regional Rail Reorganization Act; United States Court of International Trade; and rulings of the Judicial Panel on Multidistrict Litigation.) (Until 1980, the Federal Supplement contained decisions of the United States Customs Court.)

**(1) United States District Courts:**

(*Bell* v. *Hongisto* (N.D.Cal. 1972) 346 F.Supp. 1392.)
(*Allied Chemical Corporation* v. *Tug Carville* (E.D.Pa. 1972) 344 F.Supp. 1330.)
(*Beach* v. *KDI Corporation* (D.Del. 1972) 344 F.Supp. 1230.)
(*United States* v. *Liddy* (D.D.C. 1972) 354 F.Supp. 208.)

Note: States with but one district use "D." before the state or before "D.C." for the District of Columbia. In states with more than one district, the origin of the opinion is noted by a geographical prefix, e.g., in the first illustration "N.D." represents the Northern District. Divisions within the districts themselves are not normally cited.

**(2) Special Court, Regional Rail Reorganization Act:**

(*Keeler* v. *Consol. Rail Corp* (Sp.Ct., R.R.R.A. 1984) 582 F.Supp. 1546.)

**(3) United States Court of International Trade:**

(*Siaca* v. *United States* (Ct. Int. Trade 1984) 585 F.Supp. 668.)

**(4) Judicial Panel on Multidistrict Litigation:**

(*In re Career Academy Antitrust Litigation* (J.P.M.L. 1972) 342 F.Supp. 753.)

**(5) United States Customs Court:**

(*General Instrument Corporation* v. *United States* (Cust. Ct. 1973) 359 F.Supp. 1390.)

**(c) Federal Rules Decisions.**—(Presently opinions, decisions and rulings involving the Federal Rules of Civil Procedure and the Federal Rules of Criminal Procedure.)

(*Thompson* v. *Battle* (N.D.Ill. 1971) 54 F.R.D. 222.)

Where a decision is reported in both Federal Rules Decisions and Federal Supplement cite to Federal Supplement. (See *ante*, subd. (b).)

**(d) Federal Cases Cited to Advance Sheets.**—Advance sheet citations correspond to final citations.

**(e) Federal Cases Cited Prior to Advance Sheet Publication.**—Cite to the source that the opinion will be reported in using blank spaces to permit later insertion of volume and page. In addition designate the date of filing and the docket number.

(*Fox* v. *Hare* (5th Cir. July 5, 1989) _____ F.2d_____ [Dock. No. 87–3383].)

(*David* v. *Goliath* (N.D.Ga. Nov. 17, 1988) _____ F.Supp._____ [Dock. No. Civ. A–87–4432].)

(*Lyons* v. *Christian* (E.D.Pa. Mar. 31, 1984) _____ F.R.D. _____ [Dock. No. Civ. 93–4567].)

(*Pole* v. *Star* (N.D.Cal. Jun. 29, 1986) _____ F.Supp._____ [Dock. No. Civ. 85–2899] slip opn. at p. 10.)

The publisher will adjust the citation to standard style when volume and page are thereafter available.

Where a decision is reported in an early publication service such as the United States Law Week use the styles noted in section 80(c) *ante*.

**(f)** Reports of **federal courts not mentioned above,** and of **federal administrative agencies,** are dealt with in A Uniform System of Citation (14th ed. 1986) pages 35–52, 74–76, 173–177. (See also *ante*, § 72–3, and *post*, § 119.)

**§ 82. English Decisions.**—The early English decisions were reported in numerous series usually cited by the name of the reporter. The majority of these early opinions were thereafter collected and reprinted in a series called *English Reports—Full Reprint* consisting of 176 volumes with a two-volume table of cases. Since the early reporter series are not generally available no practical purpose is served in citing to them—a citation to the *English Reports* is sufficient. The notation of date is essential. Usually the report will indicate the court deciding the case. The authoring court designation is optional; if included, it appears within parentheses.

*Shatwell* v. *Hall* (1853) 152 Eng.Rep. 578
*Butter* v. *Ommaney* (1827 Ch.) 38 Eng.Rep. 731

If an opinion was not reprinted in the *English Reports—Full Reprint* then citation is to the particular reporter series that published the decision. Tables of abbreviations for these early reports are available in standard law dictionaries such as Black's, Ballentine's and Bouvier. Where an early decision is dated to a court term or regnal year convert the date to a calendar year.

Most English opinions reported after 1864 appear in a series called *Law Reports.* The series is segmented as to court and date as indicated in the table below which is reproduced by permission of the Harvard Law Review Association:

| | | |
|---|---|---|
| Privy Council | (1865–1875) | L.R. 1 P.C. to L.R. 6 P.C. |
| House of Lords | (1866–1875) | L.R. 1 H.L. to L.R. 7 H.L. |
| | (1875–1890) | 1 App. Cas. to 15 App. Cas. |
| | (1891–date) | [1891] A.C. to date. |
| Queen's and King's | (1865–1875) | L.R. 1 Q.B. to L.R. 10 Q.B. |
| Bench | (1875–1890) | 1 Q.B.D. to 25 Q.B.D. |
| | (1891–1900) | [1891] 1 Q.B. to [1900] 2 Q.B. |
| | (1901–1952) | [1901] 1 K.B. to [1952] 1 K.B. |
| | (1952–date) | [1952] 2 Q.B. to date |
| Common Pleas | (1865–1875) | L.R. 1 C.P. to L.R. 10 C.P. |
| | (1875–1880) | 1 C.P.D. to 5 C.P.D. |
| Exchequer | (1865–1875) | L.R. 1 Ex. to L.R. 10 Ex. |
| | (1875–1880) | 1 Ex. D. to 5 Ex. D. |
| Chancery | (1865–1875) | L.R. 1 Ch. to L.R. 10 Ch. |
| | | L.R. 1 Eq. to L.R. 20 Eq. |
| | (1875–1890) | 1 Ch. D. to 45 Ch. D. |
| | (1891–date) | [1891] 1 Ch. to date |
| Probate | (1865–1875) | L.R. 1 P. & D. to L.R. 3 P. & D. |
| | (1875–1890) | 1 P.D. to 15 P.D. |
| | (1891–date) | [1891] P. to date |
| Admiralty and | (1865–1875) | L.R. 1 Adm. & Eccl. to L.R. 4 |
| Ecclesiastical | | Adm. & Eccl. |
| Cases | | |
| Crown Cases | (1865–1875) | L.R. 1 Cr. Cas. Res. to |
| Reserved | | L.R. 2 Cr. Cas. Res. |
| Lords Appeals— | (1866–1875) | L.R. 1 Sc. & Div. App. to |
| Scotland | | L.R. 2 Sc. & Div. App. |

Note that the use of "L.R." is part of the citation only where noted on the table. It is essential to indicate the year of decision since some series of the *Law Reports* are renumbered each year, e.g.,

*Smith* v. *Penny* (1947) 1 K.B. 230
*Foster* v. *Robinson* (1951) 1 K.B. 149

The reporting of opinions for the *Law Reports* series is somewhat selective. Often a reported opinion not included in the *Law Reports* will be published in the *Weekly Law Reports* (1953– _____ ). The *Weekly Law Reports* is in some ways analogous to an advance sheet service and is cited as:

*Floyd* v. *Bush* (1953) 1 W.L.R. 242

Where an opinion relied upon does not appear in the *Law Reports* series or *Weekly Law Reports* cite to its publication source, often *Law Times Reports* (1859–1947), *Times Law Reports* (1884–1952), *All England Reports* (1936– _____ ) or *Law Journal Reports* (dates dependent upon court).

(*Blackwell* v. *Blackwell* (1920) 123 L.T.R. 175.)
(*Speyer Brothers* v. *Rodrigues* (1917) 34 T.L.R. 89.)
(*Keeling* v. *Pearl Assurance Co., Ltd.* (1923) All E.R. 307.)
(*Phillips* v. *Jones* (1850) 19 L.J.Q.B. 374.)

Where a decision date differs in year from the publication date of the volume in which it appears and where the volume is identified by year, note the volume date in brackets following the citation.

(*Blyth* v. *Fladgate* (1890) 1 Ch. 337 [1891].)

For the citation of reports not covered and for other examples, see A Uniform System of Citation (14th ed. 1986) pages 153–157.

§ **83. Other Nations' Reports.**—Cite to the official or primary source and, where available, parallel publications. Notation of date and jurisdiction within parentheses is essential. (For a listing of foreign reports and citation illustrations, see generally A Uniform System of Citation (14th ed. 1986) p. 157 et seq.)

(*Bouley* v. *Rochambeau* (1963 Fr.) D. Jur. 555.)

# F. General Rules of Citation

§ **84. Dating of Opinions.**—Denote the date of all opinions cited, since this information is almost always significant to the reader. The date is placed immediately after the case name within parentheses and without a comma preceding or following the parentheses.

*People* v. *Noah* (1971) 5 Cal.3d 469
*People* v. *Cardas* (1933) 137 Cal.App.Supp. 788
*Avery* v. *Midland* (1968) 390 U.S. 474
*Spurgeon* v. *Mission State Bank* (8th Cir. 1945) 151 F.2d 702
*McInnis* v. *Shapiro* (N.D.Ill. 1968) 293 F.Supp. 327
*Gressler* v. *New York Life Ins. Co.* (Utah 1945) 163 P.2d 324
*English* v. *State* (Okla.App. 1969) 462 P.2d 275
*Packard* v. *P.T.&T. Co.* (1970) 71 Cal.P.U.C. 469
*Bridges* v. *Robinson* (1959) 24 Cal.Comp.Cases 59

**Preadvance sheet citations.**—Indicate the day, month, and year of filing, and docket number to facilitate location of the opinion since volume and page numbers are not then available.
(See *ante,* §§ 69, 80(c), 81(e).)

**§ 85. Citation of Opinion in Same Volume and Citation of Companion Cases.**—When an opinion author cites another opinion which is or will be reported in the same volume, regardless of whether it is in the same or another advance sheet pamphlet, the citation should indicate the name of the case, "*ante*" if the cited opinion does or will appear earlier in the volume or "*post*" if it will appear later and the page references where available or blank spaces when not. Do not note "Cal.3d" or "Cal.App.3d," etc. or the volume number. Note that *ante* and *post* are always italicized.

> (*Suffering* v. *Clam, ante,* p. 389 [93 Cal.Rptr. 721, 482 P.2d 633].)
> In *People* v. *Choice, ante,* page 21 [100 Cal.Rptr. 100] it is noted . . . .
> (*People* v. *Snag, post,* 441, at pp. 443–444 [93 Cal.Rptr. 751].)
> (*Broken* v. *Arrow, ante,* p. _____ .)
> (*People* v. *Smart, post,* p. _____ .)

If the author has cited a same-volume opinion earlier the proper citation is: (*Smith* v. *Jones, supra, ante,* at p. 1.). Where the first citation is to an opinion that appears later in the same volume, the citation is: (*Marching* v. *Band, supra, post,* at p. 925.).

**Point Page References.**—Where the author does not have official paging and the citation involves point page references in addition to the inception page, a referral to the typed opinion paging is necessary to assist the publisher in later inserting the correct point pages for the published opinion. Either of the following styles is appropriate:

**(a) Brackets Style:**
> In *Galloping* v. *Retreat, post,* at pages _____ - _____ [typed opn. pp. 14–19] the facts were distinguishable, while in *Near* v. *Miss, ante,* at pages _____ - _____ [maj. typed opn. pp. 6–7] the circumstances were identical.
> (*In re Gentle Persuasion,* dis. opn., at p. _____ [typed dis. opn., p. 12].)

**(b) Footnote Style:**
> In the companion cases of *White* v. *Black, ante,* _____ , at pages _____ - _____ *
> and *Red* v. *Green, post,* _____ , at pages _____ - _____ ,† it is noted . . . .
> _____
> * Typed opinion pages 6–8.
> † Typed opinion pages 3–5.
>
> (*In re Zero, ante,* _____ , at p. _____ .*)
> _____
> * Typed opinion at page 12.

(See also *post,* § 98 (c) & (d) for the style of citation of a portion of an author's opinion at another place in his or her opinion.)

**§ 86. Citation of Lead, Plurality, Concurring or Dissenting Opinions.**—To cite a lead, plurality, concurring, or dissenting opinion when notation of a point page is not required, give the inception page of that opinion as well as the inception page of the report itself. If a point page is indicated do not note the inception page of the particular opinion. The name of the author of that opinion is optional but normally specified.

> The incisive analysis of this issue in *University of California Regents v. Bakke, supra,* 438 U.S. 265 at pages 319–320 (lead opn. of Justice Powell) leads us to conclude . . . .
>
> (*County Sanitation Dist. No.2 v. Los Angeles County Employees Assn., supra,* 38 Cal. 3d 564, 567 (plur. opn. of Broussard, J.).)
>
> (*California Human Resources Dept. v. Java* (1971) 402 U.S. 121, 135 [28 L.Ed.2d 666, 676, 91 S.Ct. 1347, 1356] (conc. opn. of Douglas, J.).)
>
> *Hyde v. United States* (1912) 225 U.S. 347, 391 [56 L.Ed. 1114, 1135, 32 S.Ct. 793, 808] (dis. opn. of Holmes, J.).)
>
> (*Blake v. State Personnel Board* (1972) 25 Cal.App.3d 541, 555 [102 Cal.Rptr. 50, 59] (dis. opn. of Gardner, P.J.).)
>
> (See *Hyser v. Reed* (D.C. Cir. 1963) 318 F.2d 225, 251–253 [115 App.D.C. 254, 255–256] (conc. and dis. opn. of Bazelon, C.J.).)
>
> (*Motor Coach Employees v. Lockridge, supra,* 403 U.S. 274, 302, 309 (separate dis. opns. by Douglas, J. and White, J.).)

(See *ante,* §§ 69, 80(c) & 85 for the citation of a typescript opinion before its publication and, *post,* § 101 for word symbols noting a citation's effect.)

### § 87. Indicating Headnote, Footnote or Appendix.—When an author wishes to call the reader's attention to material covered under a particular **headnote** rubric, he should place the headnote number in brackets for the first and second series of the California Official Reports and in parentheses for the third series following the page number of the text on which the headnote rubric appears.

> (*People v. Hamilton* (1969) 71 Cal.2d 176, 178 [1] [77 Cal.Rptr. 785, 454 P.2d 681].)
>
> *Estate of Germond* (1971) 4 Cal.3d 573, 579 (2), 580 (3) [94 Cal.Rptr. 153, 483 P.2d 769]
>
> (*Oakes v. McCarthy Co.* (1968) 267 Cal.App.2d 231, 267 [30] [73 Cal.Rptr. 127].)
>
> (*People v. Mancha* (1974) 39 Cal.App.3d 703, 713 (3) [114 Cal.Rptr. 392].)

Use brackets with the rubric number for other jurisdictions:

> (*State v. Sifford* (1947) 51 N.M. 430, 432 [4] [187 P.2d 540].)

Where the reference is to a **footnote** rather than to the text of the cited page, the following style is used:

> (*People v. Navarro* (1972) 7 Cal.3d 248, 267, fn. 14 [102 Cal.Rptr. 137, 497 P.2d 481].)
>
> (*Endo v. State Board of Equalization* (1956) 143 Cal.App.2d 395, 399, fn. 2 [300 P.2d 366].)

Where the reference is to an **appendix** the style is:

> (*Legislature v. Reinecke* (1972) 6 Cal.3d 595, 604–605, appen.)

(See also *post,* §§ 99, 185.)

### § 88. Notation of Prior and Subsequent History—In General.—Citations should provide information concerning the prior or subsequent history of an opinion when deemed significant to the

point for which the opinion is cited, noting, for example, when appropriate under the foregoing standard, a grant of the writ of certiorari in the United States Supreme Court or review in the California Supreme Court, an opinion subsequently written on denial of rehearing, the denial of certiorari or review in a higher court to indicate finality, etc. Whether or not the *denial* of a writ of certiorari in the United States Supreme Court, of a rehearing in a Court of Appeal or of a hearing or review or rehearing in the California Supreme Court is meaningful to the point for which the opinion is cited is a determination for the author. (See 9 Witkin, Cal. Procedure (3d ed. 1985) Appeal, §§ 775, 776, pp. 743–747; Linzer, *The Meaning of Certiorari Denials* (1979) 79 Colum. L. Rev. 1227; *Hughes Tool Co.* v. *TransWorld Airlines* (1973) 409 U.S. 363, 365, fn. 1 [34 L.Ed.2d 577, 581, 93 S.Ct. 647, 650].) It is observed, in this regard, that the frequent use of denial notations tends to dilute their weight when they are meaningful, and California appellate custom, long established, confirms that such notations are infrequent.

**§ 88.1.   History—Citation Styles.**—Where a cited opinion's history is of import, the information is provided as the examples below illustrate. (See *post,* § 88.4 relating to the notation of the status of a cause following the grant of review by the California Supreme Court but before disposition, and § 88.5 for citation styles reflecting the court's disposition following review.)

(*In re Marriage of King* (1983) 150 Cal.App.3d 304 [197 Cal.Rptr. 716] mod. 151 Cal.App.3d 356f.) [See also *post,* § 97.]

(*People* v. *Lepe* (1985) 164 Cal.App.3d 685 [211 Cal.Rptr. 432] rehg. den. Feb. 7, 1985.) [See also *post,* § 262.]

(*In re Marriage of Stephenson* (1984) 162 Cal.App.3d 1057 [209 Cal. Rptr. 383] mod. on den. rehg. 163 Cal.App.3d 680b.) [See also *post,* § 97.]

(*People* v. *Desperado* (1988) 300 Cal.App.3d 200, 210 [400 Cal.Rptr. 300] opn. filed on den. rehg., 301 Cal.App.3d 717b.) [See also *post,* § 263.]

(*Snare* v. *Drum* (Cal.App. A012345) rehg. granted Jan. 17, 1988.) [See also *post,* § 95.]

(*Danning* v. *Bank of America* (Cal.App.) rehg. granted Dec. 22, 1983, sub. opn. 151 Cal.App.3d 961 [199 Cal.Rptr. 163].)

(*People* v. *Flowers* (Cal.App. A0242244) rehg. granted Dec. 21, 1984, sub. opn. Mar. 6, 1985, nonpub.)

(*Hobbs* v. *Eichler* (1985) 164 Cal.App.3d 174 [210 Cal.Rptr. 387] hg. den. May 1, 1985.) [See also *post,* § 262.]

(*Davis* v. *Superior Court* (Cal.App. 4 Civ. 30971) hg. den. Oct. 4, 1984, and opn. ordered nonpub.)

(*County of Los Angeles* v. *Surety Insurance Co.* (1985) 165 Cal.App.3d 704 [211 Cal.Rptr. 867] review den.) [See also *post,* §§ 88.3, 262.]

(*Brown* v. *Superior Court* (Cal.App.) hg. granted June 8, 1984 (S.F. 24753).) [See also *post,* § 95.]

(*Elston* v. *City of Turlock* (Cal.App.) hg. granted Jan. 5, 1984, sub. opn. (1985) 38 Cal.3d 227 [211 Cal.Rptr. 416, 695 P.2d 713].)

(*People* v. *Avalos* (Cal.App. 2 Crim. 41017, Div. 4) hg. granted Oct. 21, 1982 (Crim. 22819) retrans. to Ct. App. with directions, Nov. 26, 1984.) [See also *post,* § 95.]

(*People* v. *Avalos* (Cal.App.) hg. granted Oct. 21, 1982 (Crim 22819) retrans. to Ct. App. with directions, Nov. 26, 1984, sub. opn. (1985) 164 Cal.App.3d 850 [211 Cal.Rptr. 15].)

(*People* v. *Sumstine* (1984) 36 Cal.3d 909 [206 Cal.Rptr. 707, 687 P.2d 904] rehg. den. Nov. 29, 1984.)

(*Ramona R.* v. *Superior Court* (1985) 37 Cal.3d 802 [210 Cal.Rptr. 204, 693 P.2d 789] opn. mod. 38 Cal.3d 453a.) [See also *post,* § 97.]

(*People* v. *Garcia* (1984) 36 Cal.3d 539 [205 Cal.Rptr. 265, 684 P.2d 826] opn. mod. on den. rehg. 37 Cal.3d 234a.) [See also *post,* § 97.]

(*People* v. *Easley* (Cal. Crim. 21117) rehg. granted Feb. 23, 1983.) [See also *post,* § 95.]

(*People* v. *Easley* (Cal.) rehg. granted Feb. 23, 1983, sub. opn. (1983) 34 Cal.3d 858 [196 Cal.Rptr. 309, 671 P.2d 813].)

(*Hardly* v. *Aware* (1983) 200 Cal.App.3d 440 [300 Cal. Rptr. 212] opn. ordered pub. by Supreme Ct. Feb. 1, 1983.)

*See Escalera* v. *New York City Housing Authority* (2d Cir. 1970) 425 F.2d 853, 861, certiorari denied 400 U.S. 853 [27 L.Ed.2d 91, 91 S.Ct. 54].

(See *Carmical* v. *Craven* (9th Cir. 1971) 457 F.2d 582, 587–588, cert. applied for June 1972, Supreme Ct. Dock. No. 71–1602.)

(*N.L.R.B.* v. *Quality Manufacturing Company* (4th Cir. 1973) 481 F.2d 1018, cert. granted Apr. 29, 1974, 416 U.S. 986 [40 L.Ed.2d 557, 94 S.Ct. 1990] (Dock. No. 73–765).)

(*Ellhamer* v. *Wilson* (N.D.Cal. 1969) 312 F.Supp. 1245, app. pending 9th Cir.)

(*Santa Barbara etc. Agency* v. *All Persons* (1957) 47 Cal.2d 699, 708 [306 P.2d 875] revd. on other grounds (1958) 357 U.S. 275 [2 L.Ed.2d 1313, 78 S.Ct. 1176].)

This issue is pending before the Supreme Court. (*People* v. *Smith,* hg. granted May 5, 1985 (S.F. 12345).)

*Mulkey* v. *Reitman* (1966) 64 Cal.2d 529, 543–544 [50 Cal.Rptr. 881, 413 P.2d 825] affirmed *sub nom. Reitman* v. *Mulkey* (1967) 387 U.S. 369 [18 L.Ed.2d 830, 87 S.Ct. 1627].

(*Roberts* v. *Roberts* (1947) 81 Cal.App.2d 871 [185 P.2d 381] disapproved on another point in *Spellens* v. *Spellens* (1957) 49 Cal.2d 210 [317 P.2d 613].)

(*Bailey* v. *Richardson* (D.D.C. Cir. 1950) 182 F.2d 46, 59 [86 App.D.C. 248] affd. by an equally divided ct. (1951) 341 U.S. 918 [95 L.Ed. 1352, 71 S.Ct. 669].)

*People* v. *Krivda* (1971) 5 Cal.3d 357 [96 Cal.Rptr. 62, 486 P.2d 1262] judgment vacated and cause remanded (1972) 409 U.S. 33 [34 L.Ed.2d 45, 93 S.Ct. 32] reiterated (1973) 8 Cal.3d 623 [105 Cal.Rptr. 521, 504 P.2d 457].

(*Robinson* v. *Merrill Lynch, Pierce, Fenner & Smith, Inc.* (N.D.Ala. 1971) 337 F.Supp. 107, 110–111, affd. *per curiam* (5th Cir. 1972) 453 F.2d 417.)

(See also § 95 for the style of noting a pending case in another appellate court, § 97 for the style of citation of a modified opinion, § 103 for the adjustment of citations to superseded opinions and opinions ordered not to be published, and §§ 104 & 88.6 for styles relating to exceptions to the noncitation rule normally applicable to unpublished opinions.)

## § 88.2.  History—Frequently Used Abbreviations.

| | |
|---|---|
| affirmed | affd. |
| affirmed by memorandum opinion | affd. mem. |
| affirmed *per curiam* | affd. *per curiam* |
| affirmed under the name of | affd. *sub nom.* |
| affirming | affg. |
| appeal dismissed | app. dism. |
| appeal pending | app. pending |
| by the court | by the ct. |
| certiorari | cert. |
| certiorari denied | cert. den. |
| certiorari granted | cert. granted |
| concurring | conc. |
| Court of Appeal | Ct. App. |
| denied | den. |
| dismissed | dism. |
| dismissed per stipulation | dism. per stip. |
| dissenting | dis. |
| effective | eff. |
| following | foll. |
| hearing denied | hg. den. |
| hearing granted | hg. granted |
| improvidently | improv. |
| instructions | instns. |
| majority | maj. |
| modified | mod. |
| nonpublished | nonpub. |
| opinion | opn. |
| partially published | par. pub. |
| petition | petn. |
| plurality | plur. |
| probable jurisdiction noted | prob. jur. noted |
| published | pub. |
| rehearing denied | rehg. den. |
| rehearing granted | rehg. granted |
| retransferred | retrans. |
| reversed | revd. |
| reversed *per curiam* | revd. *per curiam* |
| reversing | revg. |
| review denied | review den. |
| review granted | review granted |
| stipulation | stip. |
| subsequent opinion | sub. opn. |
| Supreme Court | Supreme Ct. |
| transferred | trans. |
| under the name of | *sub nom.* |
| vacated | vacated |

## § 88.3.  Grant of Review by Supreme Court—Background.—
New and amended rules of court providing for the implementation of the wide variety of review options the Supreme Court now possesses as a result of the passage of Proposition 32 on the November 1984 Ballot were adopted effective May 6, 1985. The resulting major changes in the

Supreme Court's review processes and options bring with them the need for new citation styles to reflect the court's dispositional selection and to convey to the reader the status of the cause at any point following the grant of review to finality.

Prior to May 6, 1985, the granting of a "petition for hearing" set the entire cause at large before the Supreme Court for the determination of all issues presented, leaving the underlying Court of Appeal opinion without force and effect. (See 9 Witkin, Cal. Procedure (3d ed. 1985) Appeal, § 707.) The Supreme Court's review then related not to the Court of Appeal's opinion but rather to the decision of the trial court, in appeal situations, and to the petition or application for relief in original writ and other requests directed to the appellate court. Under the "hearing granted" practice of the past, since the grant of a hearing "vacated" the Court of Appeal opinion, the citation of such opinions was limited to a notation that a petition for hearing had been granted. (E.g., "(*Tumbling* v. *Weed* (S.F. 12345, hg. granted July 10, 1984).)".) Opinions superseded by the grant of a hearing were not published in the Official Reports (Cal. Rules of Court, former rule 976 (b)), and accordingly could not be cited or relied upon as legal authority (rule 977).

Under the rules of court adopted to implement Proposition 32, the Court of Appeal's opinion on grant of *review* is no longer "dead." While that court's opinion is in the "not-to-be-published" category during the period of review, except where otherwise specifically ordered by the Supreme Court (rule 976 (d)), and is not therefore citable as precedential authority while under review (rule 977 (a)), the opinion's life continues, albeit in abeyance, subject to the will of the Supreme Court. For example: Following the grant of review of a decision of a Court of Appeal, the Supreme Court may "decide any and all issues in the cause." (Cal. Rules of Court, rule 29.2 (a).) "Under subdivision (a) [rule 29.2] the Supreme Court may determine—either immediately after granting review or at any time before completion of its opinion—that only a limited number of issues in the cause require decision by the Supreme Court . . . . If the Supreme Court decides only limited issues, other issues in the cause will be disposed of by the Court of Appeal as the Supreme Court directs . . . ." (Advisory Com. com. to rule 29.2.) The Supreme Court may specify the issues to be argued. (Rule 29.2 (b).) "Notwithstanding its specification of issues, the Supreme Court may order argument on fewer or additional issues, or on the entire cause." (*Ibid.*) It "may order action on the cause deferred until disposition of another cause pending before the court." (Rule 29.2 (c).)

"[U]nless another disposition is ordered" the Supreme Court's judgment "shall be that the judgment of the Court of Appeal is affirmed, reversed, or modified . . . ." (Rule 29.4 (a).) The "Supreme Court may decide one or more issues and transfer the cause to a Court of Appeal for decision of any remaining issues in the cause." (Rule 29.4 (b).) "The Supreme Court may dismiss review of a cause as improvidently granted and remand the cause to the Court of Appeal. On filing of the order [of dismissal and remand] in the Court of Appeal, the decision of the Court of Appeal shall become final . . . ." (Rule 29.4 (c).) "After granting review of a decision of a Court of Appeal, the Supreme Court may transfer the cause to a Court of Appeal with instructions to conduct further proceedings as the Supreme Court deems necessary." (Rule 29.4 (e).)

"After granting review, after decision, or after dismissal of review and remand as improvidently granted, the Supreme Court may order the opinion of the Court of Appeal published in whole or in part." (Rule 976 (d).) "An opinion certified for publication shall not be published, and an opinion not so certified shall be published, on an order of the Supreme Court to that effect." (Rule 976 (c)(2).)

The foregoing array of Supreme Court options, among others, many conferred by the passage of Proposition 32, require an equally broad band of citation styles and subsequent history notations to impart essential information. Illustrated below are styles designed to assist in these situations.

### § 88.4. Styles Reflecting Cause's Status During Review.

#### (a) Review granted—no instructions.[1]

(*Drifting* v. *Along* (1988) 300 Cal.App.3d 146 [400 Cal. Rptr. 201] review granted July 12, 1988 (S012345).)

#### (b) Review granted—issues limited.[2]

(. . . review granted on specified issues July 12, 1988 (S012345).)
(. . . review granted July 12, 1988 (S012345), issues on review limited Sept. 10, 1988.)

---

[1] Because in some situations it may be necessary to proceed with the publication of a bound volume before the fate or disposition of an opinion appearing in the volume's advance sheets is known, the subject opinion will be withdrawn from the bound volume and reprinted in a later volume's advance pamphlet so that its ultimate disposition can be recorded. The researcher therefore will have to consult the Cumulative Subsequent History Table to see if the opinion has been assigned a second citation which should be substituted for the first one. For example, the citation in illustration (a) above would be recast as follows:

(*Drifting* v. *Along* (1988) 308 Cal.App.3d 610 [400 Cal.Rptr. 201], review granted July 12, 1988 (S012345).)

(See Preface to the Cumulative Subsequent History Table for further particulars.)

[2] Where the notation is merely that the issues under review, or counsel's argument, or briefing, have been limited but a specification of the limitation is not provided in the citation or in the material preceding or following the citation, the reader can obtain more specific information by consulting the Cumulative Subsequent History Table.

(. . . review granted on specified issues July 12, 1988 (S012345), issues expanded Oct. 15, 1988.)

(. . . review granted on specified issues July 12, 1988 (S012345), cause ordered at large on all issues Oct. 10, 1988.)

(. . . review granted July 12, 1988 (S012345) limited to statute of frauds issue.)

(. . . review granted July 12, 1988 (S012345), review limited Aug. 30, 1988, to issues relating to validity of preliminary injunction.)

### (c) Review granted—argument (or briefing) limited.*

(. . . review granted and argument limited July 12, 1988 (S012345).)

(. . . review granted July 12, 1988 (S012345), argument limited Sept. 10, 1988.)

(. . . review granted and argument limited July 12, 1988 (S012345), argument ordered expanded Oct. 22, 1988.)

(. . . review granted and argument and briefing limited July 12, 1988 (S012345), additional briefing requested Sept. 24, 1988.)

(. . . review granted and argument limited to statute of limitations issue July 10, 1988 (S012345) argument expanded Sept. 22, 1988, to include issue of the proper standard for the assessment of fraud in property transactions.)

(. . . review granted July 12, 1988 (S012345), argument limited Sept. 10, 1988, to issue of government immunity under Ed. Code, § 44808, cause argued Dec. 4, 1988.)

### (d) Review granted—disposition deferred.

(. . . review granted July 12, 1988 (S012345), cause ordered held Sept. 10, 1988, pending disposition of *Arch* v. *Bishop* (1987) 299 Cal.App.3d 707 [399 Cal.Rptr. 300] review granted June 1, 1988 (S012333).)

(For citation of Court of Appeal opinion ordered published under Cal. Rules of Court, rule 976 (d) as an exception to the rule prohibiting publication (and therefore citation) during the course of review, see *post,* § 88.6. For noting that petition for review has merely been filed, see § 95.)

## § 88.5. Styles Reflecting Supreme Court's Disposition After Grant of Review.

### (a) Citation to Supreme Court opinion alone.

(*People* v. *Footpad* (1988) 150 Cal.3d 100 [400 Cal.Rptr. 200, 900 P.2d 800].)[3]

---

\* See footnote 2 *ante,* page 56.

[3] This citation signals to the reader that the points of law relied on by the citing author are controlled by the Supreme Court's opinion and not the opinion of the Court of Appeal that has been reviewed. The Court of Appeal's opinion may have been totally superseded where the Supreme Court decided all issues itself, or superseded only to the extent that it is inconsistent with the Supreme Court's opinion, or the Court of Appeal's opinion may have been reviewed only on limited issues. Assuming the Court of Appeal's opinion was not totally superseded and has been ordered published, but controls only the disposition of unrelated issues, no citational purpose would be served by noting that fact or by citing the Court of Appeal's opinion. Of course, if the citing author is in doubt, or feels that the Court of Appeal's opinion aids in the understanding of the case's fact pattern or issues, the better practice is to cite both opinions as illustrated, *post,* in subdivision (c).

**(b) Citation to Court of Appeal opinion alone.**

(*People* v. *Footpad* (1988) 300 Cal.App.3d 300 [400 Cal.Rptr. 500].) [4]

**(c) Citation to Supreme Court and Court of Appeal opinions.**

(*Sooth* v. *Sayer* (1988) 150 Cal.3d 100, 111 [400 Cal.Rptr. 300, 900 P.2d 600], same cause 300 Cal.App.3d 308 [395 Cal.Rptr. 700].)

(. . ., same cause 300 Cal.App.3d 308, 310–312 [395 Cal.Rptr. 700] for related issues.) [or] (. . . 700] for extensive factual description.) [or] (. . . 700] for nonconforming zoning use analysis.) [or] (. . . 700] for dis. opn. of Fairness, J.)

Where the intent is to rely on the content of a Court of Appeal opinion but the author, for whatever reason, wishes to cross-reference to the companion Supreme Court opinion, appropriate styles are:

(*Master* v. *Key* (1988) 300 Cal.App.3d 114, 119–120 [400 Cal.Rptr. 401], same cause 150 Cal.3d 22 [400 Cal.Rptr. 888, 900 P.2d 431] revg. on other grounds.) [or] . . . 431] opn. on unrelated issues.) [or] . . . 431] opn. limited to procedural issues.) [or] . . . 431] conc. in judgment only.)

In order to avoid confusion and needless title repetition, in those situations where separate opinions from the Supreme Court and the Court of Appeal in the same cause or proceeding are relied upon at a number of points in the citing author's opinion or brief, the better practice is to assign an identification title to each opinion on its first citation, e.g.,

The first premise finds support in *Alpha* v. *Wave* (1988) 225 Cal.App.3d 100 [300 Cal.Rptr. 310] (hereafter *Alpha (Ct.App.)*), while the second premise is rejected by *Alpha* v. *Wave* (1989) 100 Cal.3d 110 [350 Cal.Rptr. 500, 900 Pac.Rptr. 200] (hereafter *Alpha (Supreme)*) . . . . In *Alpha (Supreme)*, *supra*, at page 114 the court held . . . . This issue is therefore res judicata. (*Alpha (Ct. App.)*, *supra*, 225 Cal.App.3d 100.)

The practice of using roman numerals (*Alpha I, Alpha II*) as distinguishing signals where opinions with identical names are cited is better reserved for situations not related to the two-opinion disposition that can result under the new Supreme Court review procedures. (See *ante*, subd.(a), fn.3.)

**(d) Citation noting Supreme Court's review limited to specified issues.***

(*Monte* v. *Python* (1988) 150 Cal.3d 212, 222–224 [400 Cal.Rptr. 893, 900 P.2d 976] review limited to validity of suppression of evidence under Pen. Code, § 1538.5.)

**(e) Citation noting partial disposition by Supreme Court and transfer to Court of Appeal for decision of remaining issues.**

(*Harmless* v. *Error* (1988) 150 Cal.3d 21 [400 Cal.Rptr. 212, 900 P.2d 666] revg. on statute of limitations issue; cause trans. to Ct. App. for determination of merits.)
(*Hollow* v. *Victory* (1988) 150 Cal.3d 44 [400 Cal.Rptr. 250, 900 P.2d 810] revg. on statute of limitations issue; cause trans. to Ct. App. for merit determination, sub. opn. (1989) 350 Cal.App.3d 55 [410 Cal.Rptr. 808].)

---

[4] This citation recognizes the corollary to the fact pattern recited in footnote 3, *ante*. (See subdivision (c) where the intent is to cite both the Court of Appeal and Supreme Court opinions.)

* See footnotes 3 and 4 of this section.

**(f) Noting review dismissed as improvidently granted.**[5]

(*People* v. *Suspect* (1988) 350 Cal.App.3d 234 [410 Cal.Rptr. 910] review dism. as improv. granted and opn. ordered pub. by Supreme Ct., May 19, 1988.)

But, where the author deems the opinion's subsequent history immaterial:

(*People* v. *Suspect* (1988) 350 Cal.App.3d 234 [410 Cal.Rptr. 910].) [See *ante*, fns. 3 (p. 57) and 4 (p. 58).]

**(g) Transfer to Court of Appeal with instructions.**

**(1) Transfer without Supreme Court opinion.**
(*Sheer* v. *Delight* (1988) 300 Cal.App.3d 616 [400 Cal.Rptr. 401].)

But where the author deems the opinion's prior history material:

(*Sheer* v. *Delight* (1988) 300 Cal.App.3d 616 [400 Cal.Rptr. 401] opn. on trans. to Ct. App. with instns. foll. grant of review.)

And where characterization of the Supreme Court's instructions is deemed helpful:

(*Sheer* v. *Delight* (1988) 300 Cal.App.3d 616 [400 Cal.Rptr. 401] opn. foll. trans. to Ct. App. with Supreme Ct. instns. to determine cause in light of *Sparkling* v. *Cleanser* (1988) 150 Cal.3d 808 [400 Cal.Rptr. 333, 900 P.2d 888].)

(*In re Raymond H.* (B112345) review granted Nov. 28, 1990, cause trans. to Ct.App. Aug. 17, 1991, for reconsideration in light of *In re B. R.* (1990) 150 Cal.3d 100 [450 Cal.Rptr. 200, 950 P.2d 700].)

**(2) Transfer by Supreme Court opinion.**

(*Insipid* v. *Suitor* (1988) 150 Cal.3d 999 [400 Cal.Rptr. 876, 901 P.2d 222] revd. with instns. to Ct.App., see sub. opn. 310 Cal.App.3d 1010 [400 Cal.Rptr. 221].)

(*Heated* v. *Debate* (1988) 150 Cal.3d 845 [400 Cal.Rptr. 42, 901 P.2d 22] sub. opn. on remand to Ct. App. 310 Cal.App.3d 626 [405 Cal.Rptr. 243].)

(*Maltese* v. *Falcon* (1988) 150 Cal.3d 811 [400 Cal.Rptr. 777, 900 P.2d 876] judgment revd. for further proceedings in Ct. App., see sub. opn. 320 Cal.App.3d 17 [405 Cal.Rptr. 504].)

(*Hardly* v. *Ever* (1988) 150 Cal.3d 498 [400 Cal. Rptr. 801, 900 P.2d 907] judgment mod. with instns. (Cal.App. E012344) sub. Ct. App. opn. nonpub.)

**(h) Opinion of Court of Appeal ordered partially published.**

**(1) By order without Supreme Court opinion.**[6]

(*Heir* v. *Apparent* (1988) 300 Cal.App.3d 124 [400 Cal.Rptr. 300].)
(*Heir* v. *Apparent* (1988) 300 Cal.App.3d 124 [400 Cal.Rptr. 300] opn. ordered pub. by Supreme Ct. except for portions relating to attorney-client privilege.) [or]:
(*Heir* v. *Apparent* (1988) 300 Cal.App.3d 124 [400 Cal.Rptr. 300] Supreme Ct. review dism. as improv. granted and cause remanded with instns. for partial pub.)

---

[5] Because an opinion which a Court of Appeal has certified for publication loses that status on a grant of review by the Supreme Court (Cal. Rules of Court, rule 976 (d)), if the opinion is to be published the Supreme Court will so direct. (*Ibid.*)

[6] Normally, no notation of partial publication is required since the published opinion itself will advise the reader of the Supreme Court's action. Where the author deems a notation of the court's order helpful, the styles illustrated should assist in drafting appropriate citations. In many situations because of the restrictions of uniform pagination it will be necessary to republish the opinion at another place following the Supreme Court's order. ( Consult the Cumulative Subsequent History Table at the back of the most recent advance pamphlet.)

**(2) By opinion of Supreme Court.***

(*People* v. *Vindicated* (1988) 150 Cal.3d 282 [400 Cal.Rptr. 456, 900 P.2d 333] judgment Ct. App. affd. as mod., Ct. App. opn. ordered pub. except for portions relating to charge of inadequacy of counsel, 300 Cal.App.3d 799 [400 Cal.Rptr. 500].) (See also *ante,* subd. (c).)

**(3) By order preceding Supreme Court opinion (also cited).***

(*Fox* v. *Hole* (1988) 301 Cal.App.3d 666 [401 Cal.Rptr. 456] opn. ordered partially pub. Apr. 10, 1989, see same cause (1989) 150 Cal.3d 222 [402 Cal.Rptr. 502, 901 P.2d 876] for related issues.)

## § 88.6. Publication of Opinion Ordered During Review.—

Subdivision (d) of rule 976 of the California Rules of Court authorizes the Supreme Court to override, in whole or in part, the provision of that subdivision that otherwise prohibits the publication (and therefore the citation) of a Court of Appeal's opinion during the period it is under review following the court's grant of review. In those situations where the Supreme Court, in whole or in part, orders publication of a Court of Appeal's opinion it is then reviewing, the citing author should include sufficient information to advise of the cause's procedural posture to avoid ambiguity. The following style models should prove helpful in drafting citations for the many potential variations.

(*Bar* v. *None* (1987) 300 Cal.App.3d 100 [401 Cal.Rptr. 400] review granted Dec. 11, 1987 (S012345); Feb. 10, 1988, pending its review, Supreme Ct. ordered opn. pub. except for pts. II & III; Feb. 28, 1988, oral argument restricted to issues relating to novation of Dec. 12, 1986, contract. [See 150 Cal.3d 803a].)

(*Hay* v. *Stack* (1987) 300 Cal.App.3d 100 [400 Cal.Rptr. 500] review granted Dec. 31, 1987 (S012345), opn. ordered pub. except for pts. II & IV, and argument and briefing restricted to single issue whether there was a "taking" for due process purposes.)

(See also *ante,* §§ 88.4, 88.5, and *post,* §§ 95, 103.)

## § 89. Superior Court Case References.—

Titles of trial court cases are *not* italicized. Note the case title followed within parentheses by the trial court number and, where the particular court is not evident from the text, the pertinent information, e.g.,

(People v. Hood (Super. Ct. Santa Cruz County, 1986, No. 1234).)

(Gun v. Slinger (Mun. Ct. Solano County, 1986, No. 1234).)

Where the court wishes to note the case's procedural history, customary abbreviations are used when the information is cited within parentheses, e.g.,

(Star v. Wars (Super. Ct. Merced County, 1985, No. 543) order issuing injunction filed July 12, 1986.)

(Hair v. Piece (Super. Ct. L.A. County, 1984, No. 1234) petn. for writ of cert. filed Feb. 12, 1985, petn. den. by Ct.App., Second Dist., Div. Two, Mar. 10, 1985.)

(See Cal. Rules of Court, rule 977 re prohibition against citation of unpublished opinions and exceptions to the rule.)

---

* See footnote 6 on page 59.

## § 90. Parallel Citations.

**(a) Opinions of California Appellate Courts and United States Supreme Court.**—The Official Reports publication style is to indicate the official citation followed by the *usual* parallel citations in brackets for the initial reference. Parallel citations are dropped for subsequent references to the same decision to conserve space.

(*People* v. *Webb* (1967) 66 Cal.2d 107, 109 [56 Cal.Rptr. 902, 424 P.2d 342].)
    Second reference: In *People* v. *Webb, supra,* 66 Cal.2d 107, 123, it is noted. . . .
(*McLellan* v. *McLellan* (1972) 23 Cal.App.3d 343, 346 [100 Cal.Rptr. 258].)
    Second reference: (*McLellan* v. *McLellan, supra,* 23 Cal.App.3d 343, 349.)
(*Jackson* v. *Denno* (1964) 378 U.S. 368, 372 [12 L.Ed.2d 908, 84 S.Ct. 1774].)
    Second reference: (*Jackson* v. *Denno, supra,* 378 U.S. 368, 385.)

The Official Reports publication normally does not note the corresponding point pages for the parallel citations unless the opinion author does.

(*Thorn* v. *Superior Court* (1970) 1 Cal.3d 666, 675 [83 Cal.Rptr. 600, 464 P.2d 56].)

Opinion authors may omit parallel citations even for the initial reference since by contract they are provided by the publisher of the Official Reports. The publisher is not required to furnish point pages for parallel references.

**(b) Other Jurisdictions.**—The Official Reports indicate the official citation for the jurisdiction followed by the National Reporter System's citation within brackets.

(*Enlund* v. *Buske* (1971) 160 Conn. 327 [278 A.2d 815].)

Because of the practical consideration of the greater availability of the National Reporter System's regional reports it is preferable to use parallel citations with point pages noted throughout an opinion in addition to the official citation. (This practice will differ from the parallel citation style for California and United States Supreme Court decisions where parallel citations are dropped after the initial reference.)

(*Price* v. *Levin* (1967) 248 Md. 158, 162 [235 A.2d 547, 549].)
    Second reference: (*Price* v. *Levin, supra,* 248 Md. 158, 161 [235 A.2d 547, 548].)

(See also *ante,* § 76, Reports of Other States, and § 80, United States Supreme Court Decisions.)

## § 91. Opinion Titles for Citation Purposes.

—Use, as the title for a cited opinion, the *running head* adopted by the *official reports* of the jurisdiction of origin. In the interest of uniformity the official report running head is preferred over those adopted by parallel reports since often there are differences as to the first-named party, spelling, punctuation, etc. (See *ante,* § 80 (a) and *post,* § 194.)

The names of the parties are italicized but the "v." is not, e.g.,

(*People* v. *Cannady* (1972) 8 Cal.3d 379 [105 Cal.Rptr. 129, 503 P.2d 585].)

A nonadversary title is italicized in full, e.g.,

> (*Adoption of Oukes* (1971) 14 Cal.App.3d 459 [92 Cal.Rptr. 390].)
> (*In re Marriage of Coleman* (1972) 26 Cal.App.3d 56 [102 Cal.Rptr. 629]; *In re Lopez* (1969) 1 Cal.App.3d 683 [82 Cal.Rptr. 129].)

If an author, after citing an opinion (*Jones* v. *Smith*), adopts a short form of reference to the opinion, as "In *Jones,* it was stated . . . ." italics are used. (See also *ante,* § 88.5 (c).)

**Identical running heads.**—Where an author cites more than one opinion with the same running head it is recommended that the citations note, within parentheses, the real party in interest as a distinguishing mark, e.g.,

> The two pivotal decisions to be analyzed are *People* v. *Superior Court (Vega)* (1969) 272 Cal.App.2d 383 and *People* v. *Superior Court (Kiefer)* (1970) 3 Cal.3d 807.

Commencing with volume 11, California Reports, Third Series, and volume 39, California Appellate Reports, Third Series, the running heads for the *"People* v. *Superior Court"* line of cases note within parentheses the last name of the real party in interest immediately following "Superior Court."

> (*People* v. *Superior Court (Kaufman)* (1974) 12 Cal.3d 421.)

**Two opinions on single cause.**—In situations where the author deems it necessary to cite two opinions dealing with a *single cause,* as, for example, where the Supreme Court's opinion following the grant of review addresses only issues relating to procedural matters and the Supreme Court then orders publication of the Court of Appeal's opinion, which disposes of the merits, use a single running head for both, e.g.,

> (*Strong* v. *Arm* (1985) 50 Cal.3d 126, 130–135 [250 Cal.Rptr. 100, 800 P.2d 300], same cause 185 Cal.App.3d 876, 879 [252 Cal.Rptr. 400] ordered pub. *post* Supreme Ct. review.)

(See also *ante,* § 88.5 (a) through (c).)

**§ 92.  Repeating Citations.**—Experience has indicated that the choice and use of "shortcut" references must remain somewhat flexible to avoid ambiguity, awkward passages, needless and distracting repetition, and aesthetically poor copy. An adopted style should retain as much information as is deemed necessary to achieve clarity and accuracy. The guidelines that follow are designed to obtain those objectives.

(See generally *post,* §§ 93, 98, *ante,* § 80, and § 88.5 (c) re citing of opinions with same name.)

**§ 93.  Use of Case Name Alone.**—Where a decision has been initially cited in full and where the flow of the discussion is such that to repeat the citation is not helpful, and in fact distracting, the use of a short title alone is sufficient, e.g.,

> In *Smith* the court noted . . . .
> The reasoning of *Smith* is appropriate.
> The *Smith* case holds . . . .
> In *Regents of University of California* v. *Hartford Acc. & Indem. Co.* (1978) 21 Cal.3d 624 [147 Cal.Rptr. 486, 581 P2d 197] (hereafter *Regents*) . . . .
> Plaintiffs rely on *Regents, supra,* 21 Cal.3d 624, 628 for reversal.

This device should be avoided where the reference is interrupted by any intervening discussion not immediately and directly related or where a page reference is required, unless the case is a well known one in general (e.g., *Miranda*) or will be frequently cited throughout the opinion or brief. (See also *ante,* § 88.5 (c).)

### § 94. Series of Citations—Punctuation.—When two or more sources are cited in series within parentheses, the citations should be separated by semicolons, not commas, e.g.,

> (*McRae* v. *Bates* (1961) 196 Cal.App.2d 510, 513, fn.2 [16 Cal.Rptr. 565]; *Fried* v. *Municipal Court* (1949) 94 Cal.App.2d 376, 378 [210 P.2d 883]; Civ. Code, §§ 1430, 1431, 1659, 1660; 1 Witkin, Summary of Cal. Law (7th ed. 1973) Contracts, § 213, p. 243; see also 19 Cal.Jur.2d, Judgments, § 257, p. 222.)

Where two opinions dealing with a single cause are cited, separate them by a comma and not a semicolon, e.g.,

> (*Tell* v. *Tale* (1987) 100 Cal.3d 110 [300 Cal.Rptr. 300, 700 P.2d 81], same cause 200 Cal.App.3d 200 [310 Cal.Rptr. 310, 710 P.2d 222] related issues.)

In the text two or more sources cited in series may be separated either by commas *or* semicolons, e.g.,

> *Gideon* v. *Wainwright* (1963) 372 U.S. 335 [9 L.Ed.2d 799, 83 S.Ct. 792], *Hamilton* v. *Alabama* (1961) 368 U.S. 52 [7 L.Ed.2d 114, 82 S.Ct. 157], and *Douglas* v. *California* (1963) 372 U.S. 353 [9 L.Ed.2d 811, 83 S.Ct. 814] apply because . . . .

(See also *post,* § 174 re use of semicolons in series, § 168 commas in series, and *ante,* §§ 88.5 (c) & 91 for citations to dual opinions in the disposition of the same cause.)

### § 95. Notation of Pending Case in Appellate Courts.—Where an author wishes to note the procedural posture of a case pending but undecided in the appellate courts, the reference to the case should note the docket number as well as other material information, e.g.,

> An identical question relating to the status of federal retirement benefits is presently pending before our Supreme Court in *Jones* v. *Smith* (S012345, review granted June 10, 1990).
> (*Smith* v. *Lewis* (S012345, review granted June 12, 1990).)
> (*In re Marriage of Delight* (E012345, rehg. granted July 18, 1990).)
> (*Chance* v. *Slim* (B012345, app. pending).)
> (*Heavenly* v. *Fudge*) (A012345, app. pending, argued May 11, 1990).)

(*In re Allen* (F012345, order to show cause issued Oct. 11, 1990).)

(*In re Raymond H.* (B012345) review granted Nov. 28, 1990, cause trans. to Ct.App. Aug. 17, 1991, for reconsideration in light of *In re B. R.* (1990) 100 Cal.3d 100 [300 Cal.Rptr. 200, 900 P.2d 700].)

(*N.L.R.B.* v. *Quality Manufacturing Company* (4th Cir. 1990) 800 F.2d 1018, cert. granted Apr. 29, 1990, 600 U.S. 300 [500 L.Ed.2d 500, 400 S.Ct. 1990] (Dock. No. 90-765).)

(See also *ante*, §§ 88 through 88.6 for notation of prior and subsequent history, pertinent abbreviations and additional illustrations.)

## § 96. Citing Clerk's and Reporter's Transcripts.

**(a) Briefs.**—Pursuant to California Rules of Court, rule 15 (a), briefs submitted to appellate courts frequently refer to the clerk's and reporter's transcripts. The abbreviations and styles used within parentheses are: (2 C.T. pp. 17, 18.), (6 R.T. pp 19–20.), (Supp. C.T. p. 12.). For convenience, lengthy transcripts are divided into numbered or dated volumes. Numbered volumes are generally paged consecutively; dated volumes, independently. Forms of citation for them are:

(6 R.T. pp. 20001–20009.)

(R.T. Apr. 12, 1989, proceedings, pp. 21–28.)

**(b) Opinions.**—Opinion authors normally do not indicate the source or page from which an excerpt or quotation from the record is taken. Documents discussed are identified by reference to the document and not to the record. If an opinion author wishes to note that abstracted materials are from the record a general reference to the particular transcript as a whole is used and page references are avoided.

## § 97. Citation of Opinion Modification.—Opinions that are

modified are printed in the advance sheets *as modified* if the modification is received before the publisher's "cut-off" date. In this situation the usual citation is appropriate and no notation of modification is necessary. However, because of the inherent limitations under the uniform pagination format used with the publication of the Official Reports, Third Series, extensive modifications require that an opinion once published must be republished, as modified, at another place. The proper citation in this situation is to the advance sheet containing the republication and no indication of the earlier publication or of the modification is necesary.

Short modifications do not require republication of the opinion, and the modification is printed alone following the last opinion in the first available advance pamphlet after the date of the modification on an "a," "b" or "c" page. Therefore, until the modification is merged into the bound volume publication of the cited opinion, a citing author should indicate the initial citation to the opinion *and* the "a" "b" or "c" page on which the modification cited appears, e.g.,

(*People* v. *Suspect* (1988) 300 Cal.App.3d 1000, mod. 301 Cal.App.3d 297a.)

Of course if the author is not specifically citing to material affected by the modification there is no need to cite an "a" page and the citation is then only to the advance sheet containing the opinion.

Modifications not made at the time of advance-sheet publication are noted on the Cumulative Subsequent History tables toward the end of each advance pamphlet.

When a modified opinion is published in a bound volume it is always published as modified.

(See generally re modifications *ante*, § 88.1, and *post*, §§ 102, 263, 296–301.)

### § 98. Use of *Supra, Op. Cit. Supra, Ante, Post, Infra, Ibid.* and *Id.*

The short form citation styles that follow are designed to strike a sensible balance between the sometimes conflicting objectives of permitting the flow of the passage to proceed with as little concept interruption as possible and providing the reader with enough information so that the material relied upon can be readily identified and located at its source without resort to frequent frustrating backtracking.

(See also *post*, § 106 and *ante*, §§ 92, 80.)

**(a) Supra** (above) is used (1) as an informational cue that the source has been previously cited and/or (2) to act as a substitute for an earlier more complete reference. A source is considered to be previously cited if it has been cited earlier in either text or footnote but not if it merely appears in a quoted passage.

**(1) Second Reference—Different Paragraph.**—If a source has been previously cited in a different paragraph or footnote, this information is conveyed to the reader by noting, *supra,* following any subsequent reference, e.g.,

(*Reber* v. *Beckloff, supra,* 6 Cal.App.3d 341.)
(*People* v. *Scherbing, supra,* 93 Cal.App.2d 736, 741.)
(*People* v. *Roubus, supra,* 65 Cal.2d at p. 221.)
(*People* v. *Sylvestry, supra,* 112 Cal.App.3d Supp. 1, 6.)

Do not substitute the word *"supra"* for the volume and page references.

**(2) Second Reference—Same Paragraph.**—When the author has previously cited an opinion or source and desires to again cite it in the same paragraph, *supra* may be used in lieu of volume and page where the reference is to the source generally, e.g.,

Plaintiff rests her case on the authority of *Alter* v. *Michael* (1966) 64 Cal.2d 480 [50 Cal.Rptr. 553, 413 P.2d 153] . . . Defendant also relies on *Alter* v. *Michael* [or *Alter*], *supra,* for the proposition . . . .

When citing the same source in the same paragraph and a specific page reference is intended the appropriate forms are: (*Alter* v. *Michael, supra,* 64 Cal.2d at p. 483.) or (*Alter,* at p. 483 of 64 Cal.2d.) or (*Alter* v. *Michael, supra,* at p. 483.) or (*Alter, supra,* at p. 483.) or, where there is no intervening citation, (At p. 483.) or (P. 483.). For an appellate department case it would be: (*Garcia, supra,* at p. Supp. 14.). (For exceptions, see *ante,* § 93.) *Ibid.* and *id.* are also acceptable signals sometimes used in place of *supra.* See subdivisions (f) and (g), *post.*

**(b)** *Op. Cit. Supra* (work cited above) is sometimes used as a signal that the source noted has been previously cited in full earlier in the opinion. It is customarily used as a shortcut for second references to texts and periodicals, but is no longer used with opinion citations.

As a rule of thumb it is noted that the further *op. cit. supra* is removed from its parent citation the more information should accompany its use. For example, if the reference is in the same paragraph as its parent citation and is uninterrupted by intervening citations, (*Op. cit. supra.*) alone, or (*Op. cit. supra,* at p. _____ .), if a page reference is desired, is sufficient. If the reference is more than a paragraph removed from its parent citation and there are intervening citations, a more complete reference is required, e.g., (See 2 Witkin, *op. cit. supra,* at pp. 812–819) or (2 Witkin, Summary of Cal. Law, Sales, *op. cit. supra,* at p. 1137). If the reference is several pages removed from its parent and other citations intervene, it is better to repeat the citation with *supra,* e.g., (2 Witkin, Summary of Cal. Law, Sales, *supra,* at pp. 1229–1230.)

This form of citation is never used where two different works by the same author have been previously cited.

**(c)** *Ante* (before) is often used as a signal to direct the reader to what has been previously stated or discussed within the author's opinion, as where the author refers to an earlier footnote or page, e.g., (*Ante,* fn.1.) or (*Ante,* at p. 10.), or to note that a cited opinion appears or will appear *earlier* in the *same* volume as the author's opinion. No reference to report or volume is used. This citational form is frequently used in citing companion cases and in concurring and dissenting opinions when citing the majority or lead opinion, e.g., (*People* v. *Hurst, ante,* p. 123.) (Maj. opn., *ante,* pp. 126–142.). (See also *ante,* § 85.)

**(d)** *Post* (after) is used as a signal to direct the reader to what is stated later within an opinion as where the author refers to a discussion taken up thereafter or to an after–cited footnote, e.g., (*Post,* fn. 10.). *Post* is also used to note that a cited opinion appears or will appear later in the same volume the author's opinion will be published in. (See also use of *ante,* subd. (c) above and *ante,* § 85.)

**(e)** *Infra* (below).—Use is analogous to *post,* e.g., (See discussion, *infra.*).

**(f) *Ibid.*** (in the same place) is used to repeat an entire parent citation (or parent series of citations) where there are no intervening citations. This signal tells the reader that the parent citation (or parent series of citations) is considered repeated as first cited. When, however, the intended parent citation is only the last of a series of citations, neither *ibid.* nor *id.* should be used.

> The case at bench does not fall within our proscription enunciated in *Mozzetti v. Superior Court* (1971) 4 Cal.3d 699, 703 [94 Cal.Rptr. 412, 484 P.2d 84]. In that case there was no probable cause to believe the vehicle contained evidence of the crime. (*Ibid.*)

If there is a change in page, *id.* is used. (See *post,* subd. (g).) The terms *ibid.* and *id.* are used with case citations as well as with other cited sources.

**(g) *Id.*** (the same) is used to repeat the parent citation where there are no intervening citations and where there is a change of any kind. (Cf. use of *ibid.* above.)

> The court held in *Schreifer v. Industrial Acc. Com.* (1964) 61 Cal.2d 289, 290 [38 Cal.Rptr. 352, 391 P.2d 832] that the going and coming rule did not apply. It was further held that the "special mission" exception governed. (*Id.* at p. 295.)
>
> In *State v. Flynn* (1979) 92 Wis.2d 427 [285 N.W.2d 710, 718] . . . . (*Id.,* 285 N.W.2d at pp. 711, 712, 718–719.)

**§ 99. Indicating Page or Section.**—The preferred practice, except when referring to an opinion as a whole or a very brief opinion, is to give the inception page of each case *and* also the page or pages of the Official Report on which the holding, dictum or discussion appears. If the cited material extends over several pages, the term "et seq." may be used; e.g.,

> (*People v. Saddler* (1979) 24 Cal.3d 671, 677 et seq. [156 Cal.Rptr. 871, 597 P2d 130].)

If the author wishes, the headnote numbers in brackets for the first and second series of the Official Reports and in parentheses for the third series may be indicated, e.g.,

> (*People v. Ashley* (1954) 42 Cal.2d 246, 259 et seq. [10] [267 P.2d 271].)
> (*Darces v. Woods* (1984) 35 Cal.3d 871, 855–888 (5) [201 Cal.Rptr. 807, 679 P.2d 458].)

(See *ante,* § 87.)

Each of the following forms indicates a different intent on the part of the author: 4 Cal.3d 202; 4 Cal.3d 202, 209; 4 Cal.3d 202, 209, 211; 4 Cal.3d 202, 209–211; 4 Cal.3d 202, 213 et seq.

A hyphen or dash indicates that the numbers are inclusive, i.e., that any intervening numbers are included though not written, e.g., if the intent is to refer to pages 1, 2, 3, 4 and 5, it is much shorter to write "pages 1–5." The use of a comma (pages 1, 5) would indicate that there was no intent to refer to the intervening pages.

When the reference is to not more than two adjoining sections or pages, the author may use a hyphen to stress the fact that a quotation or a discussion is continued from one page to the next. It should also be noted that in the codes, and occasionally in other places, there may be lettered or decimal sections, and if the intent is to include those sections a hyphen and not a comma should be used; e.g., "Pen. Code, §§ 1201, 1202," would indicate an intent to refer to those two sections alone, whereas "Pen. Code, §§ 1201–1202," would indicate an intent to include the intervening section 1201.5 as well.

For the convenience of the readers of the Official Reports, all volumes of the Second Series commencing with 18 Cal.2d and 44 Cal.App.2d carry the inception page of the case at the top of each right-hand page immediately below the running head. The appropriate National Reporter citations appear commencing with 25 Cal.2d and 66 Cal.App.2d. Volumes of the Third Series of the Official Reports carry this information at the top of every page of the case. Commencing with volumes 33 Cal.3d and 136 Cal.App.3d the month and year of decision follow the parallel citations.

§ **100. Order of Citation.**—The order of citation is not governed by rigid rules. Citational sequences are normally structured to best support the proposition presented. In some situations an author may wish to call the reader's attention to the case deemed most pertinent first. In other circumstances the drafter may wish to note an unbroken chain of authority commencing with the date of the most recent decision, etc.

The guidelines indicated below are normally observed in the absence of an author's determination that a deviation is necessary to achieve a specific citational objective. Note that the order of citations will vary according to the type of authority, its date, the court involved and the weight of the authority.

(a) **Type of Authority.**—Constitutional citations should be given priority. When a code section or statute is cited with cases construing it, the statutory reference should precede the cases. California cases should precede those of other states unless the law of another jurisdiction is involved. When decisions from other jurisdictions are cited, federal cases should be listed first, with the others being given according to the alphabetical order of the state. References to secondary authorities should follow citations of statutes and cases.

(b) **Date.**—Several decisions of the same court should be cited in reverse chronological order, with the latest cases first. However, if a group of citations is preceded by a quotation from one of the cited cases, that case should be listed first, and the citation should always include the page of the Official Reports where the quoted language appears.

**(c) The Court.**—Decisions by the highest court of a jurisdiction should precede those of lower courts, regardless of the dates of the cases. Hence California Supreme Court cases should be listed in reverse chronological order before those of the Courts of Appeal even if the latter are more recent. Where a cause is determined in a bifurcated fashion with a separate opinion from the Supreme Court and the Court of Appeal, list the opinion relied upon most heavily first. (See also *ante,* §§ 88.5(c), 95.)

**(d) Weight.**—It is customary to cite first any cases with square holdings, next those with dictum in accord, then those that are analogous, next those with contrary holdings, and lastly those with contrary dictum. (See also *post,* § 101.)

### § 101. Indicating Effect of Citation.—There is some difference of opinion regarding the necessity of indicating the effect of a citation and the proper method to be employed. The following is intended to express the usual practice in the Official California Reports. (Compare the elaborate law review system suggested in A Uniform System of Citations (14th ed. 1986) at pp. 8–10.)

Where a case contains a square holding in accord with the proposition stated in the text, there is no need for any distinguishing words or symbols. If, however, there is merely dictum in the case, the citation should be preceded by the word **"see."** Citations of concurring and dissenting opinions, as well as lead and plurality opinions where there is no majority on the point, should also be preceded by the word "see" and should be followed by the words "conc. opn." or "dis. opn." or "conc. and dis. opn." or "lead opn." or "plur. opn." in parentheses. (See *ante,* § 86.) Secondary material should also be introduced by "see."

When the cited case deals with an analogous situation, as when there is a similar statute, and the decision is in accord, the citation should be preceded by the abbreviation **"cf."** Where an author wishes to cite cases as examples, he may precede the list with "See, e.g."

Each term such as "see" or "cf." applies to all following authorities in the group until another such term appears or the group of citations comes to an end.

The word **"accord"** may be used in connection with decisions from other jurisdictions to indicate a square holding to the same effect as the primary authority cited, but it may also be used to advantage when the author wishes to quote from a case and then to cite other supporting authorities.

If the author wishes to cite cases to the contrary, the terms **"contra"** to indicate a square holding and **"but see"** to indicate dictum to the contrary may be used. If the drafter wishes to contrast decisions, the form **"Compare . . . with . . ."** is useful.

On occasion the author may desire to indicate the facts of a case or to make an explanatory comment. While this can, of course, be done by an appropriate statement as part of the discourse, the same result may frequently be accomplished by a few words in parentheses when the citation is part of the text or in brackets when the citation is within parentheses:

> . . . and this conclusion is supported by *People* v. *Beach* (1983) 147 Cal.App.3d 612 [195 Cal.Rptr. 381] (relocation away from home community as unreasonable condition of probation).
>
> (See *Martin* v. *Dentfield School Dist.* (1983) 35 Cal.3d 294 [197 Cal.Rptr. 570, 673 P.2d 240] [employment rights of tenured school teacher on reappointment after emergency layoff].)

Punctuation styles with words and terms indicating effect are:

> (See *A* v. *B* (1961) 366 U.S. 420, 425.)
> (See § 123.)
> (*A* v. *B* (1967) 66 Cal.2d 841; see Cal. Rules of Court, rule 56 (a).)
> (See, e.g., *A* v. *B, supra, at p.* 558) or (*A* v. *B, supra,* at p. 7.)
> (See also *In re Allen* (1962) 59 Cal.2d 509.)
> (See also 4 Witkin, Summary of Cal. Law (8th ed. 1974) Torts, § 136, p. 2431.)
> (But see *A* v. *B* (1942) 21 Cal.2d 100, 104.)
> (*A* v. *B* (1942) 49 Cal.App.2d 433. And see generally, 3 Witkin, Cal. Procedure (2d ed. 1971) Pleading, § 152, p. 1825.)
> (Cf. *A* v. *B* (1953) 41 Cal.2d 628, 633, and cases there cited.)
> (9 Cal.2d, *supra,* at pp. 471–472. Cf. *Shearer* v. *Cooper* (1943) 21 Cal.2d 695.)
> (Compare *A* v. *B* (1971) 3 Cal.3d 100 with *C* v. *D* (1974) 12 Cal.3d 204.)
> (Accord, *A* v. *B* (1980) 100 Cal.3d 100; *C* v. *D* (1950) 100 Cal.App.2d 100.)
> (Contra, Kessler, *Products Liability* (1967) 76 Yale L.J. 887.)
> (E.g., *A* v. *B* (1980) 100 Cal.3d 100.)

(See also *ante,* § 100.)

## § 102. Modification Withdrawing Citation of Superseded Opinion or Opinion Ordered Not to Be Published.

—If, within jurisdictional time, an author discovers that a cited opinion has been superseded or ordered not to be published, the justice normally will modify the opinion to withdraw the inappropriate citation where other authority supports the proposition stated, or will revise the passage where the cited opinion is the sole authority relied upon. (See *post,* §§ 296–301 re modification procedures and *ante,* § 97. See also §§ 88.3–88.6 for citation status following the grant of review.) If the court has lost jurisdiction at the time the citation's infirmity is discovered then a letter should be directed to the Reporter of Decisions so that the editorial adjustment noted *post* in section 103 will be made.

## § 103. Adjustment of Citations to Superseded Opinions, Published Opinions Thereafter Ordered Not to Be Published and Opinions Following the Grant of Review.

—Opinions of the Courts of Appeal and the Supreme Court are only tentative until they become final. (See Cal. Rules of Court, rules 24 (a), 29.4; *ante,* § 88.3 and *post,*

§ 296; see also Cal. Rules of Court, rule 107, for appellate department of the superior court opinions.) However, recent opinions are frequently cited before finality. (See *ante,* § 69, preadvance pamphlet citations, § 68, advance pamphlet citations, §§ 88.4–88.6, citation noting cause's status during review and § 95, citation of pending case in appellate courts.) Where a rehearing has been granted by a Court of Appeal or by the Supreme Court the cited opinion is wholly without force as a precedent and the cause is once again at large. (*Miller & Lux, Inc.* v. *James* (1919) 180 Cal. 38, 48 [179 P.2d 174, 175]; *Morgan* v. *Stubblefield* (1972) 6 Cal.3d 606 [100 Cal.Rptr. 1, 493 P.2d 465].)

Opinions superseded by judicial action are dropped from the Official Reports and are not published in the bound volumes. (See Cal.Rules of Court, rule 976(d); *ante,* § 88.4, fn.1; and the Preface to Cum. Sub. Hist. Table in the latest Official Reports advance pamphlet.)

Additionally, the Supreme Court, pursuant to rules 976(c)(2) of the California Rules of Court, may order an opinion of a Court of Appeal or of an appellate department of a superior court that was certified for publication by the authoring court not to be published in the Official Reports. The citation of unpublished opinions is prohibited barring unusual circumstances. (Cal. Rules of Court, rule 977; *ante,* § 88.6 and *post,* § 104.) Likewise, unpublished portions of opinions ordered partially published are not citable. (Rules 976.1(b), 976(d); *ante,* § 88.6.)

Opinions of Courts of Appeal are no longer automatically vacated upon the grant of review as they were when a "hearing" was granted prior to May 6, 1985. (See *ante,* § 88.3.) However, following the grant of "review" such Court of Appeal opinions are, unless otherwise directed by the Supreme Court, not to be published and accordingly are not citable. (Cal. Rules of Court, rules 976(d), 977; *ante,* §§ 88.3, 88.6 and *post,* § 104.) Of course, the ultimate viability of the Court of Appeal's opinion, in whole or part, as well as its citability for precedential purposes following the grant of review must await and be dependent upon the determination of the Supreme Court. (See Rules of Court, rules 29.2, 29.4, 976(d), 977; *ante,* § 88.3 and *post,* § 104.)

In reporting an opinion for the bound volume, a citation in *that* opinion to a superseded opinion or an opinion not qualified under the Rules of Court to be published in the Official Reports at the time the subject bound volume is committed to "press" preferably should be adjusted to reflect the status of the cited opinion *at that time.*

Where the cited opinion is clearly no longer citable, as where the Supreme Court has ordered it unpublished, or where the opinion's *final* publication status is undetermined, as where the case is pending before the Supreme Court following the grant of review, the cited opinion's name, upon discovery of such information, will be followed by "*(Cal.)" or "*(Cal.App.)" or "*(Cal.App.Supp.)." When publication "cut-off" times allow, a reporter's footnote will be added to specify the appropriate docket number, the action of the court resulting in the opinion's permanent "noncitable" status or, in the alternative, when the cause's permanent status is not at that point known, then available information signaling the opinion's procedural posture while awaiting ultimate disposition. (See *ante,* §§ 88.3, 88.4, 88.6, 95, and *post,* § 104.) Typical editorial notations follow:

**(a) Rehearing granted.**

. . . (*A* v. *B\** (Cal.); *B* v. *C* (1988) 60 Cal.3d 501, 502 [310 Cal.Rptr. 444, 700 P.2d 801]) . . . .

*Reporter's Note: Rehearing granted, June 1, 1988 (S012345).

. . . (*A* v. *B\** (Cal.App.); *B* v. *C* (1979) 100 Cal.App.3d 166, 169 [100 Cal.Rptr. 100]) . . . .

*Reporter's Note: Rehearing granted, March 14, 1986 (E012345).

or, where an opinion on rehearing has been filed:

*Reporter's Note: Rehearing granted, March 14, 1986, for the subsequent opinion see 301 Cal.App.3d 200 [350 Cal.Rptr. 300].

or, where the opinion on rehearing was filed but not ordered published:

*Reporter's Note: Rehearing granted, March 14, 1986 (E012345). The subsequent opinion was filed April 30, 1986, but was not certified for publication.

**(b) Opinion ordered not to be published.**

. . . (*D* v. *E\** (Cal.App.)) . . . .

*Reporter's Note: Opinion (A012345) deleted upon direction of Supreme Court by order dated June 1, 1988.

**§ 104. Citation of Unpublished Opinions.**—Rule 977 of the California Rules of Court directs that opinions of the courts of appeal that are not published in the Official Reports are not to be "cited or relied on by a court or a party in any other action or proceeding except . . . when the opinion is relevant under the doctrines of law of the case, res judicata, or collateral estoppel; or . . . when the opinion is relevant to a criminal or disciplinary action or proceeding because it states reasons for a decision affecting the same defendant or respondent in another such action or proceeding."

When citing a decision falling within one of the exceptions noted, indicate the title, date of filing, district and court number, e.g.,

(*People* v. *Smith* (Jan. 1, 1988) A012345, typed opn. pp. 11–12.)[†]

[†] While *brief* authors should note pages from the typed opinion, *opinion* authors should not, since there is no readily available opinion for the reader to refer to. (See *ante,* § 96.)

(*Hill* v. *Climb* (Aug. 10, 1987) E012345 [nonpub. opn.].) [Where text does not note that the decision is unpublished.]
(*Bridal* v. *Veil* (May 1, 1986) App. Dept. Super. Ct., Santa Clara County, Civ. A No. 12345.)

An opinion once published in an advance pamphlet of the Official Reports but thereafter ordered not to be published by the Supreme Court (see Cal. Rules of Court, rule 976(c)(2)) may only be cited after the date of such an order if it falls within one of the noted exceptions.

(See also *ante,* § 88.6 and Cal. Rules of Court, rule 976.1(b)).)

# G. Secondary Materials

§ **105. Textbooks.**—Initial references must indicate volume number (where more than one), author, title, edition (if more than one) with year, section and page numbers, e.g.,

(1 Orgel, Valuation Under Eminent Domain (2d ed. 1953) p. 359.)
(4 Witkin, Summary of Cal. Law (8th ed. 1974) § 800, p. 3097.)
(2A Sutherland, Statutory Construction (4th ed. 1973) § 48.18, pp. 224–225.)
(2 Witkin, Cal. Crimes, § 603.)
(Key & Crouch, The Initiative and Referendum in California (1939) p. 442.)

In citing a text not within parentheses spell out "page" and "section," e.g.,

See Witkin, California Criminal Procedure, section 13, page 15.

It is helpful to the reader and therefore preferable to include, in addition to the foregoing essential information, the publication date for single edition works. It is recommended that chapter titles be noted, e.g.,

(1 Witkin, Cal. Procedure (3d ed. 1985) Attorneys, § 389, pp. 438–439.)
(Witkin, Cal. Evidence (2d ed. 1966) The Hearsay Rule, § 521, pp. 492–493.)

When the sections of a work are not numbered consecutively throughout, and each chapter starts with section 1, the section numbers cannot be substituted for the page numbers.

(2 Witkin, Summary of Cal. Law (8th ed. 1973) Sales, § 46, p. 1127.)

When an edition is commonly known by the name of the revising editor, substitute that name for the number of the edition, e.g.,

(8 Wigmore, Evidence (McNaughton ed. 1961) § 2286, pp. 532–537.)
(4 Wigmore, Evidence (Chadbourn ed. 1972) § 1083, p. 215.)

Some texts use as the title the name of the author and the subject connected by "on," as "Couch on Insurance." Such a text is normally cited as:

(10A Couch on Insurance (2d ed. 1982) § 42:213, p. 331.)

However, it is not improper to cite any text in that manner, e.g.,

(Bogert on Trusts (2d ed. 1964) § 451, pp. 498–499.)
2 Witkin on California Procedure (3d ed. 1985) Jurisdiction, section 324, page 741

Likewise, it is not improper to omit "on" where it appears as part of the text's title, e.g.,

> (10A Couch, Insurance (2d ed. 1982) § 42:213, p. 331.)

If the reference is to a footnote, so indicate following the page reference on which the footnote commences, e.g.,

> (Prosser & Keeton, Torts (5th ed. 1984) § 33, p. 201, fn. 78.)
> Prosser and Keeton on Torts (5th ed. 1984) section 33, page 201, footnote 78

Supplements to texts are cited as illustrated below:*

> (3 Corbin, Contracts (1971 pocket supp.) § 543D, p. 119.)
> (6 Witkin, Cal. Procedure (1983 supp.) Appeal, § 7, p. 5.)
> (5 Witkin, Summary of Cal. Law (8th ed., 1984 supp.) Constitutional Law, § 134, p. 70.)
> 5 Witkin, California Procedure (2d ed., 1983 pocket supp.) Enforcement of Judgment, section 194, page 89 assists us in that regard.

A citation to both text and supplement is noted as:

> (See Witkin, Cal. Criminal Procedure (1963) Trial, § 306, pp. 299–301; *id.* (1983 supp. pt. 1) pp. 383–387.)
> (2 Harper & James, Law of Torts (1956) § 16.15, at pp. 950–951; *id.* (1968 supp.) § 16.15, fn. 4, at pp. 48–49.)
> (5 McQuillin, Municipal Corporations (3d ed. 1981) § 17.07, pp. 292–293, (1984 pocket supp.) p. 29.)
> (Henke, Cal. Law Guide (2d ed. 1976) ch. 4, § 5.1, p. 267; *id.* (1984 cum. supp.) p. 98.)

Volume numbers are always cited in arabic numerals, *never* in roman, regardless of the publisher's designation, e.g.,

> (2 Jones, Legal Forms (10th ed. 1962) § 38.26, p. 325.) Not (II Jones . . .).
> (3 Loss, Securities Regulation (2d ed. 1961) p. 1719.)

Note that in citing textbooks in parentheses no word of a title is abbreviated except "California" which is shortened to "Cal."

### § 106. Textbooks—Subsequent References.

—When an author wishes to cite the *same* text and the *same* page or pages after his initial citation and both references are in the *same* paragraph without intervening citations, use *ibid.*:

> . . . the court concluded that the point was valid. (See 2 Nelson, Divorce and Annulment (rev. ed. 1961) §§ 15.01, 15.04, pp. 212–214, 217–219.) The next contention is based on the same legal theory (*ibid.*) and can be so considered . . . .

If an author wishes to cite *different* pages or sections after his initial citation to the text and both references are in the *same* paragraph, without intervening citations, use *id.,* e.g.,

> . . . the court based its holding on that theory (6A Corbin on Contracts (1962 ed.) § 1385, p. 46). A possible exception to that theory (*id.,* at p. 48) is raised by appellants . . . .

Where the same text is again cited but in a new paragraph or where an intervening citation appears in the same paragraph, give the author's

---

* See also *post,* section 108 for the citation of California practice handbook supplements.

name (and volume number if a multi-volume edition) with *supra* or *op. cit. supra* and the page reference.

. . . its decision in this case was supported by the majority of jurisdictions (5 Nichols on Eminent Domain (3d ed. 1969) § 21.3, pp. 21–37).

A contrary holding would have resulted in a possible confiscation of defendant's property (5 Nichols, *supra*, at p. 48).

For a discussion of defendant's contention see Fleming on Torts (3d ed. 1965) pages 491–492. This view is also held by other authorities (see, e.g., Prosser on Torts (3d ed. 1964) p. 865) but in light of the facts of this case a better solution is available to us (Fleming, *op. cit. supra*, at p. 493).

(See also *ante*, § 98.)

## § 107. Blackstone's Commentaries.—A number of editors have republished Blackstone's Commentaries on the Laws of England with annotations. These annotated editions note the page in the original edition by the use of an asterisk or "star paging" system. When citing the commentaries from these annotated reprints omit the date and edition and use the "star paging," e.g.,

2 Blackstone's Commentaries 296.
2 Blackstone, Commentaries 296.

However, if the author is citing to an annotation, it is then necessary to note the editor, date of publication, edition and page, e.g.,

(1 Cooley's Blackstone (4th ed. 1899) p. 142, fn. 4.)
(1 Jones' Blackstone (1915) p. 1314, fn. 6.)

## § 108. California Practice Handbooks, Cassettes and Videotapes.—The **textbooks** published by the California Continuing Education of the Bar are cited by volume number, if any, title, page and year of publication. Author's name and section are optional. The designation "(Cont.Ed.Bar 19 ____ )" always accompanies the citation. Since several early works in this series renumber section designations for each chapter, the use of section references without the page notation is avoided.

(Cal. Administrative Agency Practice (Cont.Ed.Bar 1970) Hearing Procedure, § 1.30, p. 26.)
(Cal. Real Estate Secured Transactions (Cont.Ed.Bar 1970) p. 21.)
(Review of Selected 1969 Code Legislation (Cont.Ed.Bar 1969) p. 205.)
(Boches & Goldfarb, Cal. Juvenile Court Practice (Cont.Ed.Bar 1968) p. 35.)
California Workmen's Compensation Practice (Cont.Ed.Bar 1963) page 553.
See 3 California Commercial Law (Cont.Ed.Bar 1966) section 3.14, page 108.
(Cal. Real Estate Sales Transactions (Cont.Ed.Bar 1967) p. 116 (hereinafter cited as CEB).) . . . (CEB § 2.18, pp. 57–59) . . . . The basis for CEB's interpretation . . . .
(2 Cal. Civil Procedure Forms Manual (Cont.Ed.Bar 1966) p. 324.)
Recent Federal Civil Practice Developments (Cont.Ed.Bar 1965) page 61, appendix B, is helpful to our analysis.

When citing an **article** within the text of a "CEB" book, the author and title of the article may be noted as, e.g.,

> See Sandler, Claims on Public Works in California Mechanics' Liens and Other Remedies (Cont.Ed.Bar 1972) sections 4.11–4.45, pages 104–120.
>
> (See Shastid, Tax Problems of Donors in Cal. Non-profit Corporations (Cont.Ed.Bar 1969) p. 145.)
>
> (Rogers & Nemerovski, Government Contracts Practice (Cont.Ed.Bar 1964) Patents and Data, § 7.6, p. 263.)

When citing a **supplement** to the text, the style is:

> (2 The Cal. Family Lawyer (Cont.Ed.Bar Supp. 1969) pp. 85–86.) [Citation is to supplement alone.]
>
> (Walker, Cal. Juvenile Court Practice (Cont.Ed.Bar Supp. 1975) § 188, pp. 50–51.) [Author of supplement noted.]
>
> (See Cal. Civil Writs (Cont.Ed.Bar 1970) §§ 5.29–5.31, pp. 82–84, *id.* (Cont.Ed.Bar Supp. 1972) pp. 10–11.) [Citation is to text and supplement.]

When the "CEB" publication takes the form of a **periodical**, however (such as the recently introduced Reporter series), the general citation style for law reviews and other periodicals is followed (*post,* §§ 109(a), 119):

> See Sacks & Levy, *Special Verdict Inconsistency Allowed* (Cont.Ed.Bar 1984) 5 Cal. Tort Rptr. pages 9–10.
>
> (Graham, *The Installment Land Contract in California: Is It Really a Mortgage?* (Cont.Ed.Bar 1981) 4 Real Prop. L. Rep. 117, 118.)

**Cassette Tapes:**

> (*Cassette,* Cal. Conservatorships (Cont.Ed.Bar 1972) tape 2, 1st half, Establishing Conservatorships.)

**Videotapes:**

> (*Videotape,* Developments in Business Law (Cont.Ed.Bar 1975).)
>
> (*Videotape,* Developments in Business Law (Cont.Ed.Bar 1975) Class Actions.) [Citation is to specific portion of subject matter covered in the tape.]

## § 109. Law Reviews and Specialized Journals, Magazines, Newspapers and Other Periodicals.

(a) **Law Reviews and Specialized Journals.**—In citing leading articles indicate author, title of article in italics, date in parentheses, volume number, name of periodical, inception page, and, where applicable, point pages.

> (McCarthy, *Trademark Franchising and Antitrust: The Trouble With Tie-Ins* (1970) 58 Cal.L.Rev. 1085.)
>
> See Putz, *Fairness and Commercial Advertising: A Review and a Proposal* (1972) 6 U.S.F. L.Rev. 215, 216.
>
> (Heyman & Twiss, *Environmental Management of Public Lands* (1971) 1 Ecology L.Q. 94.)

In textual formats, as well as within parentheses, use abbreviation forms for law review and journal references. However, no part of a title is abbreviated.

In citing articles, comments and short student notes, only the designation of "Comment" or "Note" preceding the year within parentheses, volume, publication and page need be given. It is desirable, however, to designate the title of the note or article.

> (See Comment (1972) 67 Nw.U.L.Rev. 388.)
> (Note (1972) 72 Colum.L.Rev. 415.)
> (See Comment, *Corporal Punishment in the Public Schools* (1971) 6 Harv.C.R.–C.L. L.Rev. 583.)
> (See also Note, *Administrative Discretion in Zoning* (1969) 82 Harv.L.Rev. 668, 672.)
> (*Review of Selected 1980 California Legislation* (1980) 12 Pacific L.J. 309.)

Do not use quotation marks to enclose article titles unless these marks are part of the title itself.

Where an author makes frequent reference to the same law review article needless repetition may be avoided by adopting an abbreviated reference style normally noted after the first citation, e.g.,

> (Hennessy, *Qualification of California Justice Court Judges: A Dual System* (1972) 3 Pacific L.J. 439 (hereafter *Justice Court Judges*) . . . . (See *Justice Court Judges, supra,* at p. 447.)

A partial list of frequently cited California law reviews and journals and their abbreviated forms follow. (For other law reviews and journals see, A Uniform System of Citation (14th ed. 1986) p. 93 et seq. and The Index to Legal Periodicals.) For the abbreviations of new law reviews and journals not listed in the foregoing sources, follow the publisher's citational style.

```
Beverly Hills Bar Journal ............................... Bev. Hills Bar J.
Brief Case ................................................ Brief Case
Cal Bar View ............................................ Cal Bar View
California Family Law Report ......................... Cal.Fam.L.Rep.
California Law Review .................................... Cal.L.Rev.
California Lawyer ......................................... Cal.Law.
    [previously California State Bar Journal . . . . State Bar J.; name changed
    with volume 56 (1981)]
California Western Law Review ..................... Cal. Western L.Rev.
Ecology Law Quarterly ................................ Ecology L.Q.
Glendale Law Review ................................. Glendale L.Rev.
Golden Gate Law Review ......................... Golden Gate L.Rev.
Hastings Constitutional Law Quarterly ........... Hastings Const.L.Q.
Hastings Law Journal ................................. Hastings L.J.
John F. Kennedy Law Record ................... J.F. Kennedy L.Record
Lincoln Law Review .................................. Lincoln L.Rev.
Long Beach Bar Bulletin ....................... Long Beach Bar Bull.
Los Angeles Lawyer .................................... L.A.Law.
    [previously Los Angeles Bar Bulletin . . . . L.A. Bar Bull.; then Los Angeles
    Bar Journal . . . . L.A. Bar J.; names changed with volumes 50 (1975)
    and 53 (1978) respectively]
Loyola Consumer Protection Journal ........... Loyola Consumer Prot.J.
Loyola University of Los Angeles Law Review ........... Loyola L.A. L.Rev.
Pacific Law Journal ..................................... Pacific L.J.
Pepperdine Law Review .......................... Pepperdine L.Rev.
San Diego Law Review .............................. San Diego L.Rev.
San Fernando Valley Law Review ........... San Fernando Val.L.Rev.
    [previously University of San Fernando Valley Law Review . . . . U. San
    Fernando Val.L.Rev.; name changed with volume 6 (1977)]
```

Santa Clara Law Review .................................Santa Clara L.Rev.
[previously Santa Clara Lawyer .... Santa Clara Law.; name changed with volume 16 (1975)]
Southern California Law Review ...........................So.Cal.L.Rev.
Southwestern University Law Review .........................Sw.U.L.Rev.
Stanford Law Review .......................................Stan.L.Rev.
State Bar Journal ...............................[See California Lawyer]
UCLA Law Review.........................................UCLA L.Rev.
U.C. Davis Law Review ...................................U.C. Davis L.Rev.
University of San Francisco Law Review......................U.S.F. L.Rev.
University of Southern California Tax Institute .......U.So.Cal. 1984 Tax Inst.
University of West Los Angeles Law Review ............U. West L.A. L.Rev.
Western State University Law Review .................Western St.U. L.Rev.
Whittier Law Review .....................................Whittier L.Rev.

**(b) Magazines.**–Note author (where designated), title of article in italics, date in parentheses, name of publication, and page number. Volume numbers may be given.

(See Reid, *The Presumption of Guilt* (Jan. 16, 1971) The New Republic, at pp. 15–16.)
(*The Shame of the Prisons* (Jan. 18, 1971) Time, at p. 53.)
See Main, *Only Radical Reform Can Save the Courts* (Aug. 1970) Fortune, pages 110, 153.
[12] U.S. News & World Report (Feb. 3, 1969) at page 39.*

**(c) Newspaper Articles.**–Note author's name (unless news report only), title of article in italics, name of publication, date in parentheses (month, day, year), page and column number. In citing newspapers which have separate numbering systems for each section, the section designation must be indicated; e.g.,

Reston, *The Conservative Tide,* New York Times (Nov. 1, 1972) page 41M, column 1.
*Drugs at School,* National Observer (Nov. 4, 1972) page 13, column 2.
(Waltz, *Rebuke for Trudeau on Issues,* N.Y. Times (Nov. 1, 1972) p. C3, cols. 4–6.)
[9] Wall Street Journal (Jan. 25, 1972) at page 1, column 8.*

**§ 110. Annotations in Annotated Reports.**—When the intention is to cite an annotation within parentheses but not the case to which the annotation is appended, the abbreviation "Annot." precedes the citation and the inception page of the text of the annotation is indicated. Outside parentheses the word "Annotation" precedes the relevant material. If an author wishes to note the title of the annotation cited it is set out in roman, not italics.

(Annot., Exemption of Public School Property From Assessments for Local Improvements (1967) 15 A.L.R.3d 847.)
(Annot. (1941) 130 A.L.R. 352.)
(Annot. (1951) 19 A.L.R.2d 423, 425.)
(Annot. (1960) 71 A.L.R.2d 1160, 1192, § 8 and cases cited.)

---

*Common footnote style where body of the text recites other pertinent information, i.e., title, author, subject matter.

See generally, Annotation (1967) 14 A.L.R.3d 404.
(See Annot. (1967) 13 A.L.R.3d 1251, 1254–1256, 1262.)
(Annot., Ann.Cas. 1915E 756.)

The following are the abbreviations for the more commonly cited of the annotated reports:

American and English Annotated Cases . . . . . . . . . . . . . Am. & Eng.Ann.Cas.
American Annotated Cases . . . . . . . . . . . . . . . . . . . . . . . . . . . . . . Ann.Cas.
American Decisions . . . . . . . . . . . . . . . . . . . . . . . . . . . . . . . . . . . Am.Dec.
American Law Reports . . . . . . . . . . . . . . . . . . . . . . . . . . . . . . . . . . A.L.R.
American Law Reports, Second Series . . . . . . . . . . . . . . . . . . . . . . A.L.R.2d
American Law Reports, Third Series . . . . . . . . . . . . . . . . . . . . . . . A.L.R.3d
American Law Reports, Fourth Series . . . . . . . . . . . . . . . . . . . . . A.L.R.4th
American Law Reports, Federal Series . . . . . . . . . . . . . . . . . . . . A.L.R.Fed.
American Reports . . . . . . . . . . . . . . . . . . . . . . . . . . . . . . . . . . . . . . . Am.R.
American State Reports . . . . . . . . . . . . . . . . . . . . . . . . . . . . . . . . Am.St.R.
Lawyers' Reports Annotated . . . . . . . . . . . . . . . . . . . . . . . . . . . . . . . L.R.A.
Lawyers' Reports Annotated (New Series) . . . . . . . . . . . . . . . . . . L.R.A.N.S.

(See also *ante,* § 79, annotated reports.)

References to supplements updating annotations are styled as follows:

(Annot. (1954) 38 A.L.R.2d 522, A.L.R.2d (Later Case Service 1969) p. 693.)
(See collected cases in 34 A.L.R.2d 938, 949, and Later Case Service.)
(See Annot. (1971) 40 A.L.R.3d 709, and later cases (1974 pocket supp.) p. 10.)
(See Annot. (1939) 119 A.L.R. 1399, and collection of recent California decisions, 5 A.L.R. Blue Book (1973) No. 8, pp. 370–371.)
(See Annot. 10 A.L.R.Fed 15, and later cases (1975 pocket supp.) p. 3.)

§ 111.  **Restatements.**—Note the Restatement cited and section number. References to comments and illustrations are styled as indicated:

section 100 of the Restatement Second of Trusts
the Restatement Second of Agency section 433
the Restatement of Torts section 867, comment c
the Restatement Second of Trusts (§ 96, com. d, illus. 1)
(Rest., Contracts, § 342, com. a, at p. 561.)
(Rest., Contracts, § 479, com. a, illus. 1.)
(Rest.2d Torts, §§ 302, 302A, 431.)
(Rest., Conf. of Laws, § 22.)
(See Rest., Agency, §§ 39, 76, com. c.)
(Rest.2d Trusts, *supra,* § 99, subd. 1, com. a, illus. 1, § 185, com. a.)
(Rest.2d Trusts, § 108, com. f, p. 239.)
(Rest.2d Agency (1976 in the Cts.Supp.) § 442, p. 489.)
(Rest.2d Agency (appen.) § 164, reporter's notes, pp. 249–252.)

If the author desires to include the date of the Restatement, the form is (Rest., Property, Future Interests (1936) § 157.)

When citing a draft of the Restatement that has not been approved and promulgated, the following forms are appropriate:

**(a) For a tentative draft:**

(Rest., Torts (Tent. Draft No. 3) § 103.)
(Rest.2d Torts (Tent. Draft No. 14, Apr. 15, 1969) § 695, adopted May 21, 1969, (Proceedings of ALI (46th Ann. Meeting, 1969) pp. 148–157).)

**(b) For a proposed final draft:**

(Rest., Torts (Proposed Final Draft No. 2) § 91.)

## § 112.  Model Codes.

(Model Pen. Code, § 250.3.) [When the citation is only to the statutory text of the code.]

(Model Pen. Code & Commentaries, com. 2 to § 240.7, pp. 87–89.) [When the citation is to the code and commentaries or the commentaries alone.]

(See com. Model Pen. Code, § 207.11, p. 149 (Tent. Draft No. 9, 1959).)

(See Model Pen. Code, § 305.21, com. at p. 117 (Tent. Draft No. 5, 1956).)

(See Model Pen. Code (Proposed Official Draft 1969) § 6.06.)

Model Penal Code section 305.17 at pages 102–106 (Tent. Draft No. 5, 1956)

(Model Land Development Code, Land Development Plan, § 2–101 (Tent. Draft No. 1, 1968) p. 33.)

(Model Code of Pre-Arraignment Procedure, § 1007, p. 88 (Study Draft No. 1, 1968).)

Advisory Council of Judges of the National Council on Crime and Delinquency, Model Sentencing Act, section 5, subdivisions (a) and (b) (1963)

(11 West's U. Laws Ann. (1974) Crim. L. & Proc., comrs. note, p. 61.)

(See 9A West's U. Laws Ann. (1979) U. Reciprocal Enforcement of Support (1968 rev. act) § 23.)

## § 113.  Legal Encylopedias.

§ 113. **Legal Encylopedias.**—Citations should include volume number, publication title, subject, section number and page. It is permissible, however, to omit subject and section number. Publishers often revise individual volumes between editions and authors citing to a revision should advise the reader by the use of the parenthetical expression (rev.). Where there is more than one revision, the year is added (rev. 1973).

(28 C.J.S., Domicile, § 12, p. 21.)

(3A C.J.S. (rev. 1973) Aliens, § 321, p. 221, fn. 48.)

(1 Cal.Jur.2d, Actions, § 23, pp. 467–468.)

(19 Cal.Jur. 3d (rev.) Criminal Law, § 1898, p. 216.)

(5 Cal.Jur.3d, Appellate Review, § 591, pp. 310–311.)

(1 Cal.Jur.3d, Accountants, § 5 (1984 pocket pt.) p. 25.)

13 California Jurisprudence Third, Constitutional Law, section 159, page 292

(43 Am.Jur.2d (rev.) Insurance, § 525, p. 597.)

See 4 American Jurisprudence Second, Appeal and Error, sections 345–351, pages 825–830.

**Abbreviations:**

| | |
|---|---|
| American Jurisprudence | Am.Jur. |
| American Jurisprudence Second | Am.Jur.2d |
| California Jurisprudence | Cal.Jur. |
| California Jurisprudence Second | Cal.Jur.2d |
| California Jurisprudence Third | Cal.Jur.3d |
| Corpus Juris | C.J. [Not Cor.Jur.] |
| Corpus Juris Secundum | C.J.S. |
| Cyclopedia of Law and Procedure | Cyc. |
| Ruling Case Law | R.C.L. |

**§ 114. Digests.**—Note the name of the digest, the subject reference and the section number. If desired, the volume and page number may be included, e.g.,

See cases digested in 2A McKinney's Digest, Appeal and Error, section 389.
(See McK.Dig., Indictment and Information, § 69.)
(Cal.Dig.Off.Rep.3d Ser., Adoption, § 7, p. 123.)
14A West's California Digest, Courts, section 484
(West's Cal.Dig.2d, Wills, § 341.)
(L.R.A. Dig., Pleading, § 184.)
(3 A.L.R.2d Dig., Evidence, § 106.)
11 American Law Reports Digest, Trial, section 314(4)

**American Digest System:**

(28 Century Dig., Insurance, § 84, p. 550.)
(3d Dec.Dig., Joint Adventures, § 5(1).)
(12 Gen.Dig. (4th Ser. 1970) Damages, § 62(4).)

American Digest System key numbers are cited as sections, e.g., Commerce Key No. 33, will be Commerce, § 33. Where a revised edition is involved see *ante,* section 113.

**§ 115. Dictionaries.**—Note the volume number if any, title, edition with the year, and page. Column number is sometimes noted.

(Webster's New Internat. Dict. (3d ed. 1961) p. 6.)
Webster's Third New International Dictionary (1981) page 56
Webster's New International Dictionary (2d ed. 1941) at page 18
(Webster's New Collegiate Dict. (7th ed. 1970) pp. 28–29.)
(Webster's New World Dict. (2d college ed. 1982) p. 27.)
(See Black's Law Dict. (5th ed. 1979) p. 810, col. 2.)
(Bander, Law Dict. of Practical Definitions (1966) p. 4.)
1 Schmidt, Attorney's Dictionary of Medicine (1974) page A–111
11 Oxford English Dictionary (1933) page 238
(2 Supp. to Oxford English Dict. (1976) p. 501.)
News Dictionary (Sobel ed. 1971) Crime, page 106
(17A Words and Phrases (1958) p. 63.)
(16 Words and Phrases (1984 pocket pt.) p. 5.)

**§ 116. California Jury Instructions.**—California Jury Instructions, Civil are cited as BAJI; California Jury Instructions, Criminal are cited as CALJIC and these abbreviations are favored by the editors. More descriptive forms are: (Cal.Jury Instns., Civ. (9th ed. 1977) No. 3.50) and (Cal.Jury Instns., Crim. (4th ed. 1979) No. 7.08). The numerical instruction cited is always preceded by "No." or "Nos." Since jury instructions are frequently revised, readers should be apprised, when the subject language is not provided by quotation, of the year of publication and edition.

(CALJIC No. 7.08 (4th ed. 1979).)
(BAJI No. 3.45 (6th ed. 1983 pocket pt.) pp. 8–9.)
CALJIC Nos. 3.34, 3.35 and 8.77, Fourth edition 1979, provide . . . .
(BAJI No. 9.00.7, Supp. Service, pamp. No. 2 (1984) pp. 32–33.)

Where an opinion or brief makes frequent references to jury instructions derived from the same edition the author may avoid lengthy repetition by noting the source following the initial reference, e.g.,

> BAJI Instruction No. 3.50 provides . . . . (All BAJI jury instructions referred to, unless otherwise noted, are from the 6th ed. (1977).) . . . . Jury instruc— tion No. 3.78 was refused.
> (BAJI No. 3.50 (6th ed. 1977).)*

---

> \* All BAJI instructions referred to are from the sixth edition unless otherwise noted.

## § 117. Nontextual Books, Essays, Pamphlets, Reference Book Excerpts, and Interviews.

—Note author, title (not italicized, except for essays), year of publication within parentheses (with edition if more than one) and page. Indication of the book's publisher is optional but not usually given. If more than two parties author a book, article, etc., use only the first named author and "et al."

### (a) Books.

> (Kinzer, An Episode of Anti–Catholicism (1956) pp. 15–16.)
> (Yaffe, So Sue Me (1972) p. 194.)
> (Soloman, Ancestors and Immigrants (Harv.U. Press 1956) pp. 115–116.)
> Davis, in Discretionary Justice (1971) at pages 58–60, notes . . . .
> (Rock, Hospitalization and Discharge of the Mentally Ill (1968) p. 121 (hereafter Hospitalization).)

### (b) Essays.

—When citing an individual essay contained in a volume of collected essays, note the author of the essay *and* the editor of the collection unless the editor is also the author, the title of the essay cited and the title of the collection. Essay titles are italicized. When citing collections with more than two editors, name only the first editor and use "et al." in place of the others.

> Graves, *The Deterrent Effect of Capital Punishment in Philadelphia,* in The Death Penalty in America (Bedau edit. 1964) page 315
> (Drinan, *The Inviolability of the Right To Be Born,* in Abortion and the Law (Smith edit. 1967) p. 107.)
> Antieau, *State Regulation of Contractual Relationships,* in Commentaries on the Constitution of the United States (1960) page 136. [Author is also editor.]
> (Bickel, *The Supreme Court, 1960 Term—Foreword: The Passive Virtues,* in Selected Essays on Constitutional Law (Barrett et al. edits. 1963) p. 24.)

### (c) Pamphlets.

> On Guard, A Guide for the Consumer (Cal.Dept. of Justice, information pamp. No. 3, 1972) Hints on Buying a New or Used Car, page 3.
> (Youth Service Bureaus in Cal. (Cal.Dept. of Youth Authority, pamp. 1971) table 9, p. 54.)
> A Matter of Simple Justice, The Report of the President's Task Force on Women's Rights and Responsibilities (pamp. 1970) page 4.

(See also *ante,* §§ 60, 63.)

### (d) Reference Book Excerpts.

> (Statistical Abstract of U.S. (94th ed. 1973) table 47, p. 38.)

(The World Almanac (1975) Agriculture, Nutritive Value of Foods, p. 435.)

(See also *ante,* §§ 60, 62, 64.1, and *post,* § 118.)

**(e) Interviews.**

See *Military Spendings: Impact on Business* (Interview with David Packard, Deputy Sect. of Defense) U.S. News & World Report (Aug. 3, 1970) page 44.

(See also *ante,* § 59, and *post,* § 118.)

## § 118. Miscellaneous Studies, Surveys, Reports, Hearings, Manuals, and Addresses.

(United Nations, Economic and Social Council, Note by the Sect. Gen., Capital Punishment (E/4947) (Feb. 23, 1971).)

(See generally, Universal Declaration of Human Rights, United Nations Gen. Assem. Res., 217A (111) Dec. 1948.)

United States Advisory Commission on Intergovernmental Relations, A Commission Report: State Constitutional and Statutory Restrictions on Local Government Debt (1961) at page 22 states . . . .

(Cf. President's Commission on Law Enforcement and Admin. of Justice, Task Force Rep., Corrections (1957) p. 194.)

See the Report of the National Advisory Commission on Civil Disorders (Kerner Com.) 1969, page 1.

(Crime & Delinquency in Cal.–Crime and Arrests 1970, Bur. of Crim. Stats. 1971, Refer. Tables, p. 5.)

President's Advisory Committee on Narcotic and Drug Abuse, Final Report (1963) at pages 39–43.

See Marihuana: First Report by the Select Committee on Crime, house report No. 910978, 91st Congress, 2d Session (1970) at pages 95–106.

(President's Commission on Law Enforcement and Admin. of Justice, Rep. (1967) The Challenge of Crime in a Free Society, p. 143.)

See Hearings on Senate Bill No. 1760 Before the Subcommittee on Criminal Laws and Procedures of the Senate Committee on the Judiciary on March 20, 21 and July 2, 1968 (published by G.P.O. 1970) page 21.

California Advisory Commission on Marine and Coastal Resources, Third Annual Report, California Coastal Zone Management—The Development of the Comprehensive Ocean Area Plan (1971) page 8 et. seq.

(See Hall, County Supervisorial Districting in Cal., Bur. Pub. Admin., U. Cal., 1961 Legis. Problems, No. 5, p. 35.)

See California Style Manual (3d ed. 1986) section 88.3 et seq.

(Cal. Style Manual (3d ed. 1986) § 88.3 et seq.)

(Cal. Municipal and Justice Courts Manual, Cal. Center for Jud. Ed. & Research (1974).)

(Mason, Manual of Legis. Proc. (Cal. State Printing Office 1953) p. 79.)

State Department of Social Welfare, Manual of Policies and Procedures: Eligibility and Assistance Standards, sections 22–22.3 (hereinafter SDSW Manual).

Eliminating Frivolous Appeals, Standards Relating to Criminal Appeals, American Bar Association's Project on Minimum Standards for Criminal Justice (Approved Draft 1970) page 63.

See remarks of Honorable William M. McAllister, Associate Justice of the Supreme Court of Oregon, Report of Proceedings of the National Defender Conference, National Defender Project of the National Legal Aid and Defender Association, May 14–16, 1969, pages 157, 161.

(Address, Justice for the Poor, by John N. Turner, Minister of Justice and Atty. Gen. of Canada, North Am. Judges Assn. Conf., San Francisco, Dec. 1, 1969.)

(See also *post,* § 126 re federal agency documents.)

**§ 119.    Topical Law Reporters and Services.**—The rising tide of case law, legislation, and administrative rulings and materials, as well as official and unofficial commentary relating to these sources, has spawned an accompanying expansion of valuable specialized and topical law reporters and services designed to collect, condense and editorially review these materials and the subject areas of the law they cover.

No "standard" citation form is practical, since distribution formats are varied, e.g., newsletter, looseleaf with periodic update (sometimes with annual binding), pamphlet, etc. The internal formats selected to organize these materials are equally diverse. Nevertheless, an interested reader is entitled to be led conveniently to the material cited. The author is accordingly obliged to analyze the structure of the cited service to provide essential information. After preparing a citation form, the author should challenge its appropriateness by asking, "Can the material cited be readily located with the information provided?"

Listed below are typical citations structured to impart essential information.

(1 Fed. Estate and Gift Tax Rptr. (CCH) ¶ 6407.05 (Feb. 6, 1984).)[1]

(*Delgrosso* v. *Spang & Co.* (W.D.Pa 1983) 586 F.Supp. 177, 117 Lab. Rel. Ref. Manual (Bur.Nat.Affairs) p. 3071.)

(Goff, *How to Obtain an Ex Parte Order and Avoid Improper Communication With a Judge* (Cont.Ed.Bar 1985) 7 Civ. Litigation Rptr. 69, 71.) (See also *ante,* § 108 (a).)

(See Army Corps of Engineers Regulations on Urban Studies Program, 33 C.F.R. § 264.14 (Nov. 3, 1975) Environ. Rptr. (Bur.Nat.Affairs) 3 Federal Regulations, § 131:1841 (Dec. 26, 1975).)[2]

(Green & Zell, *Federal–State Conflict in Nuclear Waste Management: The Legal Basis,* 2 Energy L. Serv. (Callaghan), Monograph 6D (May 1980), § 6D.11 Classification of Nuclear Waste, p. 12.)

. . . The notion of labor pirating (Lab. L. Rptr. (CCH) 2 State Laws, ¶ Cal. 43,015, Strikebreaking (June 8, 1984)) was recognized . . . .

(Fed. Elec. Com. Advisory Opn. No. 1980–92 (Sept. 11, 1980) Campaign Practices Rpts. (Congressional Quarterly Inc., Mar. 1981), § 4:363.)

. . . In 1 Federal Estate and Gift Tax Reporter (CCH), paragraph 6407.25 (Feb. 6, 1984), the valuation of art objects as household items and personal effects is explained in the light of Internal Revenue Service Regulation section 20.2031–6 and Review Procedure 66–49, 1966–2 CB.

(Cal. Iron Workers Employers Council, 272 NLRB No. 83 (1984), 117 Lab. Rel. Ref. Manual (Bur.Nat.Affairs) p. 1402.)

(See 1 Gov. Disclosure (Prentice–Hall) par. 30.211.4 (Nov. 1984) for brief summary of exceptions to notion of "public records" under Cal. codes.)

---

[1] Some publications use paragraph (or section) numbers as the permanent means of identification and reference, rather than page numbers.

[2] Sometimes two dates are important for a citation. Here the first dates the regulation, and the second identifies an updated version of the referenced material.

## § 120. Advance Pamphlets—Material Other Than Opinions.

—A variety of materials in the advance pamphlets (other than opinions) will sometimes be cited because the pamphlets are the only, or the most convenient, source of reference at that particular time. Such items include new California Rules of Court, court minutes, and entries in the Cumulative Subsequent History Table. A typical citation might read:

> (See Cal. Rules of Court, rule 960(c) [Off. Reps. Adv. Pamp. No. 4 (1985) Rules p. 21].)

In the foregoing example, the bracketed part of the citation is temporary only, and would be omitted from citations published after the rule has itself been routinely published elsewhere (such as in the Rules volumes of Deering's and West's Codes). (For citations to Rules of Court generally, see *ante,* § 64.)

Additional citations for these materials are noted below:

> Counsel's motion to vacate their appointment was denied. (See Mins. of Ct. App., 1st App.Dist., Div. Two, Mar. 21, 1985, A012345, Off. Reps. Adv. Pamp. No. 10 (1985) Mins., p. 17.)
>
> (By notice to counsel of July 1, 1986, the Supreme Ct. identified additional issues for review. See Supreme Ct. pages, Off. Reps. Adv. Pamp. No. 4, p. 511b.)
>
> The printing error was detected and corrected. (Off. Reps. Cum. Sub. Hist. Table, Adv. Pamp. No. 35 (1987) p. 33.)
>
> Time to grant or deny review of *Smith* v. *Jones* was extended to August 6, 1986. (Supreme Ct. Mins. July 8, 1986 [Off. Reps. Cum. Sub. Hist. Table, Adv. Pamp. No. 21 (1986) p. 167].)

# G. Federal Materials

## § 121. Federal Statutes.

—The preferable citation is to the United States Code (U.S.C.). However, the United States Code Annotated (U.S.C.A.) and the United States Code Service (U.S.C.S.) are often cited and are acceptable. It is sometimes helpful to note the year of enactment after the citation to the code, especially in referring to a code provision that is known to have been superseded. For those titles of the code not enacted into positive law the Statutes at Large are the authoritative source but need be cited only in the event of a language difference from the code.

> (7 U.S.C. § 5.) or (7 U.S.C.A. § 5.) or (7 U.S.C.S. § 5.)
>
> (29 U.S.C. § 176 (1947).)
>
> (26 U.S.C. § 2056(b)(7)(B)(v).)
>
> (44 U.S.C. § 396(a), now § 3101.)
>
> (42 U.S.C. § 2000e-2(a)(1), § 2000g et seq.)
>
> Concerning aid to needy families see the Social Security Act (42 U.S.C. § 601 et seq.).
>
> the Social Security Act as amended in 1968 (42 U.S.C. § 602(a)(23)) in material part provided . . . .

the Railroad Retirement Act of 1937, 50 Statutes at Large 309, as amended, 45 United States Code section 228b(a)4 . . . .
(Webb–Kenyon Act (37 Stat. 699, 27 U.S.C. § 122 (1913).)
Section 701 of the Civil Rights Act of 1964 (78 Stat. 253, 42 U.S.C. 2000(e)) . . . .
(61 Stat. 652, 17 U.S.C. § 203.)
(61 Stat. 652, 17 U.S.C. § 203 (1947).)
(Fair Labor Standards Act of 1938, § 13(b)(11), 29 U.S.C. §§ 213(b)(11).)
(§ 1, Sherman Antitrust Act, 15 U.S.C. § 1; §§ 2(a), 2(f), Clayton Act, as amended by the Robinson–Patman Act, 15 U.S.C. § 13.)
Title VII of the Civil Rights Act of 1964 (42 U.S.C. § 2000e et seq.) as amended by the Equal Employment Opportunity Act of 1972 (Pub.L. No. 92–261, 86 Stat. 103)

**Recent Enactments.**—Slip laws are cited by full date, public or private law number and the reference source or sources, e.g.,

(Pub.L. No. 94–126 (Nov. 12, 1975) 89 Stat. 679, 1975 U.S. Code Cong. & Admin. News, No. 11.) [Citation notes Public Law number 126, 94th Congress.]

Slip laws appear at an early date in the United States Code Congressional and Administrative News and reference to that publication's pamphlet service is encouraged.

Slip laws bear their official citation to the Statutes at Large and therefore a citation to that source should be noted even though the bound volume is not then published.

(Pub.L. No. 93–1 (Jan. 19, 1973) § 2, 87 Stat. 3.)

**Official or Popular Names.**—The use of an official or popular name in the citation of a statute will often assist in identification and may be used in abbreviated form to avoid confusion and lengthy repetitions after the statute has been first cited in full.

Respondents rely on the wording of the Wagner–O'Day Act (41 U.S.C. §§ 46–48 (1938)) (hereafter Wagner) . . . Wagner came into being as a response to . . . .

**Statutes Not in Force.**—It is permissible to cite to the Statutes at Large noting the enactment date in parentheses. (33 Stat. 724 (Feb. 20, 1905).) It is preferable, however, to note the full date, the chapter number or (commencing with the 85th Congress (1957–1958)) the public law number followed by a reference to the Statutes at Large.

(Act of Feb. 20, 1905, ch. 592, § 1–23, 33 Stat. 724.)
(Act of Aug. 27, 1958, Pub.L. No. 85–767, § 2, 72 Stat. 899.)

Citations using public or private law numbers must indicate the Congress since each Congress renumbers its laws. In the example above the number 85 designates the Congress.

**§ 122. Internal Revenue Code.**—Although the current Internal Revenue Code appears under title 26 of the United States Code which uses identical section numbering, it is customarily cited by its own name without parallel references to either the United States Code or to the

Statutes at Large.

> (§ 7237(c) of the Int.Rev. Code.)
> Internal Revenue Code of 1954, section 1012

If the reference is to the code in force no code enactment–year designation is necessary although it is frequently noted. However, if an author is comparing or contrasting earlier enactments with later provisions, code enactment dates should be indicated, e.g.,

> The predecessor of section 7237(c) of the Internal Revenue Code of 1954 was section 2557(b) of the 1939 code.

It is helpful and therefore desirable to cite the Statutes at Large as a parallel for a superseded or repealed code section.

> (Int.Rev. Code of 1939, ch. 2, § 2557(b), 53 Stat. 274–276.)
> Internal Revenue Code of 1954, section 7237(c) (formerly Int.Rev. Code of 1939, ch. 2, § 2557(b), 53 Stat. 274–276), provides . . . .

Where it is material to note that a section of the code was added after the original enactment it is not necessary to cite to "Stat.," e.g.,

> Section 1348 of the Internal Revenue Code of 1954, added by the Tax Reference Act of 1969, provides . . . .

See a Uniform System of Citation (14th ed. 1986) pages 76–78 for suitable styles when citing Internal Revenue regulations and rulings, Treasury regulations and related tax materials.

## § 123. Congressional Bills and Resolutions

**Bills:**

> (H.R. No. 11764, 86th Cong., 2d Sess. (1960) pp. 8–10.)
> (Sen. No. 1126, 87th Cong., 1st Sess. (1961) p. 2.)
> (§ 6(a) of Sen. No. 44, § 7 of H.R. No. 7155, 86th Cong., 1st Sess. (1959).)
> (Sen. No. 1126, 87th Cong., 1st Sess. (1961) (hereafter Sen. No. 1126).)

**Resolutions:**

> (Sen.Res. No. 21, 87th Cong., 2d Sess. (1962).)

After adoption, single house resolutions are cited to the Congressional Record, joint resolutions to the Statutes at Large or the Congressional Record.

> (Sen.Res. No. 10, 100th Cong., 1st Sess. (1991) 100 Cong. Rec. 100.)
> (Sen.J.Res. No. 59, 86th Cong., 1st Sess. (1959) 73 Stat. 111.)
> (H.Con.Res. No. 10, 100th Cong., 2d Sess. (1991) 150 Stat. 150.)

**Citational abbreviations:**

| | |
|---|---|
| House Bill No. 46 | H.R. No. 46 |
| Senate Bill No. 28 | Sen. No. 28 |
| House Resolution No. 5 | H.Res. No. 5 |
| House Concurrent Resolution No. 114 | H.Con.Res. No. 114 |
| Senate Resolution No. 103 | Sen.Res. No. 103 |
| Senate Concurrent Resolution No. 22 | Sen.Con.Res. No. 22 |
| House Joint Resolution No. 10 | H.J.Res. No. 10 |
| Senate Joint Resolution No. 3 | Sen.J.Res. No. 3 |

## § 124. Congressional Reports, Documents, Hearings, Debates, and Addresses.

### (a) Reports:

(H.R.Rep. No. 586, 82d Cong., 1st Sess., p. 4 (1951).)

Commencing with 1969 (91st Cong.) these reports are cited as:

(Sen.Rep. No. 92–100, 1st Sess., p. 3 (1971).) Note: The number 92 represents the Congress.

### (b) Documents:

(Engle Central Valley Project Documents, H.R. Doc. No. 246, 85th Cong., 1st Sess., pt. 2, pp. 698–702 (1957).)

(See Securities and Exchange Commission, Rep. of Special Study of Securities Markets, H.R. Doc. No. 95, 88th Cong., 1st Sess., pt. 2, pp. 355–356 (1963) (hereinafter referred to as Special Study).)

(Letter of Atty.Gen., May 10, 1962, 108 Cong. Rec. 8451, 87th Cong., 2d Sess. (1962).)

### (c) Committee Hearings:

(Hearings Before the House Com. on Interstate and Foreign Commerce on H.R. No. 4704, 65th Cong., 1st Sess., pt. 2, at pp. 3–4 (1917).)

(Hearings Before the House Com. on Post Office and Civ. Service on H.R. No. 91–17070, 1st Sess., ser. 91, pt. 22, at pp. 83–84 (1969).)

(Concerning the 1971 amendments see, 117 Cong. Rec. pp. 102–107 (daily ed. Dec. 1, 1971) remarks by Senator Proxmire.)

See the Statement of Honorable C. Douglas Dillon (hearings on H.R. No. 13270 before Sen. Com. on Finance, 91st Cong., 1st Sess., pt. 4, at p. 3342 (1969) hereafter 1969 Senate Hearings).

(Statement of Edwin S. Cohen, Asst. Sect. of the Treas. for Tax Policy, April 22, 1969, Hearings on the Subject of the Tax Reform Before the Com. on Ways and Means, 91st Cong., 1st Sess., pt. 14, 5500, 5509.)

### (d) Debates:

(Remarks of Representative Montague, 55 Cong. Rec. 4922 (1917).)

(Remarks of Congressman McCormack, 84 Cong. Rec. 10454 (1939).)

See the argument of Representative Mills before the Senate Finance Committee (90th Cong., 1st Sess. 1969) 115 Congressional Record H6982, daily edition August 6, 1969.

(Remarks of Sen. Humphrey, 106 Cong. Rec. 7266 (daily ed. Apr. 8, 1960).)

The Congressional Record is repaged in its bound edition and therefore a notation that the daily edition is the reference source is essential.

The Senate Journal (Sen. J.) and House Journal (H.R.J.) are cited only if the debates do not appear in the Congressional Record, e.g.,

(Remarks of Senator Smith, Sen. J., 100th Cong., 2d Sess. (1981) p. 1234).)

### (e) Messages to Congress:

President Nixon's Message to Congress on Revenue Sharing (117 Cong. Rec. 5811 (daily ed. Feb. 4, 1971)) . . . .

(See *ante,* this section, subd. (d).)

### (f) Addresses:

(See Radio and Tel. Address by Pres. Nixon, Aug. 15, 1971, in 1971 U.S. Code Cong. & Admin. News, No. 7, at p. 1933.)

(See *post,* § 130 concerning the citation of U.S. Code Cong. & Admin. News which differs in pagination between its advance service and the corresponding bound volume.)

### § 125. Treaties and International Agreements.—Indicate title, type of document (treaty, agreement, protocol, etc.), subject of agreement, country for identification, and date of signing. In most instances the title of the document will supply the foregoing essential information. Lengthy titles may be paraphrased. Pre–1950 treaties and agreements are generally cited to the Statutes at Large. After December 31, 1949, they are cited to United States Treaties and Other International Agreements (U.S.T.). Parallel citation to the Department of State's collection, although not essential, is frequently provided. This collection is broken into three series: Treaty Series (T.S.) 1908–1945, Executive Agreement Series (E.A.S.) 1929–1945, and Treaties and Other International Acts Series (T.I.A.S.) 1945 to date. Each document is identified by number within its series.

> (Treaty of Transit of Military Aircraft With Mexico, Apr. 1, 1941, par. 3d, 55 Stat. 1191, T.S. 971.)
> (Sudan, Guaranty of Private Investments, Agreement of Mar. 17, 1959, 10 U.S.T. 408, T.I.A.S. 4201.)

When a notation of the effective date, date of approval by the Senate, date of proclamation, etc., is material such information is placed in parentheses following the citation.

> (Education: Financing of Exchange Programs with the Republic of Korea, Agreement of Sept. 24, 1971, U.S.T. 2056, T.I.A.S. 7240 (eff. Nov. 26, 1971).)

For the citation of charters, resolutions and records of international organizations see A Uniform System of Citation (14th ed. 1986) pages 119 et seq.

### § 126. Agency Documents.—The paramount consideration in citing these sources is to give the reader sufficient information to obtain the document from the most generally accessible source. Essential information includes designation of author or authoring agency, title, date, volume and page if available. In many instances such documents can be obtained only from the originating agency.

> (Office of Research & Statistics, Soc. Sec. Admin., Dept. Health, Ed. & Welf., National Health Ins. Proposals introduced in 97th Cong., 2d Sess. (May 1981) (mimeo. rep.).)
> (See Schumer, Hospital Utilization Review and Medicare; A Survey, Office of Research & Stats., Soc. Sec. Admin., Dept. Health, Ed. & Welf., staff paper No. 8 (1971).)
> (U.S. Dept. Commerce, Statistical Abstract, table 799 at p. 533 (1966 ed.).)
> (See Administrative Procedure in Gov. Agencies, rep. of Atty. Gen. Com. on Admin., Sen. Doc. No. 186, 76th Cong., 3d Sess., pt. 13, at pp. 1–3 (1940).)

(Supplementary Rep. of the Register of Copyright on the Gen. Rev. of the U.S. Copyright Law (May 1965).)

(Letter from Sect. of the Interior Hickel to Sen. Mathias (Oct. 15, 1969) 115 Cong. Rec. 32162 (1969).)

(U.S. Dept. of Commerce, Statistical Abstract of U.S. (1969) table No. 460, p. 313; U.S. Dept. of Commerce, Survey of Current Business (July 1970) at pp. 5–10.)

(See also *ante,* § 118 re miscellaneous studies, surveys, reports, hearings, manuals and addresses, and § 60 re governmental reports.)

### § 127. Federal Administrative Rules, Regulations and Decisions.

—Generally, administrative regulations and rules are cited to the Code of Federal Regulations (C.F.R.) or to the Federal Register (Fed.Reg.) (daily supplement to C.F.R.). Where the material is not published in either (C.F.R.) or (Fed.Reg.) or is not customarily cited to those publications, indicate the agency's name (established abbreviations are permissible within parentheses), date and page. (See *ante,* § 126.) Where there is a potential for confusion as to whether an author is referring to state or federal rules and regulations, preface the citation with "United States" in the text or (U.S.) within parentheses. Regulations not currently in force are cited to the Federal Register (Fed.Reg.) even if the regulation is published in the current (C.F.R.). Subsequent history is provided parenthetically. Appropriate styles are noted below.

(Foreign Assets Control Regs. (31 C.F.R. § 500.808 (1968).)

(32 C.F.R. § 581.3(c)(5) (1968).)

Section 97.39 of the Federal Communication Commission regulations (47 C.F.R. (1971)) provides:

Department of State Public Notice 179 (26 Fed.Reg. 492 (Jan. 19, 1961)) provided:

(Off. Alien Prop., Vesting Order No. 2506, 8 Fed.Reg. 16343 (Dec. 4, 1943).)

The appropriate HEW regulation, to wit, 45 Code of Federal Regulations, section 201.3(a) (1984), provides:

(Cost of Living Council Reg. 6 C.F.R. § 105 et seq. (1972).)

On July 29, 1971, the USDA issued new regulations. (7 C.F.R. §§ 270–274; 36 Fed.Reg. 14102–14120, amended Apr. 19, 1972, 37 Fed.Reg. 7724.)

### § 128. Federal Court Rules.

—Rules controlling court procedures are cited in a style analogous to the codes. No date is generally given since it is presumed, unless otherwise noted, that the reference is to the rule in force at the citation date. However, where a rule has been recently amended, if the author does not set out the new language, it is desirable to note the amendment date to avoid the potential of readers relying on publications not yet brought current. Parallel citations are helpful and therefore encouraged. Sample styles are noted below.

(Fed. Rules Civ.Proc., rule 4, 28 U.S.C.)

rule 23 of the Federal Rules of Civil Procedure (28 U.S.C.)

(Fed. Rules Civ.Proc., rule 12(c), 28 U.S.C.)

(Fed. Rules Crim.Proc., rules 35, 37(a)(12), 18 U.S.C.)

(Rule 9(c) Fed. Rules App.Proc., as amended Oct. 1, 1972, 28 U.S.C.)

Rule 1007 of the Federal Rules of Evidence (28 U.S.C.), effective July 31, 1973, . . .
(Fed. Rules Evid., rule 804(a)(4), (b)(1), 28 U.S.C.)

## § 129. Executive Orders and Presidential Proclamations.—

Cite to the Federal Register (which publishes all orders and proclamations) or to the Code of Federal Regulations (which publishes those which are of general public interest under title 3). It is helpful to cite to parallel popular sources when available.

(Exec. Order No. 11574, 35 Fed.Reg. 19627 (Dec. 25, 1970).)
(Exec. Order No. 11615, 36 Fed.Reg. 15727 (Aug. 17, 1971) as amended, Exec. Order No. 11617, 36 Fed.Reg. 17813 (Sept. 2, 1971).)
Executive Order No. 9788, 11 Federal Register 11981 (Oct. 14, 1946), 50 United States Code Annotated, appendix, section 6, note.
(Exec. Order No. 11639, 37 Fed.Reg. 521 (Jan. 13, 1972), 1972 U.S. Code Cong. & Admin. News, p. 5495.)
Executive Order No. 11588, 3 Code of Federal Regulations 147 (1971) provides . . . .
(Pres.Proc. No. 4239, 3A C.F.R. 123 (Sept. 4, 1973).)
(Pres.Proc. No. 2592, 3 C.F.R., 1943–1948 Comp. 7 (Aug. 30, 1943).)
(Pres.Proc. No. 4155, 37 Fed.Reg. 18891 (Sept. 16, 1972), 1972 U.S. Code Cong. & Admin. News, p. 5471.)
Presidential Proclamation No. 4336, 39 Federal Register 41497, November 29, 1974, provides . . . .

## § 130. United States Code Congressional and Administrative News.—

This publication includes all public laws enacted at each session of the Congress, legislative history, proclamations, executive orders, and reorganization plans. It may be cited as a secondary source for federal statutes. Each volume is numbered according to the year of the congressional session to which it pertains. The pagination for the pamphlet service differs from that of the later bound volume with the exception that pagination to statutes now remains the same for both.

(1971 U.S. Code Cong. & Admin. News, at pp. 374–375.)
(Pub.L. No. 93—3 (Feb. 1, 1973) 1973 U.S. Code Cong. & Admin. News, p. 4.)
The legislative history is described in 1975 United States Code Congressional and Administrative News, No. 5, page 857. [Pamphlet service reference.]
(See for legis. hist., 1973 U.S. Code Cong. & Admin. News, at pp. 1217–1224.)

(See *ante,* §§ 121, 124(f) for additional illustrations.)

# CHAPTER II
## —Notes—

# CHAPTER III

# PUNCTUATION

## A. Quotations

## B. Parentheses and Brackets

## C. Italics

## D. Hyphens

### A.  Quotations

§ **131.  Correspondence With Original.**—Quoted material should correspond exactly with its original source in wording, spelling, capitalization, punctuation and citational style. Any deviations must be indicated or explained. Explanatory or other material inserted within the quotation must be placed in brackets or otherwise noted. (See *post,* § 132 et seq. for styles of noting deviations and insertions.)

§ **132.  Noting Omissions in Quoted Matter Generally.**—When an author does not quote a source in full but instead abstracts only a portion great care must be taken to convey this fact to the reader. Any break in the sequence of words or other quoted matter must be noted. However, when it is obvious from the text that what is quoted is but a broken or interrupted part of the source, a notation that a portion is missing is not necessary, e.g.,

> If the scope of the statute cannot be limited to situations to which it may constitutionally apply except "by reading into it numerous qualifications and exceptions" amounting "to a wholesale rewriting of the provision," the statute may not be saved by judicial construction but must be declared invalid. (*Fort v. Civil Service Commission* (1964) 61 Cal.2d 331, 340 [38 Cal.Rptr. 625, 392 P.2d 385].)

Ordinarily an author need not note that he is not including material from the original source which preceded or followed a sentence he is quoting since there is really no omission. However, the context may call for an indication of this information where, for example, an author is quoting a single sentence from a multi-sentenced statute, a legal document, or trial testimony.

## § 133.  Style of Noting Omissions.

**(a) Omission at beginning of quoted sentence.**—Indicate the deletion by three dots set off by a space following the last dot, or as an alternative, where the first letter of a word was not capitalized in the original, capitalize it and place it within brackets.

> "[T]he motive, as noted, is not an element of arson."
> ". . . the motive, as noted, is not an element of arson."

(See also *post*, § 139.)

**(b) Omission in the middle of quoted sentence.**—Note the omission by the use of three dots set off by a space before the first and after the last, e.g.,

> "A valid defense . . . is indicated."

Where the portion quoted ends in a punctuation mark add three dots following the mark set off by a space before the first and after the last, e.g.,

> The contract provides: "Landlord shall pay taxes, . . . and other governmental levies."

**(c) Omission following a completed quoted sentence.**—Indicate the omission of material following a completed quoted sentence by the use of three equally spaced dots following the quoted sentence's period.

> The court noted, "The facts are distinguishable. . . ."

(See also *ante*, § 132.)

**(d) Omission at end of incomplete quoted sentence.**—Note the omission by the use of three dots set off by a space *before* the first dot followed by the sentence period.

> The defendant knew "He was about to be arrested and fled . . . ."

If the quoted matter ending the author's sentence is not a complete sentence but the portion quoted ends in a punctuation mark, add two dots after the mark and the closing period, e.g.,

> The court noted, "The complaint was ignored; . . ."

If in the above example the author wishes to terminate his quote *before* the punctuation mark (;) then he uses three dots following a space (to note the deletion) and the closing period, e.g.,

> The court noted, "The complaint was ignored . . . ."

(See also *post,* §§ 142, 169.)

**(e) Omission of significant portions of intervening material between the opening and closing quotes:**

**(1) Omission within same paragraph.**—Use three dots set off by a space before the first and after the last. (See this section subd. (b).)

**(2) Omission of intervening paragraphs.**—Where the author omits one or more paragraphs between quotations he may use a quotation mark where the first missing paragraph would commence followed by a *complete* single line of evenly spaced dots, e.g.,

> "District Attorney Smith: I assume that the court is satisfied with the People's showing?
> "
> . . . . . . . . . . . . . . . . . . . . . . . . . . . . . . . . . . . . . . . . . . . .
> "The Court: I am satisfied."

(See subd.(e)(3) below, and *post,* § 140 re lengthy quotations.)

**(3) Omissions in consecutive paragraphs.**—If an author wishes to note that he is quoting a portion of one paragraph and a portion from the following paragraph but does not wish to follow the paragraph configuration of his source he may use the word "Par." or the symbol ¶ in brackets, e.g.,

> The relevant portion of the letter provides: "Williams was prepared to go forward with performance on the 23d. [¶] However, the goods were not ready for shipment until the 29th. . . . [¶] We deny that we are responsible for the delay . . . ."
> "As a general guide, those convictions which are for the same crime should be admitted sparingly . . . . [Par.] . . . One important consideration . . . is the magnified effect of such convictions."

(See also subd. (e)(2) above, and *post,* § 135, and § 140 re lengthy quotations.)

**(f) Omission of citations.**—The omission of citations may be noted in the same fashion as the omission of any other matter. (See the foregoing subdivisions for applicable styles.) However, the preferred style is to use the word "citation" or "citations" in brackets, e.g.,

> "This is the general rule. . . . However, . . ."
> [Acceptable.]
> "This is the general rule. [Citations.] However, . . ."
> [Preferred.]

"All the elements are present, including evidence of a threat . . . and prior presence in the building . . . ."

[Acceptable.]

"All the elements are present, including evidence of a threat [citations] and prior presence in the building [citation]."

[Preferred.]

**(g) Omission of footnotes.**—When the quoted matter contains footnotes which the author chooses to omit from the quotation, he may indicate this by placing "fn. omitted" or "fns. omitted" in brackets before the closing quotation marks or within parentheses after the closing quotation marks, e.g.,

". . . We follow the established rule. [Fn. omitted.]" (*A* v. *B* (1980) 100 Cal.App.3d 100.)

". . . We follow the established rule." (Fns. omitted.) (*A* v. *B* (1980) 100 Cal.App.3d 100.)

". . . We follow the established rule." (*A* v. *B* (1980) 100 Cal.App.3d 100, fns. omitted.)

(See also *post,* § 146 re including footnotes appearing in quoted matter and the style used to add footnotes to quoted matter.)

**(h) Omissions in lengthy quotations.**—(See *post,* § 140.)

**§ 134. Substitution for Omission.**—An author may omit quoted material and substitute in lieu thereof other material by enclosing the new matter in brackets where it is clear to the reader that the bracketed material is in place of what appeared in the original quote. It is not necessary to use dots to indicate the omitted wording, e.g.,

"It is provided that the Bureau of Labor Statistics of the United States Department of Labor shall determine . . . ." [Original.]

"It is provided that the [bureau] shall determine . . . ." [Adjusted.]

**§ 135. Noting Paragraphing in Original Not Followed.**—If the author wishes to note that the matter quoted was in paragraph configuration but he wishes to run on the material he may use the word "Par." or the symbol [¶] in brackets, e.g.,

"The remoteness of the prior conviction is a factor. [Par.] A special and even more difficult problem arises . . . ."

The department adopted the findings but concluded that: "1. The premises sought to be licensed are in a residential area; [¶] 2. Issuance of the license would aggravate an existing police problem; [¶] 3. All parties . . . ."

(See also *ante,* § 133(e)(3) and *post,* § 140 regarding alternate styles for lengthy quotations.)

**§ 136. Noting Error in Source Quoted.**—Even though the original contains a palpable error, it should be quoted exactly, but it should be noted that the error is intentionally quoted.

**(a) Misspelled words in quoted matter.**—Indicate by *"sic"* in brackets after the error.

> "The judgment was a bar to those preceedings [*sic*]." Word "proceedings" intended.

The practice of indicating a spelling error by spelling the word correctly and italicizing the corrected letter or letters is discouraged since the reader does not know if the italicized letter is a printer's error, was italicized in the original, or is in lieu of an undisclosed letter.

**(b) Error obvious.**—Where a passage does not "read," or the tense of a verb is incorrect or some other *obvious* flaw appears, indicate the error by *"sic"* in brackets within the quote following the error or *"sic"* within parentheses following the quotation.

> "The judgment were [*sic*] annulled."
> "By count three charged the defendant was with arson." (*Sic.*)

**(c) Error not obvious.**—Where the error is *not* obvious the author should insert in brackets within the quotation or indicate, parenthetically or by footnote, such changes or explanatory notations as are necessary to clarify the passage, e.g.,

> "Section 1234 [section 4321] of the Penal Code is not applicable."
> "Section 1234 of the Penal Code is not applicable." (The intended citation is to § 4321, not § 1234.)
> "Section 1234 [1] of the Penal Code is not applicable."

---

> [1] The intended citation was obviously to section 4321, not section 1234.

**(d) Multiple-error documents.**—When a quoted document contains many errors, such as might be found in the will or a letter of an illiterate person, it may be preferable to indicate the errors by italicizing or underlining the erroneous portions. The reader should be notified of the technique adopted by means of an explanatory parenthetical note or a footnote, e.g.,

> The testamentary document involved is set out below.[1] [Or in place of footnote 1]: (Italicized portions denote spelling and grammatical errors in the original.)
> > "May 19, 1973,
> > Fresno, California
> "I John Brown *herebye* give my *hole* estate to my wife. *Aul* other *ayers* get nothing. . . ."

---

> [1] Italicized portions denote spelling and grammatical errors in the original.

**(e) Error of omission.**—Note the error by inserting the letter or word in brackets.

> "The court[s] have followed the rule. . . ."
> "The patient then [began] hemorrhaging."

## § 137. Insertion of Explanatory Matter and Other Additions in Quotations.

—If it is necessary to insert a word or clause to explain or clarify the meaning of the quotation, or if the author wishes to add to what is quoted, place the inserted matter in brackets:

> "Such an order [denying a new trial] is not appealable."
> "The reason offered in this case [for the late filing] was . . . ."

Where the source quoted already has matter in brackets and the quoter desires to add material of his own he must note the distinction for the reader, e.g.,

> The court determined therefore, that she should not "be placed in the dilemma of awaiting 'jurisdictional' decisions . . . [of one tribunal] . . . while the clock of limitations tick[ed] in her ears." (*A* v. *B* (1990) 200 Cal.App.3d 100, 110 [first bracketed insertion added].)

Where there are several bracketed enclosures in the source quoted and the quoter desires to add several insertions of his own it is usually best to resort to an explanatory footnote, e.g., [1]Insertions added by this court are placed in brackets and underscored to distinguish them from the bracketed insertions originally appearing in the quoted material. (See *post*, § 140 for additions in lengthy quotations, § 148 for emphasis added to quoted matter, and *ante*, § 136(c) & (e).)

## § 138. Completing Citation in Quoted Matter.

—When quoting from a source which cites a case by name only, or by an incomplete reference such as "In *People* v. *Roubus, supra*," the complete citation should be inserted in brackets (unless the case has been cited in full before by the quoter), and the usual order of parentheses and brackets is reversed to indicate the insertion. For example if the original statement is: "This is the holding of *People* v. *Roubus, supra*." the citation should be adjusted as follows:

> "This is the holding of *People* v. *Roubus* [(1966) 65 Cal.2d 218 (53 Cal.Rptr. 281, 417 P.2d 876)]."
> This court reversed Smith's conviction, holding "for the reasons stated in *Agnello* [v. *United States* (1925) 269 U.S. 20 (70 L.Ed. 145, 46 S.Ct. 4)] and the explanation of that decision in *Wolder* [v. *United States* (1954) 347 U.S. 62 (98 L.Ed. 503, 74 S.Ct. 354)] . . . ."

Of course, if the author's opinion has already given the full citation in the same paragraph, the word *"supra"* is sufficient, and no additional citation need be added unless a point page is to be specified.

(See *ante*, §§ 98, 106.)

## § 139. Quoting Sentence in Middle of Author's Sentence—Capitalization.

—Where a complete sentence or the inception portion of a sentence is quoted in the middle of the author's sentence, the quoted sentence should follow copy and start with a capital letter. If the author elects not to use the capital letter he must place the first letter of the quoted sentence in brackets, e.g.,

> The court rejected the argument, stating that "For the purpose . . . ."
> The court rejected the argument, stating that "[f]or the purpose . . . ."

The former is preferred.
(See also *ante*, § 133(a).)

**§ 140. Lengthy Quotations and Adopted Opinions.**—When several paragraphs are quoted there should be quotations marks at the beginning and end of the quoted matter, and also at the beginning of *every new paragraph*. (See, e.g., *Estate of Smith* (1973) 9 Cal.3d 74, 77; see also *ante*, § 133 (e) (2) & (3), re style of noting omissions, and § 135, re noting paragraphing in original not followed.)

In the case of a particularly lengthy quotation, as where a court adopts a prior opinion or quotes extensively from a cited decision, quotation marks need not be used where the reader is informed that the matter presented is quoted. This can readily be accomplished by an explanatory note in the text before the start of the quote or by a footnote. (See, e.g., *People* v. *Cantrell* (1973) 8 Cal.3d 672, 677.) After the reader has been notified that the customary quotation marks will not be used, the author follows copy except for designations that, quoted directly from the original, would be out of context. For example, if a Supreme Court opinion adopts a lengthy quotation from a Court of Appeal case and the latter refers to "this court," the author of the Supreme Court opinion might adjust it to "[the Court of Appeal]."

If the context does not clearly apprise the reader of the point at which the lengthy quote is completed the author should use a signal to note completion before continuing with his text, e.g., [End of quote from opinion of Kirk, J.] or [We end our quotation from the Court of Appeal opinion at this point.].

If the author wishes to delete portions of a lengthy quotation or desires to make additions of his own, the following explanatory footnote styles (or situation-adjusted equivalents) may be used to apprise the reader.

**Deletion only:**
> Brackets together, in this manner [ ], without enclosing material, are used to indicate deletions from the opinion of the Court of Appeal.

**Additions only:**
> Brackets enclosing material (other than editor's added parallel citations) are, unless otherwise specified, used to indicate insertions or additions by this court.

**Deletions and additions:**
> Brackets together, in this manner [ ], without enclosing material, are used to indicate deletions from the opinion of the Court of Appeal; brackets enclosing

material (other than editor's added parallel citations) are, unless otherwise indicated, used to denote insertions or additions by this court.

If after adopting one of the explanatory footnote styles noted in the last two illustrations the author adds a new disposition sentence or paragraph to an adopted opinion, he may signal to the reader that this is not part of the quoted text by enclosing the new material in brackets following brackets together to note deletion of the adopted opinion's disposition sentence or paragraph, e.g.,

> . . . we have determined that no action lies. [ ]
> [The judgment is accordingly reversed.]

(See as illustrations *Estate of McDill* (1975) 14 Cal.3d 831, 833–834; *People* v. *Cantrell* (1973) 8 Cal.3d 672, 677; *Argonaut Ins. Co.* v. *Transport Indem. Co.* (1972) 6 Cal.3d 496, 500; *Keizer* v. *Adams* (1970) 2 Cal.3d 976, 978; and see *post,* § 146 (d) re addition of footnotes to quoted matter under this style.)

### § 141. Quoted Matter Within Quoted Matter.—Alternate in the use of double and single quotation marks, commencing with double quotes. Under this practice the quoting author reverses the quotation marks that appear in the quoted source; a double mark becomes a single mark and a single becomes a double, e.g.,

> In *Fisher* v. *Pickwick Hotel, Inc.* (1940) 42 Cal.App.2d Supp. 823, 825, it is said: "The general rule is . . . thus laid down: 'Conversion consists in the unwarranted interference by defendant with the dominion over the property of plaintiff, . . . Dominion is defined in law lexicons as "perfect or complete property or ownership in a thing" (Bouvier's Law Dict.) . . . .' "

### § 142. Quotation Marks Used With Other Punctuation.—Place the final period and the comma whether in the source quoted or the quoting author's within the closing quotation marks. Other punctuation marks are placed within quotation marks only if they are a part of the quoted matter.

> "I was advised," he stated, "to seek counsel."
> The officer's testimony was "really very weak," since the prosecutor was unable to "trace it back to its source."
> One note read, "Tax refund due . . . amount of $500 . . ."; another "I refuse to pay!"; still another "Why not waive?"
> "Who was present?" the witness was asked.
> Was the witness asked, "Who was present?"
> Was the defendant heard to say, "I confess"?
> The officer shouted, "Halt!"

(See also *post,* § 169 and *ante,* § 133 (d).)

**§ 143. Quotation Marks for Emphasis.**—An author may use quotation marks to emphasize, distinguish or point up words or phrases, e.g.,

> The so-called "better" theory is . . . .
> Defendant made a "material misstatement."
> In determining whether a "stop and frisk" is lawful, . . .

It is preferable, however, to use italics to achieve the author's purpose where it is likely the reader may interpret the quotation marks as a signal that the words within the quote marks have been taken from another source when that is not the case.

**§ 144. Strike-out Type in Quoted Material.**—When a quotation contains strike-out type, an opinion author must be especially careful to indicate to the printer that this configuration is to be followed. Otherwise it may appear to the printer that the author intended such words to be crossed out and therefore deleted from the opinion. Directions to set copy in strike-out type may be given in the same manner as directions to underscore (see *post,* § 145). The words to be set in strike-out type should have a line drawn through the middle of them and be followed by an asterisk and footnote informing the printer that strike-out type is to be used, e.g.,

> ". . . the trustee to distribute the ~~corpus of the trust~~* principal on the death of the beneficiary."

---

> * Printer: Use strike-out type.

The asterisk and its footnote explanation will be deleted for the advance sheet publication and only the strike-out type for the appropriate words will remain.

**§ 145. Distinguishing Italics From Underscoring in Quoted Material.**—When an author quotes from material which contains italics or underscoring, the reader's presumption is that copy was followed exactly and that the italics or underlining is from the original. Therefore no indication of this fact is necessary, although it may be noted if desired, e.g.,

> ". . . the tortfeasor is liable for all *consequential* damages." (Original italics.)

(See also *post,* § 147.)

However, a problem arises with opinion manuscript when underscoring is used. If an author is quoting from a passage with an underlined word or phrase, he must indicate to the printer that the underscoring is to be retained since in typewritten copy underlining directs the printer to set the type in italics. The printer may be advised that the author wants underlining and not italics by the use of an asterisk following material to be underscored with an explanatory footnote, e.g.,

". . . he pleads entrapment\* rather than diminished capacity\* . . . ."

___

\* Printer: Use underscoring, not italics.

When the opinion appears in the advance sheets the asterisks and the footnote will be deleted.

If a passage contains both underscoring and italics, the author must be careful to let the printer or in the case of briefs, the reader, know which is which. (See *post,* §§ 153–158.)

## § 146. Footnotes in Quoted Material.

**(a) Footnotes in original included.**—There are three styles for including a footnote from the original quotation and indicating that it is from that source. An author may retain the footnote's original number, regardless of the numbering of the author's own footnotes, and then place the text of the footnote at the bottom of the page. The footnote number, as well as the text, is within quotation marks, e.g.,

. . . the rule[3] was overlooked. "The earlier cases[6] held that this was not valid." But the court[4] preferred . . . .

___

[3]This rule is discussed in de Funiak on Equity, *supra,* at page 41.
"[6]These cases are reviewed in . . . ."
[4]United States Court of Appeals for the District of Columbia Circuit.

An alternative method is: At the point in the quoted text where the footnote number appears, place in brackets a new footnote number in sequence with the author's footnotes. Then word the footnote in the following style: [19]In a footnote at this point the court [or whoever is being quoted] states: "[Quote the original footnote]" or paraphrase it without quotation marks. (See, e.g., *La Manna* v. *Stewart* (1975) 13 Cal.3d 413, 419, fn. 4; *People* v. *Burnick* (1975) 14 Cal.3d 306, 324, fn. 4 [paraphrase].)

Another method is to include the text of the quoted footnote within the body of the opinion. The quoted footnote retains its original number. The opinion author includes the footnote material at the end of the quotation using introductory language such as: Footnote 6 of the quoted passage provides, e.g.,

. . . the rule[3] was overlooked. "The earlier cases[6] held that this was not valid." The court's footnote 6 provides: "These cases are reviewed in *Bear* v. *Bull* (1988) 300 Cal.App.3d 100, 101." But the court[4] preferred . . . .

___

[3]This rule is discussed in de Funiak on Equity, page 41.
[4]United States Court of Appeals for the District of Columbia Circuit.

**(b) Footnotes added to original.**—If an author wishes to add his own footnote to a quotation, the footnote is numbered consecutively with others in the opinion. The assigned number is placed in brackets in the body of the opinion to denote the addition. At the bottom of the page, the brackets are omitted and the footnote is treated like any other, e.g.,

> "The net receipts directly[3] attributable to Smith are to be paid to him." (Smith-Jones contract, p. 3.) The contract as initially signed was filed in the Shasta County Recorder's office.[4]

---

> [3]The word "directly" was added on July 10.
> [4]The record establishes that the filing took place on July 12.

(See, e.g., *City of Los Angeles* v. *Public Utilities Com.* (1975) 15 Cal.3d 680, 688, fn. 10.)

**(c) Footnotes in original deleted.**—See *ante*, section 133(g).

**(d) Footnotes added where author has adopted a major portion of another opinion.**—See *Mehl* v. *People* ex rel. *Dept. Pub. Wks.* (1975) 13 Cal.3d 710, 714, 717–718, footnotes 1–4; *People* v. *Rojas* (1975) 15 Cal.3d 540, 544–545, footnote 2, 551, footnote 7; and *ante,* section 140.

(See also *post,* § 185, re footnotes in general, § 186, re footnote numbering and style and *ante,* § 133 (g) for omission of footnotes.)

## § 147. Emphasis in Quoted Matter.

**§ 147. Emphasis in Quoted Matter.**—If the matter quoted contains words or expressions that are italicized to denote emphasis, copy should be followed exactly and the abstract quoted should adopt the original italics. No notation to the reader that the italics are from the source and are not the quoting author's is necessary since it is presumed that the quotation is identical to the original source in all regards. (See *ante,* §§ 131, 145.) If, however, the author feels that there is a potential for confusion he may add, in parentheses following the quoted passage, an expression such as (Original italics.).

> "[T]he crucial issue is the nature of *defendant's* duty." (*Gruenberg* v. *Aetna Ins. Co.* (1973) 9 Cal.3d 566, 577, original italics.)
> "The high purpose of the compensation law should not be perverted by resort to evidence *perfidiously procured."* (Original italics.) (*Smith* v. *Smith* (1980) 200 Cal.App.3d 200.)

If the author wishes to remove the emphasis in the source quoted he merely parenthetically notes: (Italics deleted.) or (Emphasis omitted.).

## § 148. Emphasis Added to Quoted Matter.

**§ 148. Emphasis Added to Quoted Matter.**—If an author adds his own emphasis to quoted matter, he must inform the reader of the change. This may be done by parenthetical notation following the quoted passage, e.g.,

> The balance of the opinion was concerned with deduction of dividends *"declared* from income . . . ." (*Safeway Stores, Inc.* v. *Franchise Tax Board* (1970) 3 Cal.3d 745, 749–753, italics added.)
>
> Section 6012, subdivision (a)(3) specifically provides that the *"gross receipts,"* should not be reduced by the cost of "materials, labor . . . or any other expense . . ." (italics added).
>
> Under this set of circumstances we decline to extend liability to "an independent contractor of the *public entity."* (§ 815.4, italics added.)
>
> The privilege can be claimed *"in any proceeding, . . ."* (*Id.* at p. 2, emphasis added.)
>
> The testimony established only that the plaintiff had "learned . . . that a *possible* change in plea was discussed." (*Id.* at p. 4, italics added.)

The notation is placed at the end of the entire quotation, not directly following the italicized word or expression.

When an author is quoting material which already contains italics and he wishes to add his own italics he must indicate which italicized portions are his and which are from the original. This may be done by a parenthetical explanatory notation placed at the end of the quotation, e.g.,

> The case is distinguished on the ground that "there the action was *solely* to prevent the doing of certain acts by such officials and by the other defendants *in the future."* (Second italics added.) (59 Cal.App.2d at p. 797.)

(See also *ante,* § 137.)

## § 149. Form and Paragraphing.

§ 149. **Form and Paragraphing.**—Quoted material should be typed and printed in the same fashion as other textual and footnote materials, i.e., the same spacing between lines and the same margins are used.

An occasional deviation from this rule is made as for example when the author is quoting a poem set out in stanzas or where the author deems a different configuration to be of importance. Where this is the situation the author should note in the margin of filed copies of opinions going to the publishers: "[Printer follow configuration.]" Otherwise the printer will space and indent the material in the usual fashion.

In order to conserve space the Official Reports use a "run on" publication style avoiding separate paragraphing for the commencement of a quotation following an introductory statement. For example, if the author notes "Penal Code section 38 provides in pertinent part:" the quoted material would be printed immediately after the colon and not in a separate paragraph regardless of whether the author uses a separate paragraph.

## B. Parentheses and Brackets

**§ 150. In General.**—Parentheses and brackets are used to indicate extraneous, explanatory and interpolated matter. Parentheses are usually employed in unquoted matter, while brackets are used in quoted passages to indicate material inserted by the person quoting. Brackets are used to indicate a second parenthetical statement within parentheses. Parentheses are used to indicate a parenthetical statement within a bracketed insertion to quoted matter.

> **Insertion by author in own text:**
> The first defendant (Smith) was found not guilty.
>
> **Insertion by author in quoted matter:**
> "The first defendant [Smith] was found not guilty."
>
> **Second parenthetical statement by author in own text:**
> The first defendant (Smith [charged with manslaughter]) was found not guilty.
>
> **Parenthetical statement within insertion to quoted matter:**
> "The first defendant [Smith (charged with manslaughter)] was found not guilty."

Alternate parentheses and brackets for multiple parenthetical expressions within parenthetical expressions commencing with the first mark, e.g.,

> The penalties imposed for those offenses (Pen. Code, § 207 [one to twenty-five years in prison (see Pen. Code, § 208)]; Pen. Code, § 261, subds. 2 & 3 [three years to life (Pen. Code, §§ 264, 671)]) are indeed severe.

## § 151. Citations.

**(a) Citations normally placed within parentheses.**—Ordinarily citations are placed within parentheses regardless of whether they appear in the middle or at the end of a sentence. Parallel citations are placed in brackets to distinguish them from the official citation. Note that where the citation is an integral part of the sentence the period follows the closing parenthesis.

> Habeas corpus ordinarily cannot serve as a second appeal (*In re Eli* (1969) 71 Cal.2d 214, 219 [77 Cal.Rptr. 665, 454 P.2d 337]), or as a substitute for an appeal (*In re Streeter* (1967) 66 Cal.2d 47, 52 [56 Cal.Rptr. 824, 423 P.2d 976]). A principal may ratify the forgery of his signature by his agent. (*Volandri* v. *Hlobil* (1959) 170 Cal.App.2d 656, 659 [339 P.2d 218].)

In the older reports citations often appeared without parentheses, e.g., "In such a case, no appeal lies. *Smith* v. *Jones* (1893) 100 Cal. 100." The modern practice favors parentheses, and the California Reports invariably use them. Under our style the above citation would be: (*Smith* v. *Jones* (1893) 100 Cal. 100.)

**(b) Citation as part of sentence—no parentheses.**—When the citation forms an integral part of the sentence, as distinguished from a parenthetical insertion, parentheses are not used. However, parallel case citations are placed in brackets.

In *Time, Inc.* v. *Hill* (1966) 385 U.S. 374 [17 L.Ed.2d 456, 87 S.Ct. 534], the United States Supreme Court considered this very question.

The leading case of *Whitfield* v. *Roth* (1974) 10 Cal.3d 874 [112 Cal.Rptr. 540, 519 P.2d 588] pronounces the rule.

In the subsequent case, *Martin* v. *Superior Court* (1917) 176 Cal. 289 [168 P. 135], involving the same parties, the same result was reached.

**§ 152. Brackets.**—Brackets are used in pairs to indicate that the matter within the brackets is: **(1)** an explanation within quotations (*ante,* § 137); **(2)** an author's insertion within a quotation (*ante,* §§ 137, 146 (b), 150); **(3)** the noting and correction of an error in a source quoted (*ante,* § 136 (a)–(c) & (e)); **(4)** a parenthetical statement within parentheses (*ante,* § 150); **(5)** a parallel citation whether in parentheses or in the body of a sentence (*ante,* §§ 151, 76, 66, fn.); **(6)** a change in paragraph configuration in a quote (*ante,* §§ 133 (e)(3), 135); **(7)** an omission in quoted matter (*ante,* §§ 133 (a), (f) and (g), 139); **(8)** a substitution for an omission in quoted matter (*ante,* § 134); **(9)** the completion of a citation within a quotation (*ante,* § 138); or **(10)** a signal in lengthy quotations (*ante,* § 140).

## C. Italics

**§ 153. In General.**—Since italics are used extensively in appellate opinions and briefs, and since the italic form can convey a variety of meanings, consistency in usage is essential. The following sections indicate approved styles.

**§ 154. Indicating Italics in Manuscript.**—Italics in manuscript should be indicated by a single straight line drawn or typed beneath each word or character to be italicized.

Under the circumstances the trial court correctly concluded that section 832 of the Civil Code does not absolve a negligent excavator.

(See *ante,* §§ 145, 147, 148, 153 and *post,* §§ 155–158.)

**§ 155. Italicizing Latin and Foreign Language Words and Phrases.**—The modern tendency is to italicize as little as possible. In legal writing many Latin and foreign words and phrases are in such common use that they have become a part of the legal idiom and no need exists to distinguish them by italicization. However, where the word or phrase is not in common usage or where tradition has established an italicized form, italics are used. (Of course, if the author intends to emphasize a word or phrase otherwise not italicized, he would use italics.)

The following lists contain many of the Latin and foreign words and phrases that are used with some frequency in the Official Reports. Where a word or phrase is listed its indicated form should be followed. (For additional guidelines consult A Uniform System of Citation (14th ed. 1986) p. 31; Chicago Style Manual (13th ed. 1982) ¶¶ 6.54–6.58; GPO Manual (1984 ed.) pp. 161–163. See also *post,* § 188.)

**The following words and abbreviations are not italicized:**

action in personam
action in rem
addendum
ad hoc
ad infinitum
ad litem
ad valorem
a fortiori
alias
alter ego
amici curiae
amicus curiae
anno Domini
ante bellum
a priori
apropos
arguendo
assumpsit
attaché
bona fide
caveat emptor
certiorari
cf.
chose
chose in action
circa
clientele
compos mentis
consortium
contra
corpus
corpus delicti
coup de grâce
data
datum
de facto
dehors
de jure
de minimis
de novo
dicta
dictum
duces tecum
e.g.
en banc
en route
ergo
errata

erratum
et al.
et cetera, etc.
et seq.
ex contractu
ex delicto
ex officio
ex parte
ex post facto
fait accompli
forum non conveniens
habeas corpus
i.e.
in camera
in extenso
in extremis
in forma pauperis
in futuro
in haec verba
in loco parentis
in pari delicto
in pari materia
in personam
in pro. per.
in propria persona
in rem
in situ
inter alia
inter vivos
interim
in terrorem
in toto
ipse dixit
ipso facto
laissez faire (n.)
laissez-faire (adj.)
lis pendens
mala in se
mala prohibita
malum in se
malum prohibitum
mandamus
mens rea
mesne profits
Messrs.
Mmes.
modus operandi
née

nil
nisi
nisi prius
nolle prosequi
nolo contendere
nom de plume
non compos mentis
non sequitur
nunc pro tunc
obiter
obiter dictum
onus
pendente lite
per annum
per capita
per diem
per se
per stirpes
petit larceny
post mortem
prima facie
pro bono
pro bono publico
pro forma
pro. per.
pro rata
pro se
pro tanto
pro tempore
propria persona
quantum meruit
quasi
quid pro quo

quo warranto
ratio decidendi
res gestae
res ipsa loquitur
res judicata
respondeat superior
resumé
scienter
seriatim
sine qua non
situs
stare decisis
status quo
status quo ante
sua sponte
subpoena
subpoena duces tecum
sub silentio
sui generis
sui juris
supersedeas
ultimatum
ultra vires
verbatim
versus
via
vice
vice versa
vis-à-vis
viva voce
viz.
voir dire

## The following words and abbreviations are italicized:

*a posteriori*
*ab ante*
*ab initio*
*ad damnum*
*ad diem*
*ad finem*
*ad idem*
*alterius*
*animo revocandi*
*animus*
*ante*
*autrefois acquit*
*autrefois convict*
*cestui que trust*
*causa mortis*
*conditio sine qua non*
*consideratum est per curiam*
*coram nobis*
*coram vobis*
*cum testamento annexo*
*cy près*
*damnum absque injuria*

*de bene esse*
*del credere*
*de son tort*
*donatio causa mortis*
*ejusdem generis*
*en masse*
*ex curia*
*expressio unius*
*ex proprio vigore*
*ff.*
*ferae naturae*
*functus officio*
*haec verba*
*ibid.*
*id.*
*idem*
*idem sonans*
*in capite*
*in curia*
*in esse*
*inclusio unius est exclusio
  alterius*

| | |
|---|---|
| *infra* | *per autre vie* |
| *in limine* | *per curiam* |
| *in perpetuum* | *post* |
| *in posse* | *post facto* |
| *in praesenti* | *post-factum* |
| *in re* | *profit à prendre* |
| *in statu quo* | *qua* |
| *interesse* | *quaere* |
| *inter se* | *quare clausum fregit* |
| *inter sese* | *quo animo* |
| *judgment non obstante veredicto* | *quoad hoc* |
| *lex domicilii* | *raison d'être* |
| *lex locus contractus* | *res nova* |
| *lex non scripta* | *sans recours* |
| *locus delicti* | *scire facias* |
| *locus in quo* | *semble* |
| *locus poenitentiae* | *sic* |
| *loc. cit.* | *stet processus* |
| *mala fide* | *sub judice* |
| *mobilia sequuntur personam* | *sub nom.* |
| *ne plus ultra* | *supra* |
| *op. cit.* | *ubi supra* |
| *op. cit. supra* | *ut infra* |
| *parens patriae* | *ut supra* |
| *pari ratione* | *vide ut supra* |
| *passim* | |

## § 156. Use of Italics With Phrases Containing Some Anglicized Words.

—It is preferable to treat a foreign language phrase as a whole and either italicize the whole or none of it, depending on whether or not the phrase as a whole has become anglicized, e.g.,

| **Italicize:** | **Do not italicize:** |
|---|---|
| *in esse* | in propria persona |
| *in statu quo* | quasi contract |
| | subpoena duces tecum |

Care must be taken to determine how much of a phrase is foreign, and only the foreign portion is to be italicized, e.g.,

administrator *de son tort*          divorce *a mensa et thoro*

## § 157. Italics for Emphasis.

—Italics are frequently employed to give emphasis or prominence to words or expressions. Whether italics should be used for emphasis, and when, are matters within the author's discretion. However, overuse of the italic form for emphasis tends to defeat the author's objective. (See *ante,* §§ 153, 154, 145, 147 and 148 for the use of italics for emphasis in quoted matter.)

## § 158. Italics With Citations.

**(a) Case names.**—Names of appellate court opinions are always italicized whether in the main text or a footnote. However, the abbreviation for versus (v.) is in roman type and where an action is brought by a party in the name of the state, the designation "ex rel." is in roman. Where an opinion is referred to by only a portion of its full running head title, italics are used. (See *ante,* §§ 93, 98(a)(2).) The title of trial court opinions are not italicized. (See *ante,* § 89.)

| | |
|---|---|
| *In re Newborn* | *In re Marriage of Smith* |
| *People* v. *Reid* | *In re D.A.S.* |
| *Jones* v. *Maloney* | a pre-*Boykin* decision |
| *People* ex rel. *Dept. Pub. Wks.* v. *Douglas* | Notwithstanding *Smith* |
| | a *Jones* instruction |

**(b) Citation cross-references.**—The cross-reference words, *ante, ibid., id., idem , infra, op. cit., post, supra,* and *op. cit. supra* are always italicized. (See *ante,* § 98 for the use of these words in citations.)

**(c) Titles of periodicals and newspaper articles.**—Titles of articles cited from professional journals, law reviews, magazines, essays and newspapers are italicized. (See *ante,* § 109 for additional illustrations.)

(McCarthy, *Trademark Franchising and Antitrust: The Trouble With Tie-Ins* (1970) 58 Cal.L.Rev. 1085.)

(See Comment, *Corporal Punishment in the Public Schools* (1971) 6 Harv. C.R-C.L. L.Rev. 583.)

(Walz, *Rebuke for Trudeau on Issues,* N.Y. Times (Nov. 1, 1972) p. C3, cols. 4–6.)

(Main, *Only Radical Reform Can Save The Courts,* Fortune (Aug. 1970) p. 110.)

**(d) Statutes and session laws.**—Do *not* italicize the following words or their abbreviations: article, chapter, clause, division, section, subdivision, subsection, title. However, if these words appear italicized in quoted matter, copy is followed. (See *ante,* §§ 147, 145.)

**(e) Subsequent history references.**—Words denoting the subsequent history of cited opinions and the abbreviated forms of these words are generally not italicized. For example, do not italicize words such as: affirmed (affd.), reversed (revd.), modified (mod.), reiterated, hearing granted (hg. granted), rehearing denied (rehg. den.), remanded with directions, certiorari granted (cert. granted), certiorari denied (cert. den.), jurisdiction noted (jur. noted), etc. However, if these words appear italicized in quoted matter, copy is followed. (See *ante,* § 147.) A few such words are italicized by tradition, e.g., *sub nom., per curiam,* etc. (See *ante,* § 88.2 for a list of frequently used abbreviations denoting subsequent history.)

## D. Hyphens

§ **159. In General.**—The present tendency is to avoid the use of hyphens except when they improve the flow of the sentence, resolve ambiguity, eliminate absurdity or assist the reader in comprehending the author's meaning. Unfortunately, rules developed by English manuals to achieve the foregoing objectives are not always consistent, exceptions abound and long-established usage of certain hyphenated forms work against uniformity. For a comprehensive collection of well-illustrated rules governing the use of the hyphen and a long alphabetically arranged guide to compounding specific words consult the GPO Manual (1984 ed.) pages 81–116. Some of the more useful guidelines are set out in the following sections.

§ **160.   Unit Modifiers.**—Where two or more words are joined to serve as a single adjective phrase before a noun they are often connected by a hyphen, e.g.,

two-year-old boy                    nonrevenue-producing plant
up-to-date theory                   ready-to-wear garment
13-day period                       agreed-upon price

It is noted, however, that where a sentence contains a unit modifier phrase or compound and the passage is readable and the meaning clear without hyphenation then hyphens should be avoided.

A civil rights bill was introduced.
This public utility rule is fundamental.
The civil service examination was held as scheduled.
Many public school districts were affected.

Adjective phrases containing an adverb ending in "ly" are never hyphenated.

highly refined material
fully discounted note

Hyphens are not used with adjective or adverbial phrases when they follow the word modified.

The up-to-date figures were admitted into evidence. [Before word.]
The figures presented to the court were up to date. [After word.]
The court by a four-to-three vote affirmed. [Before word.]
The court voted, four to three, to affirm. [After word.]

(See also *post,* § 161 for other illustrations.)

§ **161.   Compound Numbers and Units of Measurement.**—Hyphenate compound numbers from twenty-one to ninety-nine* and adjective phrases with numerical first elements. Fractions are hyphenated but no hyphen is used between the numerator and the denominator when a hyphen appears in either. Technical units of measurement are generally hyphenated. (See also *post,* §§ 189 and 190 for numeral and figure styles.)

---

*Normally these numbers would be written in figures and the examples are noted for those situations in which a deviation from normal style is appropriate. (See *post,* §§ 189, 190 (i).)

**Compound numbers:** * forty-five, one hundred and forty-five, one hundred forty-five, *but* one hundred forty.

**Adjective phrases:** an eight-hour day, 12-inch ruler, four-to-three vote, .45-caliber gun, two-sided issue, twenty-first* allegation, 60-day note, four-week vacation, (*but* four weeks' vacation), 19th-century weapon, $5-per-bushel wheat, 110-volt line, five-gallon jug, four-month continuance, five-year-old boy.

**Fractions:** five-hundredths, three-fourths, forty-five fiftieths, twenty-one thirty-fifths, half-inch, half-mile, half-hour, *but* half an inch, half an hour, half a mile, half a dozen.
He delivered three and one-half shares of stock.
He was entitled to six one-hundredths of the total.
The officer found one-half ounce of heroin.
The window was open one-third of an inch.

(See *post,* § 190 (h).)

**Technical units of measurement:** passenger-mile, board-foot, kilowatt-hour, engine-hour.

Hyphens are used in number compounds that have a common element which is expressed but once.

three- and four-foot lengths
10- to 20-unit apartment house
three- to six-pound bags
three-, four-, and five-inch openings
*but* three to four feet wide

## § 162. Miscellaneous Usage Illustrations.

### (a) Hyphens are used:

**(1) with compounds made up of nouns and prepositions:**

son-in-law, hand-to-hand, editor-in-chief,
kick-off

**(2) to avoid ambiguity of meaning:**

twenty 5-dollar bills (25 dollar bills)
a normal-school teacher (a normal school teacher)
re-treat (retreat), re-cover (recover)

**(3) to join prefixes to a capitalized word:**

| | |
|---|---|
| un-American | mid-Atlantic |
| pro-British | mid-June |
| anti-French | all-American |

**(4) to join a single capital letter to form a common word:**

| | |
|---|---|
| X-ray | I-beam |
| U-boat | V-shaped |
| T-square | |

### (b) Hyphens are not used:

**(1) with compound predicates:**
The defendant was forum shopping.
The account was profit producing.

---

*Normally these numbers would be written in figures and the examples are noted for those situations in which a deviation from normal style is appropriate. (See *post,* §§ 189, 190 (i).)

**(2) with unit modifiers which have a number or letter as a second element:**

section (a) situation          Fourth Amendment right
Class B regulation          division 3 holding

**(3) with unit modifiers in author quotes unless the compound is customarily hyphenated:**

"blue sky" law          "two pronged" rule

**(4) with compound phrases where the first word is a comparative or superlative:**

greatest income period          lowest production group

**(5) with a series of descriptive adjectives before a noun when the words are not used as a *unit* modifier:**

a poor uneducated          large brown paper bag
alien

## § 163. Official Report Usage—Hyphens Used.—Unless it appears in quoted matter and was not hyphenated in the original, hyphenate the following:

attorney-client relationship
brother-in-law
case-in-chief
co-administrator
co-executor
co-occupant
court-appointed (adj.)
cross-appeal
cross-complainant
cross-complaint
cross-defendant
cross-examination
cross-purpose
cross-reference
cross-section
ex-felon
father-child relationship
felony-murder rule (adj.)
*but:* felony murder (n.)
great-grandfather
mother-in-law

off-duty (adj.)
off-street (adj.)
on-the-scene (adj.)
out-of-state (adj.)
pre-1963
quasi-contract
quasi-community property
quasi-criminal prosecution
quasi-specific performance
rear-end collison
recross-examination
right-angle intersection
right-of-way
safe-deposit box
self-defense
self-imposed (adj.)
self-incrimination
sister-in-law
so-called
tape-recorded (adj.)
well-known (adj.)

## § 164. Official Report Usage—Hyphens Omitted.—Unless it appears in quoted matter and was hyphenated in the original do not hyphenate the following:

above quoted
above referred to
airmail
antenuptial
backlog

bailsman
bank book
bondsman
boyfriend
bylaw

coconspirator
cocounsel
codefendant
colessee
colessor
common law rule (adj.)
common law (n.)
common sense (n.)
commonsense (adj.)
cooperative
coparty
coplaintiff
cosign
cotrustor
counteraffidavit
extrahazardous
eyewitness
felony murder (n.)
*but:* felony-murder rule (adj.)
first degree murder
getaway
girlfriend
jailhouse
judgment roll

lineup
minibike
mobilehome
motor home
nonpayment
passerby
patdown
post mortem
preempt
purchase money
pretrial
redirect examination
reenter
reexamine
second degree murder
sidewalk
special circumstances
statewide
stickup
streetcar
subject matter
tortfeasor
to wit
work product

## § 165. Division of Words.

—The basic rules governing the division of words are available in Word Division, a Supplement to the Government Printing Office Style Manual. This pocket-size supplement contains the division of about 18,600 words arranged alphabetically and is a time-saving reference work. It may be purchased from the Superintendent of Documents, U.S. Government Printing Office, Washington, D.C. 20402. Another obvious aid is the dictionary, preferably Webster's Third New International Dictionary. The division of words for the advance sheets and bound volumes is determined by the printer rather than the opinion author but under the same rules. In opinion copy it is better practice to keep the division of words between lines to a minimum even though the page's appearance may suffer slightly.

## E. Commas

### § 166. In General.

—The comma is an indispensable tool in conveying intended meaning and in emphasizing or deemphasizing thought content. Rigid rules of usage often encumber rather than assist and therefore considerable latitude in style is expected. The present tendency is to avoid the comma in sentences where its use, although technically correct, adds nothing to clarity or does not enhance the even flow of the ideas presented.

Where the use of a comma becomes critical to the court's analysis or creates an ambiguity it is better to recast the sentence in a manner to avoid any interpretation problems. (See *Russell* v. *Bankers Life Co.* (1975) 46 Cal.App.3d 405, 411, 415.) The following sections indicate areas where uniformity of style is practical and the styles noted should be followed where applicable. (For the use of commas with citations see *ante,* § 85 et seq.)

**§ 167.  Commas With Names.**— Use commas before and after "Jr." and "Sr." and to separate degrees such as "M.D.," "Ph.D.," etc., following a person's name. Commas are not used when roman numerals follow the name.

> Frank Jones, Jr., appeared for the defendants.
> Walter Hunter, M.D., signed the death certificate.
> Peter Smith III appeared for appellants.

(See also *post,* § 181.)

**§ 168.  Commas in Series.**—The use of a comma before "and," "or," or "nor" when these conjunctions precede the last of a series of three or more words, phrases, letters or figures is optional unless required for clarity. If an author elects to use one style he should be consistent throughout.

> one, two, three, and four
> one, two, three and four
> *but,* one, two, three or four, and five [comma for clarity]

(See also *ante,* § 94.)

**§ 169.  Commas Inside Quotation Mark.**—Where a sentence continues following a quotation mark and a sentence comma is used at that point it should go inside the closing quote mark.

> "Counsel," said the judge, "please limit your argument."

Note in the example above that the comma before the second quote is placed before and outside the opening quotation mark.
(See also *ante,* § 133 (d) and § 142, quotation marks used with other punctuation, and *post,* § 172.)

**§ 170.  Commas With Dates.**—When the month, day and year are given, commas should be placed before and after the year. If only the month and year are noted, no commas are used.

> The accident occurred on April 10, 1973, in San Diego.
> The accident occurred in April 1973 in San Diego.

(See also *post,* § 190 (b).)

## § 171. Commas With Figures.

**(a)** Use a comma to separate numbers to avoid confusion.

Of the 100, 42 were present.
Instead of three, four appealed.

**(b)** Use a comma to separate numbers having four or more digits, e.g., 1,200; 12,000; 120,000; *but* no commas are used with such numbers when they indicate sequence:

page 1003, order 3016, section 25003, docket number 15167, S.F. No. 22861, Civ. No. 11260

**(c)** Fractions do not take commas: 60/2500

(See also *post,* §§ 189, 190.)

## § 172. Commas Following Introductory Phrases.—Commas are used following an introductory phrase before a direct quotation and before a question.

The witness testified, "I saw nobody."
The issue is, Was an easement of necessity established?
The issue is, "Was an easement of necessity established?"

(See also *ante,* § 169.)

# F. Semicolons

## § 173. In General.—Like the comma, the semicolon is a versatile tool the use of which should be guided by the author's needs and taste rather than rigid style forms. It is often used as a "full stop" pause to divide distinct thoughts joined in a single sentence; to separate long involved sentences with spur clauses; to prevent ideas, words, phrases or clauses from running together; and to obtain greater emphasis than available with the comma. In its most common use it divides a series when there is a comma in one or more sections of the series.

## § 174. Semicolons in Series.—When there is a comma in one or more sections of a series, the sections should be divided by semicolons instead of commas. There is a conflict of opinion whether a semicolon should be placed before "and" at the end of the series. For the sake of uniformity it is deemed preferable to use a semicolon before the "and." This preference is particularly applicable to citations, e.g.,

The prosecution established that defendant had discussed the matter; that he realized the same judge would determine the issues of guilt, sanity, and penalty; that he was aware of the punishments which could be imposed, including the possibility of a life imprisonment penalty; and that no promise of special treatment had been made to him.
(Cf. *People* v. *Edwards* (1969) 71 Cal.2d 1096, 1099 [80 Cal.Rptr. 633, 458 P.2d 713]; *People* v. *Henry* (1969) 65 Cal.2d 842, 845 [56 Cal.Rptr.485, 423 P.2d 557]; and *People* v. *Haven* (1963) 59 Cal.2d 713, 717 [31 Cal.Rptr. 47, 381 P.2d 927].)

(See also *ante,* § 94.)

## G. Apostrophe

**§ 175. Apostrophe With Possessives.**—The following rules indicate the apostrophe's placement in the formation of possessives.

**(a) General Rule.**—To form the possessive of singular nouns (including proper names), the general rule is to add an apostrophe and an *s,* whether or not the word itself ends in an *s* or *s-sound:*

| | |
|---|---|
| day's trip | horse's mouth |
| driver's permit | press's deadline |
| prosecutrix's testimony | administratrix's acts |
| Burns's poems | UPS's responsibility |
| Mr. Jones's lawsuit | witness's affidavit |

Optionally, add only an apostrophe to singular nouns (including proper names) that end in *two* *s*-sounding syllables:

| | |
|---|---|
| thesis' subject | oasis' area |
| Moses' beard | Jesus' name |

**(b) Plural nouns.**—To form the possessive of plural nouns (including proper names) the plurals of which end in an *s,* add an apostrophe only. For plural nouns *not* ending in an *s,* add an apostrophe *and* an *s:*

| | |
|---|---|
| doctors' reports | men's jail |
| girls' camp | women's club |
| witnesses' affidavits | geese's behavior |
| the Joneses' lawsuit | children's party |
| six months' period | oxen's burden |
| *compare:* six-month period | alumnae's ball |

**(c) Joint and individual possession.**—If the author wishes to note joint possession, the apostrophe is used with the last element of the series. If he wishes to note individual possession the apostrophe is used with each element.

Hemlock and Smart's deeds (indicates joint ownership)
Hemlock's and Smart's deeds (indicates each has individual ownership of one or more deeds)

**(d) Compound nouns.**—Place the apostrophe *s* nearest to the thing possessed.

Attorney General's report
attorney at law's oath
real parties in interest's claims
her sister-in-law's property
John Smith, Jr.'s objections
somebody else's problem

(See also *post,* § 191 re plural forms.)

**(e) Pronouns and Nouns Before Gerunds.**—Possessive pronouns such as hers, ours, theirs, yours, its, itself, and whose do not take an apostrophe. Possessive adjectives such as another's, each other's, one's, someone's, and somebody's take an apostrophe, as does a noun before a gerund, e.g., in view of Mary's leaving.

**§ 176. Apostrophe With Established Designations.**—Whether an apostrophe is to be used with the name of a firm, organization, institution, book, place, etc., depends entirely upon the official designation of the firm, organization, etc. For example, if a firm is incorporated as and uses the name: "Blacks Elevator Company" rather than "Black's Elevator Company" do not add an apostrophe. However, where the authentic title is not ascertainable from the record or otherwise use the normal possessive forms. (See *ante,* § 175.)

The GPO Manual (1984 ed.) section 8.7, page 118 suggests that the apostrophe should not be used with names of countries and other organized bodies ending in "s" or after words "more descriptive than possessive."

United States possessions
Massachusetts laws
House of Representatives committee
editors handbook
technicians guide
merchants exchange
Reporter of Decisions office

**§ 177. Apostrophe With Contracted Words or Figures.**—The apostrophe is used to note the omission of letters or figures in contracted expressions. While occasionally used with numbers, contracted word forms are disfavored in formal writings such as opinions or briefs.

| | | |
|---|---|---|
| aren't | isn't | who's (who is) |
| can't | it's (it is) | the summer of '72 |
| doesn't | o'clock | 49'ers |
| don't | they're | spirit of '76 |
| haven't | wouldn't | the '30's (also the 1930's) |

The apostrophe should not be used in the formation of abbreviations to denote omissions, e.g., avoid such abbreviation forms as sup'rs., ass'n., comm'n., comm'rs., etc.

(See also *post,* §§ 189, 190 re numerals and figures.)

**§ 178. Apostrophe With Figures, Symbols, Letters and Words Referred to as Such.**—Use an apostrophe and "s" in the formation of plurals, e.g.,

The 6's were not legible.
The m's were indicative of an altered document.
The contract was confusing because of the many hereinafter's and but's used.
He was born in the 1920's.

## H. Abbreviations

**§ 179. Abbreviations In General.**—See *ante,* pages ix-xv, for a comprehensive list of approved abbreviations.

(See also *ante,* §§ 77, 88.2, 177 and *post,* § 180.)

**§ 180.   Periods or Spaces With Organization Names.**—Both the periods and spaces in alphabetical abbreviations of governmental agencies and other organized bodies are often omitted when these entities are popularly identified by alphabetical symbols, e.g.,

AFL-CIO (union)
GM (General Motors)
MIT (Massachusetts Institute of Technology)
NLRB (National Labor Relations Board)
TVA (Tennessee Valley Authority)
UCLA (University of California at Los Angeles)
UNICEF (United Nations Children's Fund)

However, no firm rules are practical and current usage must be ascertained for the practice with regard to specific organizations. (See GPO Manual (1984 ed.) pages 135–153 for lists containing many commonly used organization abbreviations.)

It is suggested that a first reference to a popularly abbreviated designation form should be followed in the text by a spell-out in parentheses of the entity referred to, e.g., "HEW (Department of Health, Education, and Welfare) was not represented at the hearing." or "The Department of Housing and Urban Development (hereafter HUD) . . . ." or "California Industries for the Blind (CIB) . . . ." Thereafter the abbreviated form alone is used.

Abbreviations should be used consistently, that is, do not spell out an organization's name in one portion of an opinion or brief and abbreviate it in another. (See also *ante,* §§ 177, 179.)

**§ 181.   Titles or Degrees.**—These abbreviations are set with points but without spaces. Since they are commonly used in their abbreviated form, abbreviations are appropriate both within and outside of parentheses.

Jane Smith, M.D.                     Ellen Jones, D.D.S.
Jack Williams, D.V.M.                Peter Davis, M.A.
Mary Brown, C.P.A.

(See also *ante,* § 167, as to commas associated with titles; *post,* § 196, as to omission of personal titles or degrees from opinion titles.)

# CHAPTER III
## —Notes—

# CHAPTER III
## —Notes—

# MISCELLANEOUS RULES

**§ 182. Agreement of Subject and Verb.**—The following rules provide basic guidelines to assist in obtaining the agreement of subject and verb. While the guides noted below are not complete and space limitations do not permit the notation of various exceptions, it is believed they will provide a handy reference for the resolution of the more common problems.

**(a)** Singular subjects take singular verbs; plural subjects take plural verbs. While the rule is elementary errors are common. Often such mistakes can be avoided merely by taking care in the identification of the "true subject" and selecting the verb accordingly. Do not permit nouns intervening between the subject and the verb to induce the incorrect selection of the verb.

**(b)** Two or more singular subjects joined by the word "and" or the words "both . . . and . . ." take a plural verb.

However, where two or more nouns are treated as a unit and are intended to be singular in meaning a singular verb is used.

Smith and Jones is the moving company named in the complaint.

**(c)** Singular subjects followed by parenthetical expressions such as "as well as," "including," "with," "together with," "no less than," and "accompanied by" usually take singular verbs.

Fred Smith, accompanied by his two companions, was apprehended.

**(d)** Singular subjects joined by "or," "nor," "neither . . . nor," and "either . . . or" usually take a singular verb. When these words connect subjects differing in number the verb should agree with the subject closest to it.

> Neither Smith nor the other defendants were present.
> Neither the bags nor the gun was found.

The proper pairs are: "neither . . . nor" and "either . . . or."

> He had neither time nor money. [Correct.]
> He had neither time or money. [Incorrect.]

**(e)** Another, anybody, anyone, anything, each, either, everybody, everyone, neither, nobody, nothing, somebody, and someone *generally* take singular verbs.

> Neither of the defendants was present.
> Anybody is welcome.

The words "none" and "any" may be treated as either singular or plural depending upon the author's meaning.

**(f)** "Who," "that," and "which" take plural verbs with plural antecedents and singular verbs with singular antecedents.

> Plaintiff is one of the parties who were present. [Parties is the antecedent.]
> One of the witnesses who testified earlier was excused. [One is the antecedent.]
> Estoppel is the most logical of the many reasons that have been given. [Reasons is the antecedent.]

**(g)** Collective nouns and numbers denoting quantity take plural verbs when the author has in mind the component parts of the group or number, but they should take singular verbs if the author refers to the group or quantity as a unit.

This rule applies to such words as "jury," "crowd," "majority," "board," "the public," "a thousand," "one fourth of," "the whole group," etc. The word "court" almost always takes a singular verb.

Singular verb, reference to group as a whole:

> The jury has returned its verdict.
> The board has denied the application.
> The committee has the matter under submission.
> Ten pounds is the usual weight.
> Four dollars is the special admission charge.

Plural verb, reference to members or parts of group:[1]

> The jury are divided and cannot reach a verdict.
> The committee have not expressed their views.
> Ten boxes of fruit were shipped. [Individual boxes.]

When the subject of a sentence is a title, clause, quotation or some other group of words expressing a single idea, the verb is singular.

> "Juries and Their Verdicts" is an analysis of the jury system in America.
> "Clean hands" is a maxim of equity.

---

[1]Whenever the expression "members" or its equivalent may be substituted for the collective noun without impairing the author's meaning, the verb should be plural and not singular.

A corollary of the foregoing rules is that any pronouns which refer to the collective noun must also agree:

The jury has returned its verdict.
The jury were instructed that they should not . . . .

Authors should endeavor to use collective nouns consistently throughout. It is poor style for example to refer to the "jury" as a collective noun taking a singular verb in one portion of an opinion or brief and then in another to use the plural verb (denoting a reference to the individual jury members) unless it is deemed necessary by the context.

Sometimes it will be better form to use the expression "members" or equivalent substitutes in lieu of the collective noun, e.g., "The members were told," or "the jurors were instructed that they should not . . . ."

### § 183. Diagrams, Photocopies and Photographs.—It is axiomatic that the submission of a poor copy of illustrative materials will result in an inferior published reproduction. Therefore care should be exerted to see that the copy accompanying the opinion is as clear and legible as obtainable. It is suggested that photocopies of photocopies be avoided where the original or a superior source is available. In those instances where a problem of clarity arises consult the Reporter of Decisions office for suggestions as to overcoming the difficulty prior to filing the opinion.

Many times in preparing printed copy it is impractical and awkward to place a diagram, illustration or photograph on the page at which the author refers the reader to it. Therefore it is suggested that authors anticipate this problem and assist in overcoming it by including this type of material as an appendix rather than as a portion of the main text. The reader can be referred to the illustration by such parenthetical references as "(A diagram indicating the positioning of the encroachment appears as an appendix *post,* at p._____.)" or "(See appen. A for a photocopy of the deposit receipt *post,* at p._____.)" A footnote can also be employed, e.g., "We have prepared temporary apportionment plans. They are set forth in appendices to this opinion.[1] . . ."

---

[1]See *post,* pages 19 to 21.

Where a photocopy is to be cropped or a portion of a diagram or illustration is to be omitted or adjusted, special instructions should accompany opinion copies sent to the publisher.

### § 184. "Er" and "Or" Endings.—To achieve uniformity the indicated forms are preferred and are followed in the Official Reports even though an alternative ending may also be grammatically acceptable.

Manuscript copy will be adjusted accordingly for Official Report publication.

| | | | |
|---|---|---|---|
| abettor | distributor | lender | promisor |
| adjuster | examiner | lienor | relator |
| adviser | grantor | libeler | settlor |
| bailor | indemnitor | mortgagor | supervisor |
| condemner | indorser | objector | supporter |
| contemner | inspector | offeror | surveyor |
| consignor | insurer | optionor | transferor |
| conveyor | intervener | pledgor | vendor |

**§ 185.   Footnotes.**—The footnote number should be placed as near as possible to the textual material which is footnoted where this can be accomplished without serious disruption of the natural flow of the sentence, and preferably, with direct quotations, at the end of the quote. It is noted that footnotes are sometimes repetitious of material contained in the text and that this type of footnote can often be shortened or avoided entirely by careful planning and the use of complete citations within the body of the opinion or brief. For this reason, and since footnoted material has the same force and effect as the body of the opinion (*People* v. *Jackson* (1979) 95 Cal.App.3d 397, 402 [157 Cal.Rptr. 154]), some authors decline to use footnotes or use them only sparingly.

When used upon the closing of a quotation the footnote number is normally placed outside the closing quotation marks, e.g.,

The statement was "vital to the outcome."[1]

Likewise when a footnote number is used at the close of a parenthetical expression it is placed after the closing parenthesis, e.g.,

(*In re Williams* (1969) 1 Cal.3d 168 [81 Cal.Rptr. 784, 460 P.2d 984].)[11]

However, if the footnote refers to a particular citation in a series of citations within parentheses the number should then follow that citation, e.g.,

(*People* v. *Maddox* (1967) 67 Cal.2d 647 [63 Cal.Rptr. 371, 433 P.2d 163]; Gov. Code, § 37103;[4] 19 Ops.Cal.Atty.Gen.153 (1952).[5])

An asterisk may be used with a footnote to note a parenthetical, editorial or clarifying procedural matter before the text of the opinion starts. A second note of this type on any one page is identified by a dagger; and a third by a double dagger. An asterisk or dagger is used with reporter's notes. (See, e.g., *In re Spence* (1974) 36 Cal.App.3d 636, 642.)

(See also *ante,* § 146, re footnotes in quoted material.)

**§ 186.   Footnotes—Numbering and Style.**—Opinion footnotes are numbered consecutively. Majority and minority opinions are numbered independently. When the author wishes to refer to matter contained in an earlier footnote, the preferred system is to use the next footnote number and have the later footnote refer to the earlier one; e.g., the later footnote might read: "[4]See footnote 2 *ante,* page 10."

Footnotes should be typed in single spacing and should commence on the same page as the text to which they refer. Indent the first line of each footnote and double space between footnotes. Footnotes are governed by the same citational and other styles as are applicable to the text. It is specifically noted that only such abbreviations are permissible as would be allowed under text styles.

(See *ante,* § 146, re footnotes in quoted material and § 185, re footnotes generally.)

### § 187. "Guarantee" and "Guaranty."—While many authorities permit both spellings, irrespective of whether the word is used as a noun or a verb, in legal writing it is preferable to use "guarantee" as the verb and "guaranty" as the noun.

### § 188. Modern English and Other Preferred Forms.—There is no objection to the use of a Latin or other foreign language word or phrase when there is no satisfactory English equivalent, but there are many situations in which the English expression is to be preferred because it is shorter, more likely to be understood, more widely used or adopted by our codes. Frequently there are variations in spelling and the following preferred forms are suggested for the purpose of uniformity. They should be followed in all situations except where there is a quotation and the original uses another form. (For the use of italics with Latin and foreign language words and phrases, see *ante,* §§ 155, 156.)

| **Old or Questionable:** | **Preferred:** |
| --- | --- |
| administrator c.t.a. | administrator with the will |
| administrator *cum testamento annexo* | annexed |
| *animo revocandi* | intent to revoke |
| *autrefois acquit* | former acquittal |
| *autrefois convict* | former conviction or prior conviction |
| can not | cannot |
| *cestui que trust* | beneficiary |
| dehors | outside |
| en banc | in bank |
| endorsement | indorsement |
| enure | inure |
| in as much as | inasmuch as |
| in so far as | insofar as |
| *judgment non obstante veredicto* | judgment notwithstanding the verdict |
| kidnaped | kidnapped |
| kidnaping | kidnapping |
| protectable | protectible |
| res adjudicata | res judicata |
| subpena, subpoena[1] | |

---

[1] The two spellings are inconsistently used in many different code sections and no preference is noted.

**§ 189. Numerals and Figures.**—Styles vary from publication to publication, practice often being dependent upon the authority relied upon or the type of document or publication in which the figures are used. Since consistency of usage is important the following styles have been approved for the Official Reports. These styles indicate when numbers are to be spelled out and when they are to be written as figures. General rules are first indicated. These are followed by narrower rules applicable to specific circumstances. Where a conflict exists the more specific application is to be followed.*

**(a)** Follow copy exactly when quoting.

**(b)** Spell out numbers when starting sentences.

**(c)** Spell out figures one to nine when standing alone.

**(d)** Use figures for the number 10 and numbers following it when standing alone.

**(e)** Use figures with all tabular work.

**(f)** Treat alike all figures used in couples or groups, e.g., He waited eight or ten minutes (not eight or 10). Where an author has need to use several number groupings in close proximity it is usually better style for both aesthetic reasons and to aid in the flow of the material presented to treat all such groupings alike, i.e., either spell out or use figures for all. In determining whether a couple or group of figures, some of which are below 10, should be spelled out or all written as figures the following priorities should be observed:

    **(1)** If the group contains two numbers, the first number controls, e.g., He had nine to fifteen feet of rope (not 9 to 15 or nine to 15). He shortened the rope from 15 to 9 feet (not fifteen to nine or 15 to nine). The numeral one, in the context of one of many, is an exception to this rule; in such a case the one may always be spelled out, e.g., There were many conditions of probation, with 15 days in jail as one of them.

    **(2)** If the group contains more than two numbers, the majority controls, e.g., There were 2 steel bars, 12 concrete blocks, and 16 connectors. (Cf. There were two connectors, four steel bars, and sixteen concrete blocks.)

**(g)** Generally, treat alike all numbers within a given sentence, that is, all should be spelled out or written as figures, e.g., The winning time was 10 minutes 9 seconds over the 1-mile 550-yard course. Not, There were between 500 and 600 persons observing the two- and four-man crews.

**(h)** When one number follows another, use a comma to separate them, e.g., Of the 500, 300 did not vote. However, where two numbers describing the same item occur together, to avoid confusion express one of them by a figure, e.g., There were six 5-foot logs.

---

* See also *ante,* section 161, hyphens with compound numbers and units of measurement; sections 177 and 178, apostrophe with figures; and section 171, commas with figures.

**(i)** Division of figures.—Do not divide a figure at the close of a line.

**(j)** Occasionally an opinion will use a variety of numbers with reference to the same subject matter as, for example, where the discussion concerns the length of possible sentences that a trial court could have imposed in a criminal matter. Where this is the situation it is preferable to treat all such numbers alike throughout rather than to spell out some (those below 10) and use figures with the others (those 10 and over) as otherwise required by adherence to the foregoing styles.

## § 190. Numerals and Figures—Specific Applications.

**(a) Citations.**—Use arabic figures for volume, page, and date. (*People* v. *Cobb* (1971) 15 Cal.App.3d 1, 16 [93 Cal.Rptr. 152].)

**(b) Dates.**—Use figures, except for holidays (Fourth of July, Cinco de Mayo, etc.) but note: "the 4th of July" (when not referred to as a holiday).

When merely the month and day are given, the date may be "July 25" (preferred) or "July 25th" or "the 25th of July" as the author may desire, but when the year is added, use "July 25, 1974." Avoid "July 25th, 1974," "25 July 1974," or "7/25/74."

When only the month and year are given, no comma separates them, e.g., July 1974, *not* July, 1974. Where a sequence of month, day and year is not immediately followed by a period, semicolon, colon, dash, bracket or parenthesis, a comma should be inserted at that point. "He was last seen on July 10, 1974, at the Hiccup Hotel." (See also *ante*, § 170.)

When an author adds "th" etc. to the day of the month, the abbreviations are: 1st, 2d (not 2nd), 3d (not 3rd), 4th, etc.

When denoting a period of time it is optional with the author to use either the en or em dash or "to."

1970 to 1973; 1970–1973 (but not 1970–73); April to August; June to August 1973; June–August 1973; June 1, 1972, to August 1, 1973,; June 1, 1973—August 1, 1973, (em dash rather than en dash used); the 1930's, the '30's.

**(c) Time.**—Use figures for time: 4:30 p.m. (not four thirty p.m.); 10 o'clock in the evening; 10 p.m. (not 10:00 p.m.), (preferably *not* 10 o'clock p.m.); *but* nine years.

Omit spaces in a.m. and p.m. Zeroes should not be used with even hours except where precise time is material, e.g., The store opened at 10 a.m.; *but,* The bid was received at 10:00 a.m.; however, the auction was over at 9:59 a.m. (See also *ante,* § 34.)

When a reference is to a period of time composed of several subunits do not separate the subunits with commas, e.g., He was sentenced to 10 years 11 months and 2 days.

**(d) Numbers indicating sequence.**—Use figures with sequential numbers, e.g., page 4, pages 278–288 (not pages 278–88), order 9, count

2, allegation 1, section 25003, docket number 2160, item 4, part III, question 6, S.F. No. 18761, Civ. No. 10280, A012345, apartment 3. Note that commas are generally *not* used with sequential numbers. (See also *ante,* § 171.)

**(e) Measurements.**—Generally, spell out numbers below 10. Use figures for the number 10 and numbers following it. (See also *ante,* § 189, subds. (f), (g) and (j) for styles when measurements are used in groups.)

Exceptions: Use figures with tabular work. Use figures with "percent."

**(f) Money.**—Use figures: 4 cents (but not 0.4¢), $0.04, 25 cents, $0.25, $2 (not $2.00), $7.95, $179.95, $1,000 (not a thousand dollars).

Exception: For round monetary amounts of a million and over use figures with "million" or "billion" to enhance appearance and readability, e.g.,

$4 million (not $4,000,000); $4.6 million (not $4,600,000 or 4.6 million dollars), but $4,620,000; $4½ million (not four and one-half million); $950,000 to $1 million; $500,000 (not $500 thousand); a $100-a-week job; a $500 grant; $2,000–$3,000 (note the dollar sign is used with both figures).

Indefinite sums of money are spelled out, e.g., Many thousands of dollars were involved.

**(g) Decimals, percentages, and degrees.**—Use figures.

**Decimals:** 46.78, 46.780 (the additional cypher may be used where the author wishes to note the decimal was carried to three places), .09, .22-caliber gun. Exception: decimals are spelled out when beginning a sentence although usually it is better to recast the sentence to avoid such a circumstance.

**Percentages:** 2 percent, 6½ percent or 6.5 percent (not 6.5% except for tabular work), 21 percent, the bonus was between 2 and 10 percent (note the word "percent" follows the last reference), 0.10 percent, or more, of alcohol.

**Degrees:** Longitude 68° 05′ 08″ E; 90.8° to 93° above zero; 47° angle.

**(h) Fractions.**—Spell out fractions when standing alone or when followed by "of a" or "of an" or where these expressions are implied. Do not spell out a portion of a fraction and express the other part as a figure, e.g., two-thirds of a foot (not 2-thirds foot or ⅔ of a foot), three-fourths, five-hundredths, five one-hundredths, forty-five fiftieths, twenty-one thirty-fifths, half-inch, half-hour, half-mile, half an inch, half a dozen, three and one-half. (See also *ante,* § 161 for use of hyphens with fractions and additional illustrations.)

**(i) Ordinals.**—Follow section 189 (c) and (d) *ante,* e.g., first, second, third, fourth, 10th, 24th, third century, 20th century, etc. Military units other than "army" and "corps" are indicated by figures, e.g., 43d Regiment, 6th Naval District (but Seventh Army and XII Corps).

**(j) Plurals.**—These are formed by adding "'s." 10 by 12's; 20's and 30's. (See also *ante,* §§ 177, 178.)

The foregoing rules may be varied to secure emphasis, or when a different rule has been followed in quoted matter and it is desired to have uniformity in style. See also *ante,* section 189 (j). (For additional illustrations and rules controlling situations not covered see GPO Manual (1984 ed.) pp. 165–171; SPO Manual (1980 ed.) pp. 20–21.)

**§ 191.   Plural Forms.**—In compound phrases and titles, the principal word is pluralized:

assistant attorneys general
assistant chiefs of staff
attorneys general
brothers-in-law
city attorneys
courts martial
deputy attorneys general
But note: deputy county counsel

deputy district attorneys
grants-in-aid
heirs at law
inspectors general
judge advocates
notaries public
rights of way

(See also *ante,* §§ 175, 176 re formation of possessives.)

**§ 192.   Spelling Preferences Generally.**—Many words have two acceptable spellings. In order to achieve uniformity of usage for the Official Reports it is requested that authors follow the spelling preferences indicated in this manual. (See *ante,* §§ 184, 187, 188, 163, 164.) Webster's Third New International Dictionary has been selected as the authority for the determination of preferred spelling of words not otherwise covered, and if Webster's gives more than one spelling, the first is preferred. (See also GPO Manual (1984 ed.) pp. 63–72 for helpful collections of preferred and difficult spellings, spellings of anglicized and foreign words, and spellings of plural forms.)

**§ 193.   Split Infinitives.**—The preferred rule is to avoid separating the infinitive verb form. However, most authorities acknowledge that it is proper to insert an adverb or phrase between "to" and the verb in order to avoid an awkward statement, e.g., to utterly forget, to even wish, to first consider, to further complicate, to actually mention it. Usually, however, it will be found that the difficulty or supposed awkwardness can be avoided by recasting the sentence.

# CHAPTER IV
## —Notes—

# CHAPTER V

# TITLE OF CASE

## A. In General

## B. Litigation Designations

# C. Specific Titles

## A. In General

§ 194. **Types of Titles.**—The title of an opinion will differ depending upon whether it is used as the main title or as a running head.

The main title is the form used as the title of an opinion in the Official Reports. Ordinarily the same title form is the proper title for typewritten and published opinions. However, transcript and brief titles will differ from opinion titles since the usual appellate court opinion practice of using "et al." to indicate the existence of more than one plaintiff, defendant, cross-defendant, intervener, etc. after the designation of the first-named party is not followed, and all parties involved in the appeal are specified.

The running head is the title appearing at the top of the first and following pages of a published opinion and which identifies the opinion for citation purposes. Where the running head differs as between the official report of the decision and the parallel nonofficial publication, the official report running head is followed. (See *ante,* §§ 91, 80 (a).)

§ 195. **Purpose of Main Title.**—The main title, as printed in the Official Reports, is not an index to all the parties, a complete description of each one's status (as executor, trustee, etc.), nor a definitive statement of the respective positions each may have occupied as plaintiff, defendant, cross-defendant, appellant, etc. However, with the foregoing caveat noted, the title is an important informational aid designed to note the type of proceeding before the court and to assist the reader in the early identification of the parties and their trial and appellate statuses. Care in the preparation of the title is therefore essential.

(For conformity of party designations in titles, opinions and briefs, see *post,* § 211.)

§ 196. **Style of Main Title.**—The main title is always in roman, not italics. The names of the parties are in full capitals, and their trial and appellate court titles are in capitals and lowercase, e.g., GRACE JONES, Plaintiff and Appellant, v. HARRY STONE, Defendant and Respondent. When a surname contains an intermediate capital, with a prefix that is the equivalent of "the," "of," "son of," etc. (MacDonald, LaMarr, De Forrest, etc.), the initial letter is a full capital, and the rest of the prefix is in small capitals; e.g., MacDONALD, LaMARR, De FORREST. This form should be used regardless of whether the surname is written as one or two words. Personal degrees or titles (C.P.A., M.A., M.D., etc.) are not used in opinion titles. (See *post,* § 197 for title page format.)

§ 197. **Title Page Format—Typed Opinions.**—In addition to the main title (see *ante,* §§ 194–196) the inception page of the opinion should contain the title of the authoring court, and, where applicable, the division thereof; the appellate court number or numbers;‡ and, if an appeal, the trial court number. The date is added by the clerk's office at the time of filing. Since, by reason of rule 976 of the California Rules of Court, Court of Appeal and appellate department of the superior court opinions may not be published in the Official Reports unless certified for publication, a notation indicating the publication status of the opinion should be prominently displayed in large type. The customary language is "CERTIFIED FOR PUBLICATION," "CERTIFIED FOR PARTIAL PUBLICATION," and "NOT TO BE PUBLISHED." Typical title pages are:

IN THE SUPREME COURT OF CALIFORNIA*

| THE PEOPLE, | ) | |
|---|---|---|
| Plaintiff and Respondent, | ) | |
| v. | ) | S012345† |
| JOSEPH GREEN, | ) | B012345‡ |
| Defendant and Appellant. | ) | (Super. Ct. No. A-54321) |

CERTIFIED FOR PUBLICATION
[OR] CERTIFIED FOR PARTIAL PUBLICATION

IN THE COURT OF APPEAL OF THE STATE OF CALIFORNIA
FIRST APPELLATE DISTRICT
DIVISION FOUR

| WILLIAM G. LITTLE, | ) | |
|---|---|---|
| Plaintiff and Respondent, | ) | |
| v. | ) | A012345† |
| SMITH PLUMBING, INC., et al., | ) | (Super. Ct. No. 54321) |
| Defendants and Appellants. | ) | |

CERTIFIED FOR PUBLICATION

APPELLATE DEPARTMENT OF THE SUPERIOR COURT
OF THE STATE OF CALIFORNIA FOR THE COUNTY OF LOS ANGELES

| THE PEOPLE, | ) | Super. Ct. Crim. A. |
|---|---|---|
| Plaintiff and Respondent, | ) | No. 12345 |
| v. | ) | (Municipal Court for the Los |
| FRED BARN, | ) | Angeles Judicial District of |
| Defendant and Appellant. | ) | Los Angeles County No. 54321) |

(See also *post,* § 266.)

---

\* Since the Supreme Court no longer sits in departments the previous practice of routinely noting "In Bank" is discontinued. All opinions of the Supreme Court are published and therefore it is unnecessary to note "certified for publication."

† See *ante,* section 69, footnote.

‡ When the Supreme Court is reviewing a Court of Appeal decision, the appellate numbers of both courts should be provided. (See *post,* § 261 and *ante,* § 69.)

IN THE COURT OF APPEAL OF THE STATE OF CALIFORNIA
SECOND APPELLATE DISTRICT
DIVISION TWO

| | | |
|---|---|---|
| MARY LAMB et al., <br>     Plaintiffs and Appellants, <br>   v. <br> BUGGYWHIP COMPANY, <br>     Defendant and Respondent. | ) <br> ) <br> ) <br> ) <br> ) | B012345 <br> (Super. Ct. No. 54321) |
| MARY LAMB et. al., <br>     Petitioners, <br>   v. <br> THE SUPERIOR COURT OF LOS ANGELES <br> COUNTY, <br>     Respondent; <br> BUGGYWHIP COMPANY, <br>     Real Party in Interest. | ) <br> ) <br> ) <br> ) <br> ) <br> ) <br> ) <br> ) <br> ) | B012456 |

(See *Baker* v. *Supreme Court* (1984) 35 Cal.3d 663, and *post,* § 207 for proper multiple title styles where numerous cases are consolidated or coordinated for disposition by a single opinion, and § 286 for the listing of lower court numbers.)

**§ 198.  Adjustment of Opinion Titles—Reporter's Notes.—** Opinion titles are sometimes changed for bound volume publication after the opinion has first appeared in an advance pamphlet. For example, the first named appellant may not have in fact appealed and that name would therefore be dropped. (See *post,* § 200.) Where the corrected title differs materially from the title used in the advance pamphlet a reporter's note indicates the earlier title and both titles are indexed in the bound volume to avoid confusion. (See, e.g., *Swoap* v. *Superior Court* (1973) 10 Cal.3d 490, fn.*) The Cumulative Subsequent History Table at the back of the latest advance pamphlet will note significant title changes prior to the publication of the bound volume. (See also *post,* § 223 re substitution of parties.)

**§ 199.  Order of Names Remains the Same—Appeal.—**The order of names is never reversed; the plaintiff or other initiating party below is named first. In addition to the trial court designations such as "Plaintiff," "Defendant," "Petitioner," "Objector," etc., the parties are noted as being either "Appellant" or "Respondent" on an appeal, e.g.,

> JOHN JONES, Plaintiff and Appellant, v. TOM SMITH, Defendant and Respondent. [or]
> JOHN JONES, Plaintiff and Respondent, v. TOM SMITH, Defendant and Appellant.

(See Code Civ. Proc., § 902, and, for the rules relating to cross-appeals and cross-complaints, see *post,* §§ 202, 208, 209. See also *post,* § 237 for original proceeding titles, and §§ 226–258 for titles in specific types of proceedings.)

**§ 200.  Change in Practice.**—For many years it was the practice to have the main title of opinions set forth the names of the first plaintiff and the first defendant as they appeared in the complaint regardless of whether they were parties to the proceedings in the reviewing court. (For example, if John Jones and Mary Black sued Tom Smith, and Mary Black alone appealed, the title would be: JOHN JONES et al., Plaintiffs; MARY BLACK, Plaintiff and Appellant, v. TOM SMITH, Defendant and Respondent.) The Supreme Court thereafter adopted a new system, first reflected in the 1961 edition of the California Style Manual, under which only the names of those who *are* parties in the reviewing court or whose designations are *essential* to an understanding of the action will appear in the title. In the example given, the form of the title will be: MARY BLACK, Plaintiff and Appellant, v. TOM SMITH, Defendant and Respondent. The rules explaining the operation of this party-designation system are set forth in the sections that follow. (See also *ante,* § 195.)

**§ 201.  Content of Title—Appeal.**—In the case of a controversy between two persons, the main title will show the name of the plaintiff with his trial court designation (plaintiff) and his appropriate designation in the appellate court (appellant or respondent) followed by the name of the defendant with his trial and appellate court designations. (See *post,* § 218.) The title will also show any special status a party may possess as, for example, trustee, executor, minor, etc. (See *post,* § 220.) When a case involves two or more plaintiffs or defendants, only the first plaintiff or the first defendant is named (except in brief and transcript titles, see *ante,* § 194), and "et al." is used to indicate the existence of the others, unless they occupy antagonistic or opposing positions, as where one defendant is an appellant and another a respondent. (See *post,* §§ 203, 206, 219, 236 and *ante,* § 197, title page format. For the title style on death penalty appeals, see *post,* § 231.)

**§ 202.  Where Plaintiff and Defendant Both Appeal.**—When there is an appeal by both the plaintiff and defendant, both are called "Appellant" and the title then is:

> JOHN JONES, Plaintiff and Appellant, v. MARY SMITH, Defendant and Appellant.

In that it is obvious Mary Smith is respondent as to John Jones's appeal and John Jones is respondent as to Mary Smith's appeal it is not necessary to note this by the inclusion of the additional designation "Respondent."

(See, e.g., *Jones* v. *H.F. Ahmanson & Co.* (1969) 1 Cal.3d 93; see also *post,* § 203.)

**§ 203. Where Several Plaintiffs or Defendants Appeal— Appeal by Both Sets of Parties.**—Where there are several plaintiffs or several defendants, and all appeal, there is no need to state all their names, and the opinion title will show only the names of the first plaintiff and the first defendant with "et al." for the others.

JOHN JONES et al., Plaintiffs and Appellants, v. TOM SMITH et al., Defendants and Appellants.

(See, e.g., *Campbell* v. *Graham-Armstrong* (1973) 9 Cal.3d 482; see also *ante,* § 202.)

**§ 204. Appearance by Some but Not All of the Plaintiffs or Defendants—If First Person Named Appeals.**—If the first person named as plaintiff or defendant appeals, name him (with et al., if others also appeal); ignore those who do not appeal. Thus, where John Jones, Richard Doe and John Doe are plaintiffs, and only John Jones appeals, the title will be:

JOHN JONES, Plaintiff and Appellant, v. TOM SMITH, Defendant and Respondent.

But if John Jones *and* John Doe appeal, the title will be:

JOHN JONES et al., Plaintiffs and Appellants, v. TOM SMITH, Defendant and Respondent.

If Tom Smith also appeals, the title will be:

JOHN JONES et al., Plaintiffs and Appellants, v. TOM SMITH, Defendant and Appellant.

(See also *ante,* § 200 and *post,* § 205.)

**§ 205. If First Person Named Is Not a Party to the Appeal.**— Where the first person named in the complaint or petition as plaintiff or defendant does not appeal from an adverse decision, but others do, the name of the first person is omitted, and the name of the next person who appeals is substituted. In the following examples, assume that the plaintiffs in the trial court were Al Able, Ben Black and Carl Cable and that the defendants were Roy Row, Sam Smith and Tom Tait.

**(a)** If the decision below is in favor of the defendants and against the plaintiffs, and if the first named plaintiff (Al Able) does not appeal, the title will be:

BEN BLACK et al., Plaintiffs and Appellants, v. ROY ROW et al., Defendants and Respondents.

**(b)** If the judgment below allows a recovery by the first named plaintiff (Al Able) but denies relief to the other plaintiffs, who appeal, the title will likewise be:

> BEN BLACK et al., Plaintiffs and Appellants, v. ROY ROW et al., Defendants and Respondents.

**(c)** If the judgment below is in favor of the plaintiffs and against the defendants, and the first named defendant (Roy Row) does not appeal, the title will be:

> AL ABLE et al., Plaintiffs and Respondents, v. SAM SMITH et al., Defendants and Appellants.

**(d)** If the action was dismissed as to the first named defendant (Roy Row) and the remaining defendants appeal from an adverse judgment, the title will be:

> AL ABLE et al., Plaintiffs and Respondents, v. SAM SMITH et al., Defendants and Appellants.

It will be noted that the effect of the foregoing style is to eliminate from the main title the names of persons who are not parties to the appeal. (But see *post,* §§ 243 [interpleader]; 256 [third party claims]; and 257 [third party lien claimants] for exceptional situations where the name of a nonparty is retained as essential for identification of the proceeding.) The style does not, however, operate to eliminate the names of parties affected by the appeal merely because they fail to make an appearance in support of or in opposition to the trial court's decision. For example, if Al Able appealed from a judgment in favor of defendants Roy Row, Sam Smith and Tom Tait, it would make no difference in the title whether Roy Row filed a brief, joined in his codefendant's brief, or failed to appear, in each instance the title would be:

> AL ABLE, Plaintiff and Appellant, v. ROY ROW et al., Defendants and Respondents.

(For rules governing the substitution of parties, see *post,* § 223.)

### § 206. Where Some Plaintiffs (or Some Defendants) Are Appellants and Some Are Respondents.

—When there is an appeal by some of the plaintiffs or defendants and the others are respondents, use the fact-applicable designations "Plaintiff and Respondent," "Plaintiff and Appellant," "Defendant and Respondent," and "Defendant and Appellant." (See, e.g., *Crocker-Citizens National Bank* v. *Younger* (1971) 4 Cal.3d 202.) The necessity for distinguishing between different sets of plaintiffs or defendants usually arises in cases where cross-pleadings have been filed, and it may then be necessary to use the designations of "Plaintiff, Cross-defendant and Appellant," or "Plaintiff, Cross-defendant and Respondent," or "Defendant, Cross-complainant and Appellant," or "Defendant, Cross-complainant and Respondent," or (where the appeal involves only the judgment on the cross-complaint) "Cross-complainant and Appellant" or "Cross-complainant and Respondent" or "Cross-defendant and Appellant" or "Cross-defendant and Respondent." The terms "cross-appellant" and "cross-respondent" are never used in appellate titles and should be avoided in the body of opinions. (See *post*, §§ 207–208.)

**§ 207. Consolidated and Coordinated Cases.**—When two or more *separate* actions are consolidated in the trial court or at the reviewing court level, the opinion should set out the title of each action regardless of whether there is a single judgment for all or a number of separate judgments and regardless of whether the matters have been given one or more numbers, unless the titles are identical *in all respects.* If, for example, a party plaintiff is an appellant in one case and a respondent in the other or the defendants in one action differ from those in the other, both titles must be set out. However, where titles are absolutely identical, repetition is meaningless and should be avoided, and it is sufficient to note the appellate court numbers (if more than one) and, in appeals, the trial court numbers. (See, e.g., *Estate of Desmond* (1973) 34 Cal.App.3d 139.)

In instances where there are more than four cases and no confusion as to the designation of parties and counsel will result it is preferable to use only the title of the first case with a parenthetical reference to the other consolidated cases which are listed in a footnote. (See, e.g., *Pasillas* v. *Agricultural Labor Relations Bd.* (1984) 156 Cal.App.3d 312; *Englund* v. *Chavez* (1972) 8 Cal.3d 572; *Seibert* v. *Sears, Roebuck & Co.* (1975) 45 Cal.App.3d 1; *People* v. *Yniquez* (1974) 42 Cal.App.3d Supp. 13.)

Opinions determining multiple cases coming before reviewing courts under the statutes and rules of court (Code Civ. Proc., §§ 404–404.8; Cal. Rules of Court, rules 1501–1550), which permit the coordination of civil actions pending in different courts where there are common questions of law or fact, use the title styles for consolidated cases as outlined above. Do not adopt as the title for such opinions the titles of convenience often assigned under such circumstances in the trial courts to identify the coordinated group, e.g., "Cases Relating to Crash of Flight 1040."

Avoid the use of double titles where in reality there is only *one* case with cross-pleadings, as by cross-complaint. (See, e.g., § 208 and §§ 206, 209 for the form of title where cross-pleadings in the same action are involved and Code Civ. Proc., §§ 426.10-428.80.)

Since it is obvious from the face of an opinion containing more than one title that either there has been a consolidation at the trial or appellate level or that the court is considering the cases together, the former practice of noting "(Consolidated Cases.)" is discontinued as superfluous. In almost all instances the body of the opinion recites the procedural aspects of the matter.

**§ 208. One Case—Cross-complaint; Intervention.**—When there is in reality only one case, and a second title has been inserted by someone merely because there has been a cross-complaint, or because an intervener has appeared, only one title should be used and there should be no repetition of names because a person is both a plaintiff and a cross-defendant or both a defendant and a cross-complainant, etc. For example, suppose the transcript is entitled "JOHN JONES, Plaintiff and Respondent, v. TOM SMITH and FRED BROWN, Defendants and Appellants. TOM SMITH and FRED BROWN, Cross-complainants and Appellants, v. JOHN JONES, Cross-defendant and Respondent." This is a false double title and, where the appeal is not challenging the lower court's ruling on the cross-complaint, the opinion title should be reduced to the following form:

> JOHN JONES, Plaintiff and Respondent, v. TOM SMITH et al., Defendants and Appellants.

Where, however, the appeal is directed at the lower court's ruling on *both* the complaint and cross-complaint the title in the above example would be:

> JOHN JONES, Plaintiff, Cross-defendant and Respondent, v. TOM SMITH et al., Defendants, Cross-complainants and Appellants.

(See, e.g., *Cornell* v. *Sennes* (1971) 18 Cal.App.3d 126.)

In situations in which the appeal concerns *only* the ruling on the cross-complaint, the preferred style is to name the cross-complainant first and drop the trial court designations of "plaintiff" and "defendant." The form of the title then is:

> TOM SMITH et al., Cross-complainants and Appellants, v. JOHN JONES, Cross-defendant and Respondent.

(See also *post,* § 209(d).)

A double title should not be used merely because a new party or parties have been brought into the case whether by a cross-complaint, intervention or otherwise.

(See also *ante,* § 207 and *post,* §§ 209, 244.)

By virtue of the Legislature's adoption of the recommendation of the California Law Revision Commission concerning the forms of pleading, the counterclaim has been abolished and "A party against whom a cause of action has been asserted in a complaint or cross-complaint may file a cross-complaint setting forth either or both of the following: (a) Any cause of action he has against any of the parties who filed the complaint or cross-complaint against him. . . . (b) Any cause of action he has against a person alleged to be liable thereon, whether or not such a person is already a party to the action, if the cause of action asserted in his cross-complaint (1) arises out of the same transaction, occurrence, or series of transactions or occurrences as the cause brought against him or (2) asserts a claim, right, or interest in the property or controversy which is the subject of the cause brought against him." (Code Civ. Proc., § 428.10.)

Additionally the rules concerning the joinder of parties and causes of action have been substantially liberalized. (Code Civ. Proc., §§ 428.20, 428.30; 5 Witkin, Cal. Procedure (3d ed. 1985) Pleading, §§ 1089–1101, pp. 511–522; Marshall, *New Developments in Pleading* (1972) 48 L.A. Bar Bull. 9.)

Since the potential for joining causes of action and parties made possible by the described reform legislation has substantially increased, the opinion title preparer will occasionally be faced with the problem of preparing titles involving complex combinations of party litigants. While the task of producing the correct title under such circumstances might seem complex in theory, if the formula for listing parties described *post* in section 209 is applied the correct title will result.

Under the operative pleading practice in rare instances it may be necessary to list two or more groups on the "plaintiff's side" of the versus (v.) symbol, for example, if plaintiff A sues defendant B and B cross-complains against A naming C, D, and E as additional cross-defendants and A in turn cross-complains joining F and G as cross-complainants and A, F, and G appeal, the form of the title would be:

> A, Plaintiff, Cross-complainant and Appellant; F et al., Cross-complainants and Appellants, v. B, Defendant, Cross-complainant and Respondent; C et al., Cross-defendants and Respondents.

### § 209. One Case—Cross-complaint—Grouping of Litigants.—

Having determined there is but one case and therefore that a single title is appropriate it is necessary to group all parties with *identical* trial *and* appellate designations and to list each group separately.

Assume, for example, a case in which A sues B, C, and D.

D answers and cross-complains against A, B, and C.

D's cross-complaint additionally names E et al. as parties cross-defendant.

**(a)** If D appeals from a judgment against him on both A's complaint and D's cross-complaint the title is:

> A, Plaintiff, Cross-defendant and Respondent, v. B et al., Defendants, Cross-defendants and Respondents; D, Defendant, Cross-complainant and Appellant; E et al., Cross-defendants and Respondents.

**(b)** If A appeals from a judgment against him on his complaint and D appeals from a judgment against him on his cross-complaint the title is:

A, Plaintiff, Cross-defendant and Appellant, v. B et al., Defendants, Cross-defendants and Respondents; D, Defendant, Cross-complainant and Appellant; E et al., Cross-defendants and Respondents.

**(c)** If A appeals from a judgment against him on his complaint and D loses on his cross-complaint but elects not to appeal from the ruling the title is:

A, Plaintiff and Appellant, v. B et al., Defendants and Respondents.

In this situation the cross-complaint is not involved and the title reverts to the simple A v. B situation.

**(d)** If D obtains a judgment against A and B et al. on his cross-complaint but appeals from the judgment insofar as it denies him recovery as to E et al., and assuming the appeal concerns *only* the ruling on the cross-complaint, the title is:

D, Cross-complainant and Appellant, v. E et al., Cross-defendants and Respondents.

(See, e.g., *Mehl* v. *The People* ex rel *Dept. Pub. Wks.* (1975) 13 Cal.3d 710; *Sea-Land Service, Inc.* v. *Matson Terminal Co.* (1967) 253 Cal.App.2d 885; see also *ante,* § 208.)

Because of the large number of variables, illustration of even a small fraction of the potential titles is impractical. However, the foregoing principles are constant, and with care in the determination of the facts and by assigning parties with *identical* trial *and* appellate designations to their respective groups the proper title will result even where there are complexities such as multiple cross-complaints. (See *ante,* § 208.) Often the necessary information can be obtained rapidly from the clerk's transcript by consulting the trial court's judgment and the notice or notices of appeal. In more complex situations it may be necessary to examine the entire procedural history of the case, where, for example, there have been dismissals, substitutions or multiple judgments. A perusal of the clerk's transcript index will generally alert the title preparer to unusual circumstances.

Care in the preparation of appellate court opinion titles in the first instance avoids nomenclature inconsistencies between party designations used in the title and those used in the opinion text, and obviates the need for a later examination of the record to bring about a correct title when problems appear. (See also *post,* §§ 210, 211.)

## B. Litigation Designations

**§ 210. Appeals—Selection of Party's Designation.—** In most instances, it is preferable, in briefs and opinions, to use the trial court terminology (or individual names) in referring to the parties, i.e., plaintiff, defendant, etc. Ordinarily, the problems to be discussed arose in the trial court, and it is easier to follow the discourse if the writer retains the trial court designations when stating the facts and discussing the issues. On the other hand it may be simpler to use the reviewing court designations in cases where the point at issue involves the proceedings in that court, as where the question concerns a motion to dismiss the appeal. The designation of a party consistently throughout, especially in cases involving numerous parties, assists the reader in following the flow of material presented without the mental interruptions often otherwise necessary to identify the party's standing. It is therefore poor style to identify the same party successively as "plaintiff," "respondent," "condemner," etc.

(See also *post,* § 211 for conformity of title and opinion body references; § 253 for the designation of parties in special proceedings; § 238 for Family Law Act titles; §§ 230, 240, 249-251 for conservatorship, guardianship and probate proceedings and § 237 for original proceedings.)

### § 211. Conformity of Party Descriptions in Titles, Opinions and Briefs.—In order to assist in the early identification of the parties involved, avoid confusion and achieve consistency in reference, opinion and brief authors should, where practicable, conform party designations adopted for the title with those used in the body of the opinion or brief.

Similarly, briefs seeking review before the Supreme Court, briefs on the merits following the grant of review, as well as opinions following the grant of review should retain the titles and party designations applicable in the Court of Appeal under the guidelines provided by this manual. Consistency of title and party references during the entire appellate process is essential to provide continuity of identification at each level of briefing, to facilitate the tracking of a cause or proceeding throughout its appellate court life and to avoid needless confusion.

(See also *ante,* §§ 209, last par., 210.)

### § 212. Corporations.—Do not abbreviate any word forming a part of a corporate name unless the word is used in abbreviated form by the corporation; e.g., if the corporation's title is Ajax Gas and Electric Company, do not abbreviate to Ajax Gas & Elec. Co. If on the other hand, the corporate title contains abbreviations, that configuration should be maintained, e.g., Directors Guild of Cal., Inc., should not be changed to Directors Guild of California, Incorporated.

It is not necessary to note parenthetically that the entity designated is a corporation, since that fact is usually apparent from the title or will appear, where material, in the body of the opinion.

As a style matter, the word "The" preceding a corporate name is dropped. (See *post,* §§ 219, 259 and *ante,* §§ 26, 27.)

## § 213. Damaging Disclosures—Appellate Court Policy of Nonidentification of Innocent Parties.

—Recognizing that the publication of the names of innocent victims of sex crimes and the names of minors who, without blame, are caught up in the type of case where damaging disclosures are made serves no useful legal or social purposes, the Supreme Court has issued the following policy memorandum to all appellate courts: "To prevent the publication of damaging disclosures concerning sex-crime victims and minors innocently involved in appellate court proceedings it is requested that the names of these persons be omitted from all appellate court opinions whenever their best interests would be served by anonymity." Customarily, expressions such as "the complaining witness," "the mother," "a 10-year-old girl," "the prosecutrix," "C.D. testified," "the girl (Heidi)," "the victim (Mary)," and "Susan B." are substituted.

Clerk's and reporter's transcripts as well as briefs reflect the true names of parties and the foregoing nondisclosure policy does not extend to them in the absence of protective legislation.

(See also *post,* § 214 and §§ 241, 245, 246 re nonidentification of minors in juvenile court and collateral proceedings; cf. § 226.)

## § 214. Damaging Disclosures—Nondisclosure of Minor's Identity.

—The prevailing California appellate court practice is to not disclose the identity of minors in either the title or body of opinions reviewing proceedings under the Juvenile Court Law. (See *In re M.G.S.* (1968) 267 Cal.App.2d 329, 340, fn. 4; *T.N.G. v. Superior Court* (1971) 4 Cal.3d 767, 770, fn. 1; see also *ante,* § 213.) This practice has been adopted in collateral proceedings as well. (See *post,* §§ 241, 245.)

The preferred reference style is to identify the minor by the use of his or her first name followed by an initial for the last name although the use of initials alone is common and acceptable. If the minor's first name is so unusual as to defeat the objective of anonymity then the minor's initials should be used. The term "Anonymous" or other fictitious designations should be avoided.

It is noted that in order to carry out this nondisclosure policy it is usually necessary to suppress the identity of parents and others bearing the minor's last name. (See *post,* §§ 226, 246.)

Where the minor seeks relief in a collateral proceeding such as a petition for a writ of mandate to compel the juvenile court to reconsider its determination that he was not amenable to its treatment, the nondisclosure title is not used where relief is denied. (Cf. *Jimmy H.* v. *Superior Court* (1970) 3 Cal.3d 709 [relief granted] with *Bryan* v. *Superior Court* (1972) 7 Cal.3d 575 [relief denied].)

It is additionally noted that the foregoing nondisclosure policy has no application to situations where the minor is not dealt with under the Juvenile Court Law but is held to answer as an adult in a criminal proceeding. (See *People* v. *Arauz* (1970) 5 Cal.App.3d 523; but cf. *People* v. *Joe T.* (1975) 48 Cal.App.3d 114, 121 where the criminal proceeding was a nullity and the matter was remanded to the juvenile court.)

**§ 215. Government Officers.**—When suit is brought by or against a government officer in his *official capacity,* the title should so note: JOHN JONES, as City Treasurer, etc., or, as County Auditor, etc., or, as Insurance Commissioner, etc., or, as Attorney General, etc., or, as Director of Finance, etc., e.g.,

> FRED GREEN, as Attorney General, etc., Plaintiff and Respondent, v. BONANZA BANK, as Trustee, etc., Defendant and Appellant.

(See also *post,* § 223 where there has been a change of governmental officers during the course of litigation and § 252 for quo warranto proceeding titles.)

**§ 216. Governmental Bodies.**—Ordinarily the name itself will indicate the character of the particular body, and it is unnecessary to add any explanatory wording such as "a municipal corporation," "an irrigation district," etc.

When an action involves a state board or department rather than the State of California generally, the title should show the name of the particular body, rather than the name of the State of California. (See, e.g., *Nightingale* v. *State Personnel Board* (1972) 7 Cal.3d 507; *Subsequent Injuries Fund* v. *Workmen's Comp. App. Bd.* (1970) 2 Cal.3d 56; *City of Los Angeles* v. *Public Utilities Commission* (1972) 7 Cal.3d 331; cf. *post,* § 225.)

**§ 217. Individual Doing Business in Firm Name.**—When the plaintiff or defendant is doing business under a fictitious name, that fact is usually ignored. Thus, if defendant Tom Smith is sued as "Tom Smith, doing business under the name of Smith Realty Co.," the title is merely,

> JOHN JONES, Plaintiff and Appellant, v. TOM SMITH, Defendant and Respondent.

Do *not* use "etc." to indicate the fictitious name.

(See *post,* § 219, for the style of designating partnerships or unincorporated associations.)

**§ 218. Natural Persons—Single Plaintiff and Defendant.**—In the simple case involving two persons, the title is:

JOHN JONES, Plaintiff and Appellant, v. TOM SMITH, Defendant and Respondent.                     [or]
JOHN JONES, Plaintiff and Respondent, v. TOM SMITH, Defendant and Appellant.

The fact that a person has used an alias or is "also known" under a different name or names is to be disregarded. Do not use "etc." to indicate an alias. When it appears from the pleadings or other reliable documentation that a person sues or is sued by an alias or that his name is misspelled, his correct name should be used, not the inaccurate name or the alias.

(See also *post,* § 232 and *ante,* §§ 217, 201.)

### § 219. Partnerships or Unincorporated Associations.—"Any
partnership or other unincorporated association, whether organized for profit or not, may sue and be sued in the name which it has assumed or by which it is known." (Code Civ. Proc., § 388, subd. (a).) Where the first named party is a partnership or unincorporated association it is not necessary to note its character as a partnership, nonprofit corporation, national banking association, etc., since this information is usually apparent from the title or will appear, where material, in the body of the opinion. Where the partnership or association is named first followed by the names of its members, use the firm's name and "et al." (AJAX PROPERTIES et al.). If the first named party is a member of the entity it is not necessary to note that a partnership or association is involved (TOM SMITH et al.) (See also *ante,* §§ 217, 201.) As a style matter, the word "The" preceding a partnership or unincorporated association's name is dropped. (See *ante,* § 26 and *post,* § 259.)

### § 220. Persons Acting in a Representative Capacity.—If the
action involves a person who is suing or being sued in a representative capacity, the title should indicate that fact. Use "etc." with the designation of the person's status, e.g., "JOHN JONES, as Administrator, etc.," "as Executor, etc.," "as City Treasurer, etc.," "as Attorney General, etc.," "as County Auditor, etc.," "as Trustee, etc.," "as Trustee in Bankruptcy, etc.," "as Special Administrator, etc.," "as Supervisor, etc.," etc.

It is noted, however, that where the action is that of a minor or a person under a disability the title normally bears the name of the minor, incompetent or ward and *not* that of his representative. (See *post,* §§ 221, 222; *In re Marriage of Higgason* (1973) 10 Cal.3d 476, 484; *Dixon* v. *Cardoza* (1895) 106 Cal. 506, 507 and *Estate of Cochems* (1952) 110 Cal.App.2d 27, 29; see also *post,* §§ 230, 240 for the designation of representatives in conservatorship and guardianship proceedings and § 224 for the style of class actions.)

If a person also appears in his individual capacity, the designation is, "PETER SMITH, Individually and as Executor, etc." Where the Party is appearing individually and additionally brings an action as a guardian of a minor or incompetent no notation is normally made and "et al." is used to represent the unnamed minor or incompetent, e.g., "PETER SMITH et al." (See *post,* §§ 221, 222, 249, and *ante,* § 201.)

### § 221. Persons Under a Disability—Minors.—"A minor may enforce his rights by civil action, or other legal proceedings, in the same manner as a person of full age, except that a guardian must conduct the same." (Civ. Code, § 42; Code Civ. Proc., § 372.) In most instances the minor and not the guardian is the *party* and the title should bear the name of the minor and not that of the guardian or conservator. (See 4 Witkin, Cal. Procedure (3d ed. 1985) Pleading, § 60, pp. 99–100; *In re Marriage of Higgason* (1973) 10 Cal.3d 476, 484; *ante,* § 220.) The appropriate title style therefore is:

> TOM SMITH, a Minor, etc., Plaintiff and Respondent, v. AJAX CORPORATION, Defendant and Appellant.

The "etc." is used in place of "by X, his guardian ad litem."

Where the suit is *against* a minor, even though a guardian or conservator has previously been appointed, the minor is the proper party and the title would note: FRED GREEN, a Minor, Defendant and Respondent. Again, the guardian is not mentioned.

Care must be exercised in determining who the party litigant is since in some situations involving minors and others under a disability an action may be brought by a third party in his own name even though he does so *on behalf* of the minor who is the real party in interest. For example, Civil Code section 4426 permits an action to nullify a marriage, under the conditions specified, by either the minor *or* his parent, guardian, or other person having charge of the minor. In probate proceedings concerning the administration of the estates of insane and incompetent persons the guardian or conservator may be authorized to bring the action in his own name. (See, e.g., *post,* §§ 230, 240.) In such situations the Legislature has prescribed by whom such litigation may be commenced and the title should follow the facts. If such an action is commenced by a guardian or conservator indicate his representative status. (See *ante,* § 220.) Do not indicate the relationship of the party litigant to the minor in situations where the action is brought by a relative. For example, a title in a proceeding to nullify a marriage commenced by a minor's parent (John Kirham) would be:

> In re the Marriage of MARY and JAMES SMITH. JOHN KIRHAM, Appellant, v. JAMES SMITH, Respondent.

(See 4 Witkin, Cal. Procedure (3d ed. 1985) Pleading, § 129, p. 161, §§ 835–837, pp. 280–283; 5 Witkin, Cal. Procedure, *supra,* Pleading, § 846, pp. 291–293.)

Other examples of situations where an action may be brought by *or* on behalf of a minor are: minor against father for support, and minor for support and to establish parentage. (See 5 Witkin, Cal. Procedure, *supra,* Pleading, § 846, pp. 291–292.)

Where the right of action is really that of the parent, although involving the minor, the parent is the party and the child would not be mentioned in the title. Such is the situation where a parent has a statutory right of recovery from a third party because of injury to his minor child. (See Code Civ. Proc., § 376.) Of course, the injured minor has an independent right of action for those damages he or she incurred, and if such an action is joined with that of the parent the title should bear the name of the first named plaintiff and "et al." Although the right of action for personal injuries to a minor is the parents' under usual circumstances, there are situations where the minor may seek recovery in his own name, as for example, where the child is emancipated. (See 4 Witkin, Cal. Procedure, *supra,* Pleading, § 151, pp. 177–178.)

By reason of the amendment of Civil Code section 25 in 1971 "minors are all persons under 18 years of age."

(See also *post,* § 226, adoptions; §§ 230, 240 for the styles governing conservatorship and guardianship proceedings; §§ 245, 246 for juvenile court proceedings; § 241 for habeas corpus proceedings involving minors and *ante,* §§ 213, 214, for use of anonymous references.)

## § 222. Persons Under a Disability—Incompetent Persons.—

"When a minor, an incompetent person, or a person for whom a conservator has been appointed is a party, such person shall appear either by a guardian or conservator of the estate or by a guardian ad litem appointed by the court in which the action or proceeding is pending,..." (Code Civ. Proc., § 372.) Usually the incompetent person and not the guardian *is the party* and the title should bear the name of the incompetent and not that of the guardian or conservator. (See *ante,* § 221; 4 Witkin, Cal. Procedure (3d ed. 1985) Pleading, § 60, pp. 99–100; *In re Marriage of Higgason* (1973) 10 Cal.3d 476, 484; *post,* §§ 230, 240.) A typical title is:

MARY ADAMS, an Incompetent Person, etc., Plaintiff and Respondent, v. HAROLD BURNS, Defendant and Appellant.

The guardian is not mentioned. The "etc." is used in place of "by X, her guardian."

Care must be exercised in determining who the actual party litigant is since in some situations the guardian may be permitted to bring the action *on behalf of* his ward. (See *ante,* § 221 and *post,* §§ 230, 240 governing conservatorship and guardianship proceeding title styles.)

Where the issue before the appellate court is whether the party is or is not incompetent, do not use the designation "an Incompetent Person" following the individual's name.

**§ 223.   Substitution of Parties.**—When there has been a substitution of a party during the pendency of an appeal or other proceeding before the reviewing courts because of death, transfer of interest, bankruptcy, liquidation, receivership, or other cause, the name of the original party is dropped from the title and the name of the substituted party inserted. The fact of substitution is not noted for title purposes although this procedural feature is often described in the text of the decision. Where an opinion has been reported in the advance sheets under the original party's name the title is corrected for the bound volume and a reporter's note is used: "This case was previously entitled *A* v. *B*." The opinion is then indexed under both its advance sheet and corrected bound volume titles. (See *ante,* § 198.)

Substitution of parties in pending appeals is made in and by the trial court and upon presentation of a certified copy of the order of substitution the appellate court makes a similar order and adjusts its records. (See Cal. Rules of Court, rule 48(a).) Substitution of parties in proceedings initiated in the appellate courts, e.g., original proceedings, is normally made upon order of the appellate court following application or stipulation.

Where a public official is a party, without regard to the individual that holds the office, the incumbent and not his predecessor should be named in the title, although the action is sometimes continued by the successor in the name of his predecessor. (See Code Civ. Proc., § 385; *Weadon* v. *Shahen* (1942) 50 Cal.App.2d 254, 259-260; see also *ante,* § 215.)

When a party has transferred his interest in the subject matter of an action and his successor elects to continue the action in the name of the original party, there is usually no need for any change in the title of the case. (See *Stark* v. *Shaw* (1957) 155 Cal.App.2d 171, 182, Code Civ. Proc., § 385, subd. (a).) In preparing brief and transcript titles it may become necessary, however, to name both the transferor and the assignee if the transferor retains, or seeks to assert, some rights in the controversy. The opinion title under this set of facts would name the first party with "et al."

When litigation is continued by a substituted party in a representative capacity, the status of the representative should be set forth, e.g., as Trustee, as Trustee in Bankruptcy, as Receiver, as Executor, as Administrator, as Liquidator, etc. (See *ante,* § 220.)

**§ 224.   Suit by One on Behalf of a Class.**—Where a person sues on behalf of himself and a class of persons similarly situated, it is not necessary to note this fact, and the title follows the style of an ordinary action. (See Code Civ. Proc., § 382; *Jones* v. *H.F. Ahmanson & Co.* (1969) 1 Cal.3d 93, 101; *Garrett* v. *Coast & Southern Fed. Sav. & Loan Assn.* (1973) 9 Cal.3d 731, 735; *Vasquez* v. *Superior Court* (1971) 4 Cal.3d 800 (original proceeding).)

**§ 225. Suit in the Name of the State or the People; Intervention.**—When litigation is initiated by a private individual, governmental official or branch of the state in the name of the state, the relator's name is given with "ex rel." The form of the title is:

> THE PEOPLE ex rel. DEPARTMENT OF TRANSPORTATION, Plaintiff and Appellant, v. MARY MOOR, Defendant and Respondent.
>
> THE PEOPLE ex rel. JOHN JONES, as Attorney General, etc., Plaintiff and Respondent, v. COUNTY OF SAN MATEO et al., Defendants and Appellants.

(See also *post,* § 252, quo warranto proceedings; Code Civ. Proc., § 731; cf. *ante,* § 216.)

(For additional style examples see: *People* ex rel. *Younger* v. *County of El Dorado* (1971) 5 Cal.3d 480; *People* ex rel. *Cranston* v. *Bonelli* (1971) 15 Cal.App.3d 129; *People* ex rel. *Dept. Pub. Wks.* v. *Volz* (1972) 25 Cal.App.3d 480; *People* ex rel. *Dept. Pub. Wks.* v. *Shasta Pipe etc. Co.* (1968) 264 Cal.App.2d 520.)

An appearance in intervention in the name of the state or the people by a private individual, governmental official or branch of the state is styled in the same fashion. (See, e.g., *Environmental Defense Fund, Inc.* v. *Coastside County Water Dist.* (1972) 27 Cal.App.3d 695.)

## C. Specific Titles

**§ 226. Adoption Proceedings.**—When an appeal is taken to review an order or judgment following a petition for adoption the usual form of title is:

> Adoption of JOHN INFANT, a Minor. EDITH MOTHER, Plaintiff and Appellant, v. SONYA ADOPTER, Defendant and Respondent.

(See *Adoption of R. R. R.* (1971) 18 Cal.App.3d 973 for title style where one natural parent supports adoption while the other opposes it.)

Where the opinion contains disclosures that are detrimental to the child or the contesting parties the appellate court policy of protecting against the injurious effects of such disclosures would recommend the use of an anonymous style title, e.g.,

> Adoption of JOHN I., a Minor. EDITH M., Plaintiff and Appellant, v. SONYA A., Defendant and Respondent.

Party references in the body of the opinion should be consistent with the anonymous style title.

(See, e.g., *C.V.C.* v. *Superior Court* (1973) 29 Cal.App.3d 909 and *ante,* §§ 213, 214 re appellate nondisclosure policy.)

If the ruling contested is collateral to the adoption proceedings or if relief is sought by way of a petition for a writ of habeas corpus, mandate or prohibition, the usual title for such proceedings is followed. (See *San Diego County Dept. of Pub. Welfare* v. *Superior Court* (1972) 7 Cal.3d 1 [prohibition, mandate and habeas corpus]; *County of Los Angeles* v. *Superior Court* (1969) 2 Cal.App.3d 1059 [prohibition and mandate]; *C.V.C.* v. *Superior Court* (1973) 29 Cal. App.3d 909 [mandate]; *Smith* v. *Superior Court* (1974) 41 Cal.App.3d 109 [mandate]; see also, *In re Richard M.* (1975) 14 Cal.3d 783 [habeas corpus proceeding to obtain custody].)

**§ 227. Arbitration Proceedings.**—In the superior court, arbitration proceedings are ordinarily controversial, and the title should be an adversary title. (See *ante*, § 196 et seq.) The "In re" form, which implies an in rem or ex parte proceeding, is therefore not appropriate. The title should follow the general rules for ordinary appeals in civil actions. (See, e.g., *San Luis Obispo Bay Properties, Inc.* v. *Pacific Gas & Elec. Co.* (1972) 28 Cal.App.3d 556.)

Proceedings commenced in the appellate courts seeking relief by writ, as, for example, where a party petitions for a writ of mandate to set aside a trial court order vacating an arbitration award, follow the title styles applicable to original proceedings. (See *post*, § 237; *National Indemnity Co.* v. *Superior Court* (1972) 27 Cal.App.3d 345.)

**§ 228. Cases Which Normally Originate as Nonadversary Proceedings—In General, and Dissolution, Liquidation and Conservation Proceedings.**—There are a number of types of cases, somewhat similiar in nature to probate proceedings, which originate in a lower court as nonadversary proceedings but later become contested. In these cases there should be a double title, i.e., the nonadversary title followed by the adversary title, e.g.,

> In re Establishment of THE SQUIB as a Newspaper of General Circulation. FRED EDITOR, Petitioner and Respondent, v. AL OBJECTOR, Contestant and Appellant.

(See, e.g., *In re La Opinion* (1970) 10 Cal.App.3d 1012.)

> In re AARD VARK, a Minor, etc., et al., for Change of Name. AARD VARK, a Minor, etc., et al., Petitioners and Respondents, v. SPARK VARK, Objector and Appellant.

(See, e.g., *In re Worms* (1967) 252 Cal.App.2d 130.)

> In re JOHN BEAN to Establish Fact of Death of MARY BEAN, Deceased. JOHN BEAN et al., Petitioners and Respondents, v. JOSEPH SPROUT, as State Controller, Objector and Appellant.

(See, e.g., *In re Lewis* (1969) 271 Cal.App.2d 371.)

Similar double title styles are used with voluntary dissolution, liquidation and conservation statutory proceedings involving such organizations as banks, building and loan associations, charitable associations and corporations, insurance companies, etc. (See, e.g., *In re Veterans' Industries, Inc.* (1970) 8 Cal.App.3d 902 [voluntary dissolution]; *In re Metropolitan Baptist Church of Richmond, Inc.* (1975) 48 Cal.App.3d 850 [voluntary dissolution]; *In re American Reserve Ins. Co.* (1983) 138 Cal.App.3d 906 [liquidation]; *In re Bank of San Pedro* (1934) 1 Cal.2d 675 [conservation of assets]; *In re Cole's Check Service, Inc.* (1963) 215 Cal.App.2d 332 [trust funds set aside pursuant to Fin. Code, § 12300.3].)

### § 229.  Citizenship and Naturalization.—The form of title on appeal is:

> In re JOHN ALIEN for Citizenship. JOHN ALIEN, Petitioner and Appellant, v. UNITED STATES DEPARTMENT OF JUSTICE, IMMIGRATION AND NATURALIZATION SERVICE, Objector and Respondent.

> In re JOHN ALIEN on Naturalization. JOHN ALIEN, Petitioner and Appellant, v. UNITED STATES DEPARTMENT OF JUSTICE, IMMIGRATION AND NATURALIZATION SERVICE, Objector and Respondent.

Whether a case is entitled "for Citizenship" or "on Naturalization" will depend upon the wording of the title in the trial court.

### § 230.  Conservatorship Proceedings.

**(a)  Conservatorship of the Estate.**—When the case involves only the conservatorship of the *estate* and not the *person,* use:

> Conservatorship of the Estate of JANE SPADE.

Disregard the lengthy titles often employed in the superior courts, e.g., "In the Matter of the Conservatorship of JANE SPADE," or "In the Matter of Conservatorship of the Estate of JANE SPADE." The adversary title should be added in all cases. Where the petitioner appeals, the form of title is:

> Conservatorship of the Estate of JANE SPADE. RALPH BROWN, as Conservator, etc., Petitioner and Appellant, v. MARY BLACK, Objector and Respondent.

**(b)  Conservatorship of the Person.**—When the case involves only the conservatorship of the person, use:

> Conservatorship of the Person of JANE SPADE.

The adversary title follows.

**(c)  Conservatorship of Person and Estate.**—Use:

> Conservatorship of the Person and Estate of JANE SPADE.

The adversary title follows. (See, e.g., *Conservatorship of Lambert* (1983) 143 Cal.App.3d 239.) (See *post,* §§ 236, 240 *ante,* §§ 221, 222 re persons under a disability, § 220 re persons acting in a representative capacity. See *Place* v. *Trent* (1972) 27 Cal.App.3d 526, for the designation of parties when the action before the court concerns conservatorship property but is not part of the conservatorship proceedings.)

**§ 231. Criminal Proceedings—In General.**—In the ordinary criminal prosecution the plaintiff's name is shortened to "The People." Defendants are designated in the same manner as in ordinary civil actions. (See Pen. Code, §§ 684, 685.)

The usual form of title is:

> THE PEOPLE, Plaintiff and Respondent, v. JOHN JONES, Defendant and Appellant. Or [where more than one defendant is involved], THE PEOPLE, Plaintiff and Respondent, v. JANE SMITH et al, Defendants and Respondents.

If the first named defendant does not appeal, his name is omitted, and the title will show instead the name of the first defendant who does appeal. (See *ante,* §§ 200, 201, 205.)

As in civil cases, the titles are never reversed, and the plaintiff's name is always first, regardless of which party takes the appeal.

In death penalty cases, the current practice is to name all defendants who are involved in the appeal. (See *People* v. *Howk* (1961) 56 Cal.2d 687.)

**§ 232. Criminal Proceedings—Alias v. True Name.**—Where the prosecution uses an alias of the defendant, and his true name is afterwards discovered, the main title should carry his true name, not the alias, e.g.,

> THE PEOPLE, Plaintiff and Respondent, v. JOHN TRUE NAME, Defendant and Appellant.

(See Pen. Code, §§ 953, 959, subd. 4, 989, and *ante,* § 218.)

**§ 233. Criminal Proceedings—Coram Nobis and Coram Vobis.\***—In a *coram nobis* or *coram vobis* proceeding, where the defendant seeks to vacate a judgment against him, the proceeding is "properly regarded 'as a part of the proceedings in the case to which it refers' rather than as 'a new adversary suit'" (*In re Paiva* (1948) 31 Cal.2d 503, 509–510) and therefore takes the title of the case in which the judgment was obtained, as:

> THE PEOPLE, Plaintiff and Respondent, v. JOHN SMITH, Defendant and Appellant.

Do *not* use "In re JOHN SMITH on Coram Nobis" or "JOHN SMITH, Petitioner, v. THE PEOPLE, Respondent."

**§ 233.1 Criminal Proceedings—Certified Court Reporters.**—Titles for opinions concerning appellate court enforcement actions directed to the preparation and delivery of transcripts use a double title. The style is:

> In re TARDY PEN, a Certified Shorthand Reporter, Respondent. THE PEOPLE, Plaintiff and Respondent, v. NORMAN ACCUSED, Defendant and Appellant.

---

\* The writ of *coram vobis* is essentially identical to the writ of *coram nobis* except that the latter is addressed to the court in which the petitioner was convicted. (*People* v. *Welch* (1964) 61 Cal.2d 786.)

## § 234. Disciplinary Proceedings—Attorneys.

**(a) Review of Disciplinary Proceedings Originating With State Bar.**—When an attorney petitions the Supreme Court to review a decision of the State Bar recommending disbarment, suspension from practice or other discipline, the form of title is:

ARTHUR ATTORNEY, Petitioner, v. THE STATE BAR OF CALIFORNIA, Respondent.

(See Cal. Rules of Court, rule 952; *Sevin* v. *State Bar* (1973) 8 Cal.3d 641. See also, *In re Walker* (1948) 32 Cal.2d 488 for rare situation where Supreme Court exercises its disciplinary powers without prior recommendation from the State Bar.)

**(b) Proceedings on Conviction of Crime.**—The forms of title for opinions concerning the imposition of discipline following an attorney's conviction of a crime are:

In re ARTHUR ATTORNEY on Disbarment.
or
In re ARTHUR ATTORNEY on Suspension. [or] . . . on Interim Suspension.†
or
In re ARTHUR ATTORNEY on Reprimand.

The title normally reflects the discipline imposed by the court, but where the Supreme Court refers the matter to the State Bar for hearing, report and recommendation, the title reflects the recommended discipline of the State Bar rather than the discipline actually imposed where there is a difference. (See Cal. Rules of Court, rule 951 (c); *In re Jones* (1971) 5 Cal.3d 390.)

The attorney in a conviction reference proceeding seeking review of the State Bar's report and recommendation normally is designated as petitioner in the body of the opinion although the attorney's document is denominated "Written Objections and Brief in Support." (See Cal. Rules of Court, rule 951 (d).)

(See *post,* § 254 for the title style of nondisciplinary State Bar proceedings.)

## § 235. Disciplinary and Retirement Proceedings—Judges.—

When a judge, by petition, seeks a writ to review a recommendation of the Commission on Judicial Performance,* the style of title is:

JOHN JONES, a Judge of the Municipal Court, Petitioner, v. COMMISSION ON JUDICIAL PERFORMANCE, Respondent.

(See Cal. Rules of Court, rule 919 (b); *Gonzales* v. *Commission on Judicial Performance* (1983) 33 Cal.3d 359; *Roberts* v. *Commission on*

---

* Legislative proposition No. 7 approved at the election of November 2, 1976, changed the name of "Commission on Judicial Qualifications" to "Commission on Judicial Performance."

† See Business and Professions Code sections 6100, 6102.

*Judicial Performance* (1983) 33 Cal.3d 739; *Geiler* v. *Commission on Judicial Qualifications* (1973) 10 Cal.3d 270.)

Where no petition for writ of review is filed the form of opinion title following the Supreme Court's review of the commission's report and recommendation is:

In re JOHN JONES, a Judge of the Municipal Court, on Censure.
or
In re JOHN JONES, a Judge of the Superior Court, on Removal.
or
In re JOHN JONES, a Judge of the Municipal Court, on Retirement.

The title normally reflects the commission's recommendation rather than the discipline imposed or action taken where there is a difference. (See Cal. Rules of Court, rule 919 (c); *In re Stevens* (1982) 31 Cal.3d 403; *In re Fisher* (1982) 31 Cal.3d 919.)

## § 236. Estates, Conservatorships, Guardianships—Double Titles—Single Titles.

**(a) Double Titles.**—Since every estate, conservatorship and guardianship case has a dual aspect, two titles are necessary, the estate, conservatorship or guardianship title and the title of the adversary proceeding between the parties, e.g.,:

Estate of ALLEN APPLE, Deceased.
MARY GRAPE, as Executrix, etc., et al., Petitioners and Respondents, v. FINE CHARITY et al., Objectors and Appellants; FRED BENEFICIARY, Claimant and Respondent.

In probate proceedings use "Estate of JOHN JONES, Deceased." for the first title. The lengthier title: "In the Matter of the Estate of JOHN JONES, Deceased." often appearing on superior court printed forms and transcripts is not followed. (See *ante*, § 230, for conservatorship titles; *post*, § 240, for guardianship titles and §§ 249–251, for specific probate titles.)

**(b) Single Titles.**—Where the action brought by or against the executor or conservator is not part of the probate or conservatorship proceedings but rather is an independent civil action, as where an executor or conservator files a complaint to enforce a contract entered into between the decedent or conservatee and third parties, the title style would be:

HARRIET GREY, as Executrix, etc., Plaintiff and Respondent, v. BARTHOLOMEW BRUT, Defendant and Appellant.

Since an estate is not recognized as a legal entity, and therefore cannot sue or be sued, it is improper to name "The Estate of John Jones" as a party. (See 4 Witkin, Cal. Procedure (3d ed. 1985) Pleading, § 57, pp. 96–97; *Tanner* v. *Estate of Best* (1940) 40 Cal.App.2d 442, 445.)

## § 237. Extraordinary Writ Proceedings—Original Proceedings Commenced in Appellate Courts and Appeals Following Original Proceedings Commenced in Trial Courts.

**(a)** In an **original proceeding** *commenced in an appellate court* the parties are to be designated simply as "Petitioner," "Respondent," and "Real Party in Interest," e.g.,

> NANCY ADAMS, Petitioner, v. THE SUPERIOR COURT OF LOS ANGELES COUNTY, Respondent; THE PEOPLE, Real Party in Interest.

(See Cal. Rules of Court, rule 56(a); Code Civ. Proc., § 1107; *Guidi* v. *Superior Court* (1973) 10 Cal.3d 1; *Morand* v. *Superior Court* (1974) 38 Cal.App.3d 347.)

**(1) Certiorari.**—Since certiorari is directed to a court or tribunal, and not to the judge or tribunal members, it is improper to name the judge or tribunal members in the title. (See 8 Witkin, Cal. Procedure (3d ed. 1985) Extraordinary Writs, §§ 148–149, pp. 789–791.) The form of title is:

> NORTHERN POWER, Petitioner, v. PUBLIC UTILITIES COMMISSION, Respondent; PACIFIC GAS AND ELECTRIC COMPANY, Real Party in Interest.

(See, e.g., *City of Los Angeles* v. *Public Utilities Commission* (1972) 7 Cal. 331.)

**(2) Mandamus and Prohibition.**—In mandamus and prohibition proceedings the judge or tribunal members may be proper parties, but the main party is the court or tribunal, hence the first respondent named should be the court or tribunal. Real parties in interest in such proceedings should be noted, e.g.,

> JOHN SMITH, Petitioner, v. THE SUPERIOR COURT OF LOS ANGELES COUNTY et al., Respondents; TOM BROWN et al., Real Parties in Interest.

(See, e.g., *Drumgo* v. *Superior Court* (1973) 8 Cal.3d 930 [mandamus]; *County of Sacramento* v. *Superior Court* (1972) 8 Cal.3d 479 [prohibition]; see also 8 Witkin, Cal. Procedure, *supra,* Extraordinary Writs, §§ 148, 149, pp. 789–791.)

**(b)** Upon **appeal** from a decision of the trial court denying or granting an application for a writ in an original proceeding, the parties are to be designated in the same manner as appeals in ordinary civil and criminal cases, with the addition of the name of the real party or parties in interest where appropriate; e.g.,

> JOHN SMITH, Plaintiff and Appellant, v. NANCY BLACK, as County Auditor, etc., Defendant and Respondent; BUSTER BROWN, Real Party in Interest and Respondent.

The foregoing style was adopted to avoid the confusion that would otherwise result where a party is a "respondent" in the lower court and a "respondent" or "appellant" on the appeal. For example, if the respondent below is the appellant on appeal his appellate designation, if not adjusted, would be "respondent and appellant." If he is the respondent on appeal, his unadjusted designation would be "respondent and respondent." (See also *post,* § 253.)

(See as style formats *Bekiaris* v. *Board of Education* (1972) 6 Cal.3d 575; *Friends of Mammoth* v. *Board of Supervisors* (1972) 8 Cal.3d 247.)

### § 238. Family Law Act Proceedings—Appeal.—Due to the major changes in divorce law concepts brought about by the 1969 enactment of the California Family Law Act, opinion and brief titles previously used in divorce proceedings are no longer appropriate.

Under the California Rules of Court developed by the Judicial Council to establish practice and procedure under the Family Law Act it has been determined that "The party initiating the proceeding is the petitioner, and the other party is the respondent. . . ." (Cal. Rules of Court, rule 1210 (eff. Jan. 1, 1970); see also form of petition (marriage) rule 1281.)

In view of the party reference confusion that would result because of the designation of a party as "respondent" in the lower court and the traditional designations of "appellant" and "respondent" on appeal, opinion and brief titles for this line of cases drop the lower court designations of "petitioner" and "respondent" entirely, retaining only appellate court descriptions. An opinion or brief title on appeal in such a case then would read:

> In re the Marriage of JANE and FRED JONES. JANE JONES, Respondent, v. FRED JONES, Appellant.

The party initiating the proceedings in the court below would be the first named party in the appellate adversary title regardless of whether that party is appellant or respondent on the appeal. (See *ante,* § 199.) The initiating party in the court below in the suggested title set out above would be Jane Jones.

Since references in the body of an opinion or brief to a party who was a respondent below as "respondent" might cause confusion and awkward explanations to distinguish between appellate and trial court statuses, it is suggested that authors refer to parties in the body of such opinions and briefs as "husband" and "wife" rather than as "respondent" and "appellant," or "petitioner" and "respondent."

If both sides appeal counsel for each should be identified respectively as: "for Appellant Husband" and "for Appellant Wife."

Later proceedings in a case commenced under the divorce and separation law applicable prior to the adoption of the California Family Law Act retain the title pertinent to the earlier proceedings where judgment was obtained under the earlier law, e.g., a proceeding commenced in 1986 to modify a decree for separate maintenance obtained in 1968 would take the 1968 title. (See, e.g., *Ganschow* v. *Ganschow* (1975) 14 Cal.3d 150; *Faught* v. *Faught* (1973) 30 Cal.App.3d 875.)

On the other hand, if the proceeding was commenced before the California Family Law Act became effective but judgment was thereafter obtained pursuant to the new law, use the Family Law Act style of title. (See *In re Marriage of Nicolaides* (1974) 39 Cal.App.3d 192.)

**Appeals Concerning Joined Parties:**

California Rules of Court, rules 1250–1256 provide for the joinder of parties who claim an interest in a proceeding brought under the Family Law Act.

Where the petitioner or respondent *below,* normally the husband or wife, petitions for the joinder of a party (see rule 1252 (a)) the style of title on an appeal concerning the issue of joinder or the resolution of the joined party's claim is:

> In re the Marriage of JANE and FRED JONES.
> JANE JONES, Respondent, v. FRED JONES, Respondent;
> NORMA HEATH et al., Appellants.

In the illustration Jane Jones petitioned to join Norma Heath and others who appealed from the trial court's order following joinder. (See, e.g., *In re the Marriage of Sommers* (1975) 53 Cal.App.3d 509.)

Where the party petitioning for joinder and relief is not the husband or wife (see rules 1252 (b) & (c)) the style of title is:

> In re the Marriage of JANE and FRED JONES.
> MARY GRANDPARENT et al., Appellant, v. JANE JONES et al., Respondents.

In this illustration Mary Grandparent and others petitioned to be joined seeking custody of the Jones' minor children, and appeal from the trial court's order denying their petition. (See, e.g., *In re Marriage of Meier* (1975) 51 Cal.App.3d 120.)

For titles involving appeals from orders or judgments in dissolution proceedings concerning entitlement to pension plan benefits, see *In re Marriage of Williams* (1985) 163 Cal.App.3d 753, California Rules of Court, rule 1256 and Civil Code section 4351 and following.

**§ 239.  Forfeiture of Bail Proceedings.**—In a proceeding to forfeit or set aside the forfeiture of bail posted in a criminal matter the usual style of title is:

> THE PEOPLE, Plaintiff and Respondent, v. BONDING INSURANCE CO., Defendant and Appellant.

The proceeding does not take the title of the criminal action to which it is collateral. Forfeiture proceedings of this type ordinarily are civil in nature.

(See *People* v. *United Bonding Ins. Co.* (1969) 272 Cal.App.2d 441, 442; *People* v. *North Beach Bonding Co.* (1974) 36 Cal.App.3d 663.)

## § 240. Guardianship Proceedings.

**(a) Guardianship of Estate.**—When the case involves only the guardianship of the *estate* and not of the person, use:

Estate of ADAM JONES, a Minor.
or
Estate of ADAM JONES, an Incompetent Person.
or
Estate of ADAM JONES, an Insane Person.

Disregard the lengthy titles often used in the superior courts, e.g., "In the Matter of the Estate of ADAM JONES, an Insane Person." The adversary title should be added in all cases. (See *ante,* §§ 230, 236; Code Civ. Proc., § 372.)

Where the objector appeals the style of title is:

Estate of ADAM JONES, a Minor. EDITH RAY, as Guardian, etc., Petitioner and Respondent, v. FRED GREEN, Objector and Appellant.

**(b) Guardianship of Person.**—When the case involves only the guardianship of the *person,* use:

Guardianship of ADAM JONES, a Minor.
or
Guardianship of ADAM JONES, an Incompetent Person.
or
Guardianship of ADAM JONES, an Insane Person.

The adversary title follows. (See, e.g., *Guardianship of Marino* (1973) 30 Cal.App.3d 952.)

**(c) Guardianship of Both Person and Estate.**—When the case involves the guardianship of both the *person* and *estate,* use:

Guardianship of the Person and Estate of ADAM JONES, a Minor.
or
Guardianship of the Person and Estate of ADAM JONES, an Incompetent Person.
or
Guardianship of the Person and Estate of ADAM JONES, an Insane Person.

The adversary title follows. Where the guardianship of more than one person is involved use "Guardianships of the Persons and Estates of." (See, e.g., *Guardianship of Barassi* (1968) 265 Cal.App.2d 282; see *ante,* §§ 221, 222 re persons under a disability, § 220 re persons acting in a representative capacity, and § 236 for the designation of parties when the action before the court is not a part of the guardianship proceedings.)

## § 241. Habeas Corpus Proceedings.—Use "In re JOHN JONES on Habeas Corpus." for the ordinary title. Never use "Ex Parte" or "In the Matter of the Application of," or "On Application of," or "Petition of."

The title is not affected by the fact that the People appeal from a superior court order "discharging a defendant or otherwise granting all or any part of the relief sought, . . ." (See Pen. Code, § 1506.) The basic title, "In re JOHN JONES on Habeas Corpus." is used without noting a secondary appellate title regardless of whether the proceeding is criminal or civil in nature. (See, e.g., *In re Pickett* (1972) 25 Cal.App.3d 1158; *In re Martha* (1954) 122 Cal.App.2d 654.)

When the proceeding is brought on behalf of another the form of title indicates only the name of the real party in interest and not that of the applicant.

When the writ is sought by a minor or on behalf of a minor and is collateral to a juvenile court proceeding or contains detrimental disclosures, the appellate court policy of protecting against the injurious effects of such disclosures would encourage the use of an anonymous title, e.g.,

In re RICHARD T., a Minor, on Habeas Corpus.

(See also *ante,* §§ 213, 214; *In re D.A.S.* (1971) 15 Cal.App.3d 283; *In re Richard M.* (1975) 14 Cal.3d 783.)

## § 242. In Rem Proceedings—Escheat and Forfeiture.—

**(a) Escheat.**—In ordinary escheat actions the form of title follows that used in general civil actions.

THE STATE OF CALIFORNIA, Plaintiff and Appellant, v. UNION BANK, Defendant and Respondent.

(See, e.g., *State of California v. Pacific Far East Line, Inc.* (1968) 261 Cal.App.2d 609.)

If the state seeks the escheat of property belonging to an estate, and action is taken in the probate court, the title will follow the rules for probate proceedings, and there will be a double title, i.e., an estate title and an adversary title, e.g.,

Estate of FRED BORN, Deceased.
THE STATE OF CALIFORNIA, Plaintiff and Respondent, v. TOM SMITH, as Executor, etc., Defendant and Appellant.

(See *ante,* § 236 and for other examples, *Estate of Horman* (1971) 5 Cal.3d 62 [claimant and objector used]; *Estate of Tischler* (1971) 20 Cal.App.3d 137 [plaintiff, objector, and claimant used].)

Where a party by an original proceeding seeks to require or prevent escheat in an estate proceeding the title styles governing original proceedings are followed. (See *ante,* § 237; *Mannheim v. Superior Court* (1970) 3 Cal.3d 678.)

**(b) Forfeiture of Illegally Used Property.**—In actions to declare a forfeiture the first named defendant is usually the *thing* proceeded against. While the *thing* proceeded against cannot take action, it should continue to be designated as a defendant, e.g.:

> THE PEOPLE, Plaintiff and Appellant, v. ONE PURSE SEINE NET, Defendant; JOHN FISHERMAN, Defendant and Respondent.

**§ 243. Interpleader.**—In interpleader cases the plaintiff-interpleader (obligor) is usually merely a stakeholder who has no interest on the appeal, having deposited money or delivered property as directed by the court below. The plaintiff-interpleader is normally discharged and it is then merely necessary in preparing the appellate title to identify and distinguish the rival defendants. The name of the plaintiff-interpleader is retained without an appellate court designation merely to identify the procedural origin of the appeal. The usual style of title is:

> OLD FAITHFUL INSURANCE CO., Plaintiff, v. TOM SMITH, Defendant and Appellant; JACK BLACK, Defendant and Respondent.

(See e.g., *California State Auto. Assn. Inter-Ins. Bureau v. Jackson* (1973) 9 Cal.3d 859.)

If, however, the plaintiff-interpleader is not discharged or not *fully* discharged, as for example, in an action for partial interpleader where the plaintiff is discharged only to the extent of the funds deposited or the property delivered and he remains liable for a deficiency, or where the court requires additional deposits, or where the validity of the order of discharge is challenged, then the plaintiff-interpleader usually remains a party on appeal and is assigned an appellate designation. The typical forms of title are:

> OLD FAITHFUL INSURANCE CO., Plaintiff and Respondent, v. TOM SMITH, Defendant and Appellant; JACK BLACK, Defendant and Respondent. [or]
> OLD FAITHFUL INSURANCE CO., Plaintiff and Appellant, v. TOM SMITH, Defendant and Respondent; JACK BLACK, Defendant and Respondent.

Where the interpleader action is commenced by way of cross-complaint (see Code Civ. Proc., § 386) the same principles are applicable, that is, if the defendant is discharged below he is named for identification only; if he remains a party his appellate status is noted. (See, e.g., *City of Glendale* v. *Roseglen Constr., Inc.* (1970) 10 Cal.App.3d 777; see also *ante*, §§ 206, 208, 209 for titles on cross-complaints.)

**§ 244. Intervention.**

**(a) Appeal.**—In cases of intervention, the order of names is Plaintiff, Defendant and Intervener, e.g.,

> JOHN JONES, Plaintiff and Appellant, v. TOM SMITH, Defendant and Respondent; RITA GREEN, Intervener and Appellant.

(See *Drinnon* v. *Oliver* (1972) 24 Cal.App.3d 571.)

A party who moves for leave to intervene is termed a "Movant" until his motion is granted, at which time he becomes an "Intervener." In the example cited, if Rita Green had appealed from an order denying leave to intervene, she would have been named as "Movant and Appellant." (See, e.g., *Continental Vinyl Products Corp.* v. *Mead Corp.* (1972) 27 Cal.App.3d 543; *post,* § 283.)

Where the appeal is from a judgment determining a dispute between the defendant (or plaintiff) and the intervener and where the plaintiff (or defendant) is not a party to the appeal, retain the nonparty's name in the opinion title for identification purposes; the form of title is:

> JOHN JONES, Plaintiff, v. TOM SMITH, Defendant and Respondent; RITA GREEN, Intervener and Appellant.

(See, e.g., *Wright* v. *Standard Engineering Corp.* (1972) 28 Cal.App.3d 244; see also *ante,* § 208 and *post,* § 256.)

**(b) Original Proceedings.**—Where an appellate court has permitted intervention in a pending original proceeding, title styles are:

> JOHN JONES, Petitioner, v. THE SUPERIOR COURT OF ORANGE COUNTY, Respondent; RONDA ROSE, Real Party in Interest; PETER SMITH, Intervener.
> NANCY NOON et al., Petitioner, v. FRED FOX et al., Respondents; BART BLACK, Intervener.

(Where a matter started as an original proceeding in the trial court and an appeal follows, see subd. (a) and *ante,* § 237.)

**§ 245. Juvenile Court Proceedings.**—Where an appeal is taken from an order made in a juvenile court proceeding to have a minor adjudged a ward or dependent of the court, a double title form is used:

> In re THOMAS J., a Person Coming Under the Juvenile Court Law. HAROLD HELP, as Chief Probation Officer, etc., Plaintiff and Respondent, v. RITA J., Defendant and Appellant.

Proceedings below are normally commenced by filing a petition under section 300, 601 or 602 of the Welfare and Institutions Code. In a section 300 proceeding normally the parent (or guardian) is the responding party whereas in a 601 or 602 proceeding the minor is the answering party.*

Proceedings which are supplemental to the wardship proceeding may be commenced under the provisions of sections 777 and 778 and the title would be adjusted accordingly. For example, where a parent or other person having an interest in a child who is a ward of the juvenile court or the ward himself appeals from an order following a petition

---

* A section 300 proceeding to declare a minor a dependent is filed in the name of the county's chief probation officer or the county welfare department. (See Cal. Rules of Court, rule 1308 (a); Welf. & Inst. Code, §§ 215, 272.) A section 601 wardship proceeding is filed by the county's chief probation officer while a section 602 wardship proceeding is filed by the prosecuting attorney in the name of the People (use "The People v." in the secondary title). (See Welf. & Inst. Code, § 650.)

to the juvenile court under section 778 to change or set aside one of its order, the basic form of title is:

> In re MARY C., a Person Coming Under the Juvenile Court Law. SUSAN C., Plaintiff and Appellant, v. SAN BERNARDINO COUNTY WELFARE DEPARTMENT, Defendant and Respondent.

The respondent normally is the public entity having custodial care of the juvenile at the time the action was commenced.

A supplemental proceeding under section 777 is initiated by the probation officer and would follow the style first noted in this section. (See *In re Arthur N.* (1976) 16 Cal.3d 226, 228.)

(See *ante,* § 214 for the appellate court practice of not disclosing the identities of minors in detrimental situations and *post,* § 246 for extraordinary writ proceedings in juvenile court matters, see also *ante,* § 241 re habeas corpus proceedings.)

### § 246. Juvenile Court Proceedings—Extraordinary Writs.—

Petitions to test the validity of orders of the juvenile court, as for example, by application for writs of mandate, prohibition or habeas corpus, follow the usual styles for such proceedings. (See *ante,* § 237, extraordinary writ proceedings; § 241, habeas corpus proceedings.)

Such collateral proceedings should use the anonymous title forms in those instances where opinion authors deem it appropriate to carry out the appellate court's protective nondisclosure policy in matters concerning minors. (See *ante,* §§ 213, 214, 245; *T.N.G.* v. *Superior Court* (1971) 4 Cal.3d 767 [mandate]; *In re William M.* (1970) 3 Cal.3d 16 [habeas corpus]; *In re Arthur N.* (1974) 36 Cal.App.3d 935 [habeas corpus].)

### § 247. Notices of Appeal—Proceedings Seeking Late Filing.—

Where a petitioner seeks an order permitting him to file a late notice of appeal, litigation designations of parties for opinion titles differ depending upon whether relief is granted or denied. When relief is granted the style of title is that used in ordinary appeals, e.g.,

> THE PEOPLE, Plaintiff and Respondent, v. JOHN JONES, Defendant and Appellant.

When relief is denied, however, the style of title is:

> THE PEOPLE, Plaintiff and Respondent, v. JOHN JONES, Defendant and Petitioner.

(See, e.g., *People* v. *Ribero* (1971) 4 Cal.3d 55 [relief granted]; *People* v. *Rodriguez* (1971) 4 Cal.3d 73 [relief denied].)

### § 248. Parental Custody and Control Proceedings.—

Proceedings under Civil Code section 232 to have minors declared free from parental control usually take title styles as illustrated:

> In re MARY B. et al., Minors. AGNES A., Petitioner and Respondent, v. FRED B. et al., Objectors and Appellants.
> In re MARY BROWN et al., Minors. AGNES AUNT, Petitioner and Respondent, v. FRED BROWN et al., Objectors and Appellants.
> In re ROBERT J., a Minor. KERN COUNTY WELFARE DEPARTMENT, Petitioner and Respondent, v. MARSHA J. et al., Objectors and Appellants.

(See *In re Morrow* (1970) 9 Cal.App.3d 39. See also *ante,* § 214, for appellate nondisclosure policy and *In re Eugene W.* (1972) 29 Cal.App.3d 623.)

**§ 249.  Probate Proceedings.**—The party to be named first is the party who initiates the particular proceeding in the probate court, i.e., the party who seeks relief or court confirmation by petition, application or motion. (See, e.g., petitions listed in Prob. Code, § 1200.5.) Ordinarily the initiating party is referred to as "Petitioner" and the adversary party is identified as "Objector" or "Claimant" depending upon which designation most nearly reflects the facts. Normal appellate court designations are added. (See *ante,* § 236 for title form.)

In some instances, the substitution of the term "Claimant" or "Contestant" for "Petitioner" is appropriate where such terms prove more descriptive of the party than the less specific expression "Petitioner." The reader will recognize that the first named party initiated the proceeding below.

Where more than one petition was before the court below and the appeal is from multiple orders or a single order determining all the petitions, the party whose petition was filed first in time should be the first named party for title purposes, except where the author deems a different arrangement important. Of course, if the appeal concerns only the ruling from the order or orders relating to just one of the petitions, the title would merely indicate the parties to that petition.

As with all titles, authors should, in the interests of clarity and consistency, endeavor to assign party designations in the opinion conforming to the party descriptions used in the title. (See *ante,* § 210.)

Other than the styles noted above, follow the usual rules as to name, status and designation of parties.

Where an individual appears in a representative capacity such as executor, trustee, etc., that fact should be indicated. (See *ante,* § 220.) Where a party appears for himself *and* in a representative capacity the word "individually" is first noted and the representative status follows, e.g., PETER SMITH, Individually and as Administrator, etc., Petitioner and Respondent. (See *ante,* § 220.)

**§ 250.  Probate Proceedings—Will Contests.**—Procedurally, will contests are usually divided into three categories: Contests before probate (Prob. Code, § 370); after probate (Prob. Code, § 380); and by complaint in intervention (Code Civ. Proc., § 387).

**(a) Contests Before Probate.**—The issue is normally presented by the filing of a petition for the probate of the will and by written opposition of the contestant. While under section 371 of the Probate Code, *on the trial* of the contest, the contestant is plaintiff and the petitioner seeking probate is defendant, the more descriptive title retains the designation, "Petitioner" for the petitioning proponent and "Contestant" for the objector. Where the petitioner appeals, the form of title is:

> Estate of A, Deceased. B, Petitioner and Appellant, v. C, Contestant and Respondent.

When there is an appearance (independent from petitioner's) by parties supporting the will (normally the will's beneficiaries), the form of title is:

> Estate of A, Deceased. B, Petitioner and Appellant, v. C, Contestant and Respondent; D et al., Claimants and Appellants.

If in the above situation B, usually the party seeking appointment as executor or administrator with the will annexed, files no notice of appeal or doesn't join in the appeal of D et al., then B becomes "Petitioner and Respondent."

**(b) Contests After Probate.**—Where the will has been admitted to probate, normally the "Contestant" is the initiating party (see Prob. Code, § 380) and the proponent is usually described as "Claimant" or "Objector" depending upon which of these terms most nearly fits the facts.

Where a party is an executor or administrator with the will annexed note his status as "X, as Executor With the Will Annexed, etc.," or "A, as Administrator, etc." (See *ante,* §220.) Where there are parties who do not have identical trial *and* appellate court designations, each nonidentical group must be seperately listed. (See *ante,* § 209.) Suppose, for example, in the Estate of A, the contestant (C) files his petition to revoke the will; the beneficiaries under the will (B et al.) appear in support of the will, while other parties (D et al.) who will take if the will is revoked, but who did not initiate the contest, appear in support of revocation. Assume that the trial court revokes the will. Under this pattern the appropriate title is:

> Estate of A, Deceased. C, Contestant and Respondent, v. B et al., Claimants and Appellants; D et al., Claimants and Respondents.

**(c) Contests by Intervention.**—In situations where a party with sufficient interest to contest a will intervenes in a pending contest proceeding initiated by another party, the following style of title, or a variation, depending upon the facts, is appropriate:

> Estate of A, Deceased. B, Petitioner and Respondent, v. C et al., Contestants and Appellants; D, Intervener and Appellant.

**§ 251. Probate Proceedings—Inheritance Tax Reports— Appeals.**—Usually the appeal follows as a challenge to an order overruling or sustaining objections to an inheritance tax report and fixing the inheritance tax accordingly. The form of title is:

> Estate of A, Deceased. B, as State Controller, Petitioner and Respondent, v. C, as Executor, etc., Objector and Appellant.

(See, e.g., *Estate of Bielec* (1972) 8 Cal.3d 213.)

The appellate designations would vary in the above illustration if the State Controller appealed; the title would then be:

> Estate of A, Deceased. B, as State Controller, Petitioner and Appellant, v. C, as Executor, etc., Objector and Respondent.

(See, e.g., *Estate of Nunn* (1974) 10 Cal.3d 799.)

Though the passage of Proposition 6 at the June 8, 1982, Primary Election resulted in the repeal of the state's then current inheritance and gift tax laws, litigation relating to earlier deaths will result in a continuation of this line of titles for some time.

**§ 252. Quo Warranto Proceedings.**—Where the action is commenced by the Attorney General follow the style noted *ante,* in section 215 (government officers). Actions brought in the name of the people upon the relation of a private party follow the style noted *ante,* in section 225. (See, e.g., *People* ex rel. *Fund American Companies* v. *California Ins. Co.* (1974) 43 Cal.App.3d 423.)

Occasionally a quo warranto proceeding will be instituted by a legislative body of a county, city and county, or municipal corporation. (See Code Civ. Proc., § 811.) The style of title for such a proceeding is:

> COUNTY OF RIVERSIDE ex rel. BOARD OF SUPERVISORS, Plaintiff and Appellant, v. JOHN GREEN et al., Defendants and Respondents.

**§ 253. Special Proceedings—Designation of Parties— Appellate Practice.**—The Code of Civil Procedure defines a "special proceeding" in a negative manner: "An action is an ordinary proceeding in a court of justice by which one party prosecutes another for the enforcement or protection of a right, the redress or prevention of a wrong, or the punishment of a public offense." (§ 22.) "Every other remedy is a special proceeding." (§ 23.) Ordinarily parties to "special proceedings" in the trial court are designated as "plaintiff" and "defendant" as suggested by Code of Civil Procedure section 1063. In these situations an appeal title would follow the customary and ordinary appellate style. (See *ante,* § 201, et seq.)

However, there are a number of special proceedings where the initiating party in the trial court is customarily designated as "petitioner" and his opponent is called "respondent." Original proceedings, for example, fall in this class. When an appeal is taken in such a proceeding a confusion potential arises if the party designations below are carried on into the titles of transcripts, briefs and opinions. Resultant designations would be "Petitioner and Respondent," or "Respondent and Respondent," or "Respondent and Appellant." In order to avoid such confusing designations the petitioner below should be called "Plaintiff" and his opponent "Defendant."

(See also *ante,* §§ 237, 210.)

**§ 254. State Bar Proceedings—Nondisciplinary.**—Titles of opinions determining petitions to review actions of the Board of Governors of the State Bar or of any board or committee appointed by it and authorized to make a determination pursuant to the State Bar Act should designate the petitioner and the described respondent. Typical titles for such opinions would be:

FRED JONES, Petitioner, v. THE STATE BAR OF CALIFORNIA, Respondent.
FRED JONES, Petitioner, v. COMMITTEE OF BAR EXAMINERS OF THE STATE BAR OF CALIFORNIA et al., Respondents.

(See Cal. Rules of Court, rule 952 (c); *Hersh* v. *State Bar* (1972) 7 Cal.3d 241; *Bib'le* v. *Committee of Bar Examiners* (1980) 26 Cal.3d 548; see *ante,* § 234 for title styles in disciplinary proceedings.)

**§ 255. Supersedeas—Application For.**—When a petition for a writ of supersedeas is filed to stay proceedings pending appeal, the petition, and any opinion rendered, should carry the title and number of the action in which the appeal is taken. It should *not* be entitled in the name of the applicant against the trial court. Proper forms of title are:

AL ABLE, Plaintiff and Appellant, v. RONDA ROW, Defendant and Respondent.
AL ABLE, Plaintiff and Respondent, v. RONDA ROW, Defendant and Appellant.

(See Cal. Rules of Court, rule 49; *California Table Grape Com.* v. *Dispoto* (1971) 14 Cal.App.3d 314.)

**§ 256. Third Party Claims.**—In attachment cases, a third party may enter the litigation and claim a prior right to the property attached. While this is in the nature of intervention, the party should be designated as "Third Party Claimant" if necessary to distinguish between him and the other parties, e.g.,

JOHN JONES, Plaintiff and Respondent, v. TOM SMITH, Defendant and Respondent; JANE BROWN, Third Party Claimant and Appellant.

(See e.g., *Ataka America, Inc.* v. *Crateo, Inc.* (1973) 30 Cal.App.3d 315.)

If the dispute on appeal is only between the plaintiff (or defendant) and the third party, retain the nonaffected party's name in the title for identification purposes, e.g.,

> JOHN JONES, Plaintiff and Respondent, v. TOM SMITH, Defendant; JANE BROWN, Third Party Claimant and Appellant.

(See also *ante,* § 244 (a), intervention; cf. *post,* § 257.)

**§ 257. Third Party Lien Claimants.**—In some situations a third party will seek to establish a lien on a cause of action or on any judgment subsequently obtained as where a judgment creditor seeks to obtain a lien on his debtor's cause of action or where, in a personal injury action, an insurer seeks to recover on a subrogated claim for workers' compensation benefits the insurer paid to its insured's employee. Such claims are in the nature of intervention and should be so treated. In such cases it is sufficient to distinguish the third party from the others who appear by adding the words "Claimant and" to his designation as appellant or respondent, e.g.,

> JOHN JONES, Plaintiff and Appellant, v. TOM SMITH, Defendant and Respondent; BLANK INSURANCE COMPANY, Claimant and Appellant.

If the dispute on appeal is only between the plaintiff (or defendant) and the third party, retain the nonaffected party's name in the title for identification purposes. (Cf. *ante,* § 256.) (See, e.g., *Takehara* v. *H. C. Muddox Co.* (1972) 8 Cal.3d 168; *Roseburg Loggers, Inc.* v. *U.S. Plywood-Champion Papers, Inc.* (1975) 14 Cal.3d 742; *Del Conte Masonry Co.* v. *Lewis* (1971) 16 Cal.App.3d 678; cf. *ante,* § 244, intervention.)

**§ 258. Workers' Compensation Proceedings.**—Opinions determining petitions to review decisions of the Workers' Compensation Appeals Board take the following title form:

> _____, Petitioner, v. WORKERS' COMPENSATION APPEALS BOARD and [list here other party respondent], Respondents.

If there is more than one party respondent in addition to the board the form of title is:

> _____, Petitioner, v. WORKERS' COMPENSATION APPEALS BOARD, [next named respondent] et al., Respondents.

Because the Workers' Compensation Appeals Board and the same insurance companies are involved in a great number of these cases, the name of a respondent other than the board should always be given and not included in the term "et al.," as is the usual style. (See for typical titles, *Wilson* v. *Workers' Comp. Appeals Bd.* (1976) 16 Cal.3d 181; *Muznik* v. *Workers' Comp. Appeals Bd.* (1975) 51 Cal.App.3d 622.)

**§ 259. Use of "THE" With Party Designations in Titles.**—With the exceptions noted below, as a matter of style, the word "THE" as the first word of a party litigant's name is not used with the name of a corporation, partnership, association, city or other entity.

**Exceptions:**

> THE APPELLATE DEPARTMENT OF THE SUPERIOR COURT OF _____
> COUNTY
> THE COURT OF APPEAL, _____ APPELLATE DISTRICT
> THE ENTERPRISE [with in rem proceedings]
> THE JUSTICE COURT FOR THE _____ JUDICIAL DISTRICT OF
> _____ COUNTY
> THE MUNICIPAL COURT FOR THE _____ JUDICIAL DISTRICT OF
> _____ COUNTY
> THE PEOPLE
> THE PEOPLE ex rel. _____
> THE REGENTS OF THE UNIVERSITY OF CALIFORNIA
> THE SMALL CLAIMS DIVISION FOR THE GLENDALE JUDICIAL DISTRICT
> OF LOS ANGELES COUNTY
> THE STATE BAR OF CALIFORNIA
> THE STATE OF CALIFORNIA
> THE SUPERIOR COURT OF _____ COUNTY

(See *ante,* §§ 26, 27, 212, 219.)

# CHAPTER V.
## —Notes—

# CHAPTER VI

# EDITORIAL INFORMATION

## A. In General

## B. Listing of Counsel

## C. Designation of Trial Judge

## D. Names of Justices on Opinions

## E. Discontinuance of Use of "Pro Tem." and "Pro Tempore"

## F. Modification of Opinions

## G. Partial Publication

## A. In General

**§ 260. Editorial Format of Official Reports.**—The contract for the publication of the Official Reports entered into between the State of California and the successful bidder, presently the Bancroft-Whitney Company, now requires that bound volumes and advance sheets be printed substantially in the appearance, manner and style of volume 25, California Reports, Third Series; volume 100, California Appellate

Reports Third Series; and the official advance sheets published during the year 1979. A new publication contract, under terms and conditions yet to be finalized, is expected to become operative on November 1, 1986. (See Gov. Code, §§ 68902–68904.)

The format and styles, physical and editorial, contractually prescribed under the operative publication contract are incorporated herein by reference. While many of these matters were spelled out in detail in earlier editions it was felt that much of this information is of limited assistance to most users of the manual and the bulk of these materials have therefore been deleted.

## § 261. Furnishing Opinion Editorial Information—In General.

—In order to provide the publisher with essential editorial information to complete the publication of an opinion for the Official Reports the authoring justice's staff should list the appearances of counsel (see *post,* §§ 268-284) and designate, in appeals;* the trial court, the trial court number,the Court of Appeal number for Supreme Court opinions and the trial court judge or judges whose ruling or rulings are challenged. (See *post,* § 285 and *ante,* § 197.) Where the appeal is from several rulings made by different judges, indicate the names of all judges whose decisions are challenged; e.g., "Superior Court of Kern County, No. 12345, Mary Jones and Fred Barn, Judges." However, do not indicate a judge's name where his ruling is not being contested, as for example, where he merely continued the matter or sat on an immaterial preliminary motion. Typical editorial information pages follow.

CERTIFIED FOR PUBLICATION

IN THE COURT OF APPEAL OF THE STATE OF CALIFORNIA
SECOND APPELLATE DISTRICT
DIVISION FIVE

| | |
|---|---|
| THE PEOPLE, ) | |
| Plaintiff and Respondent, ) | |
| v. ) | B012345† |
| HARRY HORN, ) | (Super. Ct. No. A 654321) |
| Defendant and Appellant. ) | |

APPEAL from a judgment of the Superior Court of Los Angeles County, William B. Green, Judge. Affirmed.

Rodney H. Fan, under appointment by the Court of Appeal, for Defendant and Appellant.

Sidney L. Star, Attorney General, Linda Horn, Chief Assistant Attorney General, R. Lee Look, Assistant Attorney General, and Hans C. Strom, Deputy Attorney General, for Plaintiff and Respondent.

---

* Neither trial court number nor trial court judge are specified in original proceedings commenced in the reviewing courts. However, where the Supreme Court is reviewing a Court of Appeal's decision, the Court of Appeal's number should be provided. (See *post,* § 286.)

† See *ante,* sections 69, footnote and 197.

IN THE COURT OF APPEAL OF THE STATE OF CALIFORNIA
FIRST APPELLATE DISTRICT
DIVISION ONE

| | |
|---|---|
| ANN A. SMITH et al., ) | |
| Plaintiffs and Respondents, ) | |
| v. ) | A012345* |
| SOUTHERN PACIFIC COMPANY, ) | (Super. Ct. No. A 654321) |
| Defendant and Appellant; ) | |
| PUBLIC EMPLOYEES RETIREMENT SYSTEM, ) | |
| Intervener and Appellant. ) | |

APPEAL from a judgment of the Superior Court of the City and County of San Francisco, Mary M. Mars, Judge. Affirmed.

John Jones and Douglas E. Seven for Defendant and Appellant.

Frank Forrest, Attorney General, June Jacobs, Assistant Attorney General, and Arthur Orr, Deputy Attorney General, for Intervener and Appellant.

No appearance for Plaintiffs and Respondents.

........................................................................................................................

IN THE COURT OF APPEAL OF THE STATE OF CALIFORNIA
SECOND APPELLATE DISTRICT
DIVISION FIVE

| | |
|---|---|
| JAMES CASTRO, ) | |
| Petitioner, ) | |
| v. ) | |
| THE SUPERIOR COURT OF SANTA ) | |
| BARBARA COUNTY, ) | B012345* |
| Respondent; ) | |
| CHARLES ENT et al., ) | |
| Real Parties in Interest. ) | |

ORIGINAL PROCEEDING; application for a writ of mandate. Writ denied.

Richard Roe for Petitioner.

No appearance for Respondent.

Flower, Flower & Seed and Lotta Seed for Real Parties in Interest.

**§ 262. Notation of Denial of Rehearing or Review.**—When a petition for a rehearing or review has been filed and denied, the Reporter of Decisions office in reporting the opinion for the bound volume makes a notation of this procedural fact at the end of the official report of the opinion. The names of justices voting to grant a petition are specified. Notice of the denial of a rehearing is sent to the Reporter's office by the clerk's office of the particular Court of Appeal. Information concerning Supreme Court determinations is obtained from that court's minutes. (See *ante,* §§ 88 & 88.1.)

_____

\* See *ante,* section 69.

## § 263. Opinion on Denial of Rehearing—Uniform Pagination.

—Occasionally a court will issue a supplemental opinion on denial of a rehearing. Where such an opinion is short and can fit in the blank space at the end of the advance sheet report of the primary opinion, then the supplemental opinion is reported on an "a" page in the advance sheets and will appear at the last page of the bound volume report of the case. However, if the supplemental opinion is lengthy, in order to preserve the uniform pagination system the primary opinion and the opinion on denial of rehearing will be reprinted together at another place. Then, in the bound volume, the primary opinion will be deleted where it first appeared in the advance sheets. The subscribers are notified that an opinion on denial of rehearing has been written and whether a reprinting will be necessary by an entry on the Cumulative Subsequent History Table. (See *ante*, § 97.)

## § 264. Opinion Galleys—Proofreading and Queries.

—Pursuant to California Rules of Court, rule 976 (e), each opinion is edited for publication by the Reporter of Decisions. The reporter's office makes necessary revisions, additions and adjustments to the editorial materials and notes style, printing and other errors perceived on galley proofs, which are then submitted as adjusted to the court which authored the opinion for examination, proofreading, correction and final bound-volume approval. Because of a small staff, a high volume of published opinions and the consequential necessity of reading rapidly, not all the printing and other errors that a slower reading would disclose are caught. Incorrectly printed passages which read correctly are often difficult and many times impossible to detect. Therefore the reporter's office must rely on the careful proofreading of each justice's staff to ensure fidelity of publication.

In many instances queries are noted on forwarded galleys. The query could concern the title of the opinion, the listing of counsel, the wording or construction of a sentence or paragraph, conflicting references to a party, the correctness of a citation or a variety of other procedural or substantive matters. In all instances before a query is noted, available sources of information are exhausted in order to impose as slight a burden as possible on busy court staffs. *Please answer all queries presented* to avoid costly follow-up phone calls. The use of a colored pencil rather than a lead pencil in reply to these queries and in noting other galley changes and corrections is requested. It is axiomatic that no substantive changes may be made after a decision is final. (See Cal. Rules of Court, rule 24 (a) and *post*, § 296.)

## § 265. Opinion Galleys—Return of Proofread and Corrected Galleys—Time.

—A date for return of a galley proof is prominently noted on the title page of an edited opinion forwarded to the originating court. The return of a submitted galley proof within the noted time is essential to meet tight publication schedules. Should an opinion not be returned within the indicated time please advise the Reporter of Decisions office of the expected return date.

(See also *ante,* § 264.)

**§ 266.  Appellate Department of the Superior Court Opinions Certified for Publication.**—In addition to the editorial information furnished with all appellate court opinions to be published (see *ante,* § 261), an opinion of an appellate department of a superior court submitted to the Reporter of Decisions for publication should indicate that it is certified for publication (see *ante,* § 197). It should also specify that a copy was forwarded to the appropriate Court of Appeal upon the judgment becoming final as to the appellate department to allow the Court of Appeal, at its election, to transfer the cause to itself on its own motion. (See Cal. Rules of Court, rules 106, 976(c), 62(a), (b) and 107(b).)

When the period for transfer by the Court of Appeal on its own motion has expired (see Cal. Rules of Court, rule 62(b)), or prior thereto if the Court of Appeal has denied transfer before expiration of that period, the clerk of the appellate department should foward to the Reporter of Decisions a letter indicating: (1) that a copy of the opinion stamped "Certified for Publication" was submitted to the appropriate Court of Appeal noting the date of submission; (2) the date of receipt of the opinion by the Court of Appeal; and (3) that the Court of Appeal either filed an order declining to take the case over, noting the date of such order, or, that the Court of Appeal has not acted on the matter within its jurisdictional time.

Upon receipt of such a letter from the clerk the reporter will then proceed with publication procedures. If, however, the Court of Appeal has transferred the cause to itself, the appellate department clerk should advise the Reporter of Decisions of the opinion's status.

**§ 267.  Memorials—Procedure for Publication.**—Memorials are published, upon court direction, in the next bound volume of the Official Reports following the completion of the publication procedures outlined below. Where a justice was in office at the time of demise the memorial is normally published in the bound volume in which that justice's final opinions will appear. The "In Memoriam" is published immediately following the last reported opinion of the particular volume. The justice's name is indexed in the table of cases as: "Jones, Hon. John J., Memorial for" and "In Memoriam—Hon. John J. Jones."

Customarily the "In Memoriam" is introduced editorially by a dated history of all courts that the justice sat upon, a notation of the date and place of the memorial and an identification of the clerk, reporter and bailiff in attendance. (See, e.g., 8 Cal.3d 955; 30 Cal.3d 921; 23 Cal.App.3d 1107.)

The procedure for publication is as follows:

1. Collect the editorial information noted above.
2. Edit the memorial for publication.
3. Forward the collected information and the edited memorial to the Reporter of Decisions.
4. The Reporter of Decisions then prepares the memorial for galley publication. When the memorial is printed a sufficient number of preliminary galleys will be returned to the originating court so that the court can distribute one galley to each of the parties participating in the memorial service for approval. When the court has obtained the approval of all parties a dated galley with all adjustments indicated is returned to the Reporter of Decisions office with a notation "O.K. to print as adjusted."

## B. Listing of Counsel

**§ 268. Collection of Information—Source.**—In order to obtain accuracy in the listing of counsel for the Official Reports in the first instance and thereby avoid the costly resetting of advance sheet copy to make adjustments, it is essential that the opinion author's staff or other court personnel preparing editorial materials carefully examine all filings and pertinent correspondence in the original record, since that record is the only complete and reliable source of necessary information. In this regard, it is noted that some records, previously used by the reporter's office to verify counsel listings are no longer available to that office. (See also *post,* § 269.)

**§ 269. Listing of Individuals and Firms.**—An opinion published in the Official Reports editorially lists the names of all attorneys and firms of attorneys who appeared of record in the appellate court proceeding. The filing of a brief or other document or the adoption of a filed brief or participation at oral argument constitutes an appearance for listing purposes. Give the names of individuals and firms as spelled on the briefs of counsel, except where there is an obvious error. If the briefs differ as to spelling, consult the State Bar's roster, a current edition of one of the California attorneys directories or the telephone directory. If, however, the difference is merely that an attorney's name is spelled in full on one brief and is abbreviated on another, give preference to the full spelling.

Where a brief is signed in a firm name "by" an associate or a member of the firm, as "Jones & Smith by John Jones," substitute "and" for "by" and show counsel as "Jones & Smith and John Jones for" etc.

Most firms use the sign "&" and not the word "and," but some do not, and some use both in the same name, as "Jones & Smith and Black." Where the sign is used on one brief and the word on another, use the sign; otherwise follow the signature as shown on the briefs of counsel.

Do not use the words "of counsel" in listing attorneys, regardless of whether those words appear on the briefs.

Include *all* attorneys who sign or formally adopt a brief. Do not rely alone on the list of counsel on the inception page of a brief, since the names of participating attorneys frequently appear only on the signature page at the back of a brief, e.g., the cover may indicate "Black & Blue and John Blue for" etc. The signature page of the brief may additionally note "Black & Blue and John Blue, by Fred Green." Fred Green's name must be added and the listing would then be, "Black & Blue, John Blue and Fred Green for" etc.

Where a party files several briefs, whether on the merits or relating to preliminary motions, etc., all must be examined since frequently there are changes of firm names and participating attorneys between briefs. New names are added to the appearances noted from the earlier briefs. If the briefs show a change in a firm name while the appeal or proceeding is pending, show *both* versions of the firm name. (See, e.g., *Bareno* v. *Employers Life Ins. Co.* (1972) 7 Cal.3d 875, 877.)

Consult the court's minutes for the date of argument since the case may have been argued by counsel who did not sign a brief.

When a Court of Appeal decision is reviewed by the Supreme Court, appearances by counsel in both courts are listed in the Official Report publication of any resulting opinion of the Supreme Court.

Where the Court of Appeal's opinion in the cause or proceeding survives the Supreme Court's review, in whole or in part, *appearances* by counsel in *both* courts are listed. Likewise any appearances by counsel in either court are listed even though the Supreme Court may later have dismissed review as improvidently granted and remanded the cause to the Court of Appeal. (See *ante,* § 88.3 et seq.)

The foregoing practices are premised on the proposition that the primary purpose of listing counsel in reporting an opinion for the Official Reports is to chronicle "appearances" in broad categories, e.g., "for Defendants and Appellants" or "for Plaintiffs and Respondents" or "as Amici Curiae on behalf of Defendants and Appellants," etc., and not to sort out and identify what particular party litigant, within a broad category, counsel appeared for or to identify whether the appearance was limited to specific issues. (See also *ante,* § 279.)

An attorney who appeared only in the trial court is not listed. Do not list nonattorneys unless the party appeared in propria persona.

Once an attorney has made an appearance in the reviewing court his name is listed in reporting the decision and cannot be withdrawn at a later date either unilaterally or by stipulation. (See also *post,* § 281 re substitution of attorneys.)

**§ 270. Sequence of Names—Appeals.**—Regardless of whether the appellant was the plaintiff, defendant, intervener, etc., in the trial court, counsel are to be named in the following order:

1. Counsel for appellants.
2. Counsel for amici curiae on behalf of appellants.
3. Counsel for respondents.
4. Counsel for amici curiae on behalf of respondents.

(See, e.g., *Rivera* v. *City of Fresno* (1971) 6 Cal.3d 132, 134.)

If plaintiff and defendant both appeal, show first the counsel for plaintiff and then the counsel for defendant.

If there is an appeal by an intervener alone, his counsel will be listed first as counsel for appellant; but if there is also an appeal by plaintiff or defendant, or both, counsel for the intervener will be listed after the counsel for the other appellants. The same rule applies to a third party claimant or a real party in interest.

Where there is no appearance for a party on appeal, that fact should be noted; e.g., "No appearance for Defendant and Respondent."

Where the amicus curiae does not appear in support of any particular litigant's position or where the amicus curiae's support status is not clear, list counsel for the amicus curiae last.

(See also *post,* § 272 re amici curiae.)

**§ 271. Sequence of Names—Original Proceedings Commenced in Appellate Court.**—Counsel are to be named in the following order:

1. Counsel for petitioning party, i.e., the initiating party seeking relief.
2. Counsel for amicus curiae on behalf of petitioner.
3. Counsel for respondent.
4. Counsel for amicus curiae on behalf of respondent.
5. Counsel for real party in interest.
6. Counsel for amicus curiae on behalf of real party in interest.

(See, e.g., *Randone* v. *Appellate Department* (1971) 5 Cal.3d 536, 539.)

Where there is no appearance for a party, as is frequently the case where a court is a respondent, that fact should be noted, e.g., "No appearance for Respondent."

Where the proceeding seeking a writ was commenced in the trial court and the pending matter is an appeal from the trial court ruling, follow the rules for the listing of counsel in appeals.

(See *ante,* § 270.) (See also *post,* § 272, re amici curiae.)

**§ 272.  Amici Curiae.**—Where counsel appears as amicus curiae in support of a party to the litigation and an appeal is involved, the style is:

> John Jones as Amicus Curiae on behalf of (designate trial court status, i.e., Defendant, Plaintiff, or Real Party in Interest) and (designate appellate court status, i.e., Appellant or Respondent).

Where the matter before the court is an original proceeding commenced in the appellate court no trial court designation is noted and the style is:

> John Jones as Amicus Curiae on behalf of (designate status, i.e., Petitioner, Respondent, or Real Party in Interest).

In the case of an appearance by two or more individuals or by a firm, use the form "Amici Curiae," e.g.,

> Jones, Jones and Smith and Alma Smith as Amici Curiae on behalf of . . . .

Where counsel does not appear in support of any particular litigant's position or where the amicus curiae's support status is not clear, the form is:

> John Jones as Amicus Curiae.

(See *ante,* § 270 re sequence of listing counsel.)

Where an individual appears as an amicus curiae at the invitation of the court the form is:

> John Jones as Amicus Curiae, upon the request of the Supreme Court. (Or ", upon the request of Chief Justice Black" or ", upon the request of the Court of Appeal.")

Where counsel are attorneys for the state, a city or a county, that designation should be shown, e.g., "as Attorney General," "Deputy Attorney General," "City Attorney," "District Attorney," "County Counsel," etc. (See *post,* § 273.) In the case of city and county officers, the name of the city or county should be placed in parentheses after the designation of each chief officer, but not after the names of the deputies:

> John Jones, District Attorney (Tulare), Tom Blue, Deputy District Attorney, Mary Brown, District Attorney (Merced) and Jack Black, District Attorney (Kern), as Amici Curiae on behalf of Appellant.

(See, e.g., *Young v. Gnoss* (1972) 7 Cal.3d 18, 20.)

**§ 273.  Official Titles of Public Attorneys.**—In order to avoid space-consuming recitations of the frequently changed and often lengthy titles of official attorneys for state, county, city and other governmental agencies, the Official Reports do not note those formal titles.

Traditionally, however, a limited number of short titles, more descriptive than official, are indicated, e.g.,

> Attorney General, District Attorney, City Attorney, Public Defender, and County Counsel.

All assistants and deputies of these officers are noted as such: e.g., Assistant Attorney General, Deputy Attorney General, Deputy Public Defender, Chief Deputy State Public Defender, Deputy State Public Defender, etc. If more than one assistant or deputy appears, one pluralized designation is used; e.g., Assistant Attorneys General, Deputy District Attorneys, Deputy Public Defenders. Since "counsel" is both singular and plural, two or more deputies should be referred to as "Deputy County Counsel."

**Illustrations:**

> John Blue, Attorney General, Mary Tan, Chief Assistant Attorney General, N. Fred Green, Assistant Attorney General, Edmund Red and Charles Buff, Deputy Attorneys General, for Plaintiffs and Appellants.
>
> Ben Black, State Public Defender, Betty Blue and Barry Brown, Deputy State Public Defenders.
>
> Martha Moore, County Counsel, Douglas Dude, Jr., and Martin Moon, Deputy County Counsel, for Defendant and Respondent.

(See also *post,* § 274 where there has been a change of the official attorney during the pendency of appellate court proceedings.)

### § 274. Change of Official Attorney During Pendency of Appellate Court Proceedings.—Where there is a change of an official attorney while an action is pending in the appellate courts, give both names only where both have *appeared* of record. For purposes of listing counsel an appearance has traditionally been considered to be the filing of a brief or other document or the adoption of a filed brief or participation at oral argument. The mere holding of an official office during the pendency of the appellate proceeding is not an appearance.

**Illustrations:**

(1) Where a brief has been filed on behalf of a party to an appellate court proceeding by John First, Attorney General, but no brief is thereafter filed nor oral argument made by new Attorney General Jane Second, through her deputies, then only Attorney General First's name and the names of participating deputies would be listed as counsel even though the case may be decided while Jane Second is Attorney General.

(2) Where *both* Attorneys General, through their deputies, file briefs, then both names are listed. An example of proper designations would be "John First and Jane Second, Attorneys General, Helen Help and Harry Support, Chief Assistant Attorneys General, Mary Smart and William Bright, Deputy Attorneys General, for Plaintiff and Respondent."

(3) Where a brief had been filed by Attorney General First and no briefs are filed by Attorney General Second but Attorney General Second, through her deputies, argues a case, that is considered to be an appearance and both Attorneys General are then listed with any participating assistants and deputies.

(4) A waiver of oral argument is not considered an appearance.

(5) Finally, where an appeal or other appellate court proceeding was commenced while Attorney General First was in office, but no Attorney General briefs were filed during that period, his name should not appear as counsel.

(See also *post,* § 281.)

**§ 275. Criminal Cases—For General.**—In criminal cases the appeal is usually handled solely by the Attorney General and his staff, and the district attorney's name should not appear unless he actually does some work on the appeal, i.e., unless his name appears on a brief or he appears at oral argument.

**§ 276. Criminal Cases—Court-appointed Counsel.**—Where counsel is appointed by an appellate court in a criminal case, the fact of appointment is noted; e.g.,

> John Jones, under appointment by the Supreme Court [or Court of Appeal], for Defendant and Appellant.
> Mary Jones, under appointment by the Supreme Court, and Andrew Foot, under appointment by the Court of Appeal, for Defendant and Appellant.
> Lisa Green and John Jones, under appointments by the Supreme Court [or Court of Appeal], for Defendants and Appellants.

When the same attorney is appointed in both the Court of Appeal and the Supreme Court, use,

> Mary Jones, under appointment by the Supreme Court, for Defendant and Appellant.

Where the State Public Defender is appointed, the fact of appointment is noted in the following fashion:

> John Black, State Public Defender, under appointment by the Supreme Court, [or Court of Appeal] and Martha Blue, Deputy State Public Defender, for Defendant and Appellant.

Where the State Public Defender is not appointed by the court but a defendant is nevertheless represented by that office follow the style noted *ante* in section 273. (See Gov. Code, § 15421.)

Where the participating attorney is not a staff member of the State Public Defender's Office but is a panel attorney working with that office, list his name following that office's participating members.

(See also *post,* § 277 for where the defendant is or was in pro. per. and had or has court-appointed counsel.)

**§ 277. Party in Propria Persona.**—When a party appears as attorney for himself, or for himself and others, or for himself as executor, receiver, etc., the words "in pro. per." should follow his name, e.g.,

William Tell, in pro. per., for Defendant and Appellant.

When an attorney appears for himself or for himself and others, and he is one of several attorneys, his name should always be placed before those of the other attorneys to show that he alone is appearing in propria persona, e.g.,

James Sharp, in pro. per., and Harvey Plant for Plaintiffs and Respondents.
Jane Heath, in pro. per., and for Defendants and Appellants.

Where a party who is not an attorney appears for himself and later counsel is retained or appointed by an appellate court, the forms are:

Mary Green, in pro. per., and Peter Attorney for Plaintiff and Respondent.
Mary Green, in pro. per., and Peter Attorney, under appointment by the Supreme Court [or Court of Appeal], for Defendant and Appellant.

(See also *post,* § 278.)

**§ 278. Nonattorneys.**—Other than the "in propria persona" exception noted *ante* in section 277, do not list nonattorneys even though they may have argued a case with the appellate court's permission or assisted other attorneys in the preparation of appellate court briefs. This section precludes the listing of law student trainees participating in the Practical Training of Law Students program authorized by State Bar rules. (See State Bar Rules for Pract. Training of Law Students.) When a nonattorney worked on a matter pending in an appellate court and thereafter is admitted to practice, his or her name is listed only in the event of an appearance of record in the matter *after* admission to the bar.

(See *ante,* §§ 269, 274 as to what acts constitute an appearance of record.)

**§ 279. Use of Names of Clients in Listing Counsel.**—In general in specifying whom counsel represents, *do not* add the formal names of parties litigant but merely their status designations, as "for Plaintiff and Appellant," "for Defendant and Respondent," "for Intervener and Appellant," "for Petitioner," [original proceeding in reviewing court], "for Respondent," [original proceeding in reviewing court], etc.

Where two or more parties have identical designations in the reviewing court (as where both are plaintiffs and appellants) list their counsel consecutively notwithstanding the fact that each party may have obtained independent representation. For example, if plaintiff and appellant John Smith is represented by the law firm of Black and Blue by

Mary Punch, while plaintiff and appellant Buster Brown is represented by Heel & Toe by Ted Toe, the counsel listing would be:

> Black and Blue, Mary Punch, Heel & Toe, and Ted Toe for Plaintiffs and Appellants.

Where two parties or groups of parties, while both within the same category (as where both are defendants and appellants), have diametrically opposite or unrelated interests in the case and are seeking to establish opposing or unrelated theories, it may be necessary to name the parties in order to differentiate between the attorneys. It then is proper to list the counsel "for Plaintiffs and Appellants Jones et al.," and "for Plaintiffs and Appellants Smith et al." The foregoing exception does not apply to appeals by both plaintiff and defendant, for then the parties can be designated as "Plaintiff and Appellant" and "Defendant and Appellant."

(See *Legislature* v. *Reinecke* (1973) 10 Cal.3d 396, 398, *ante,* § 269, and *post,* § 280.)

### § 280.  Opinion Covering Two Cases.

—When an opinion involves two cases and the plaintiff is appellant in one but respondent in the other, or where one case is an appeal and the other an original proceeding, or where incompatible and therefore confusing designations would otherwise result, it is necessary to list counsel as "for Plaintiff and Respondent in No. B012345" or "for Plaintiff and Appellant in No. B012399," etc.

(See for illustrations *Legislature* v. *Reinecke* (1973) 10 Cal.3d 396, 398; *County of Alameda* v. *Carleson* (1971) 5 Cal.3d 730, 734; *Felix* v. *Workmen's Comp. Appeals Bd.* (1974) 41 Cal.App.3d 759, 761; *People* v. *Orrante* (1962) 201 Cal.App.2d 553, 554–555.)

### § 281.  Substitution of Attorneys.

—Where an attorney has filed a brief in the appellate court or appeared at argument and thereafter there is a substitution or withdrawal of attorneys pursuant to California Rules of Court, rule 48 (b), list as counsel for the Official Reports *both* the retiring attorney and the substituted attorney. This is the practice regardless of whether the attorneys involved agree between themselves to a different listing arrangement. (See also *post,* § 282 and *ante,* §§ 269, 274.)

### § 282.  Motion for Substitution.

—On motions for substitution of counsel on appeal show counsel as follows: "John Smith for Movant" (party making motion) and "Jack Black in Opposition." Do not name the counsel for the remaining parties to the appeal (the appellant or respondent) unless they actually take part in the hearing of the motion, as they ordinarily do not appear and are not interested in the motion or its disposition. (See also Cal. Rules of Court, rules 48(b), 41, 42.)

**§ 283. Counsel on Intervention.**—Where a person seeks to intervene in an action to which he is not a party, he is called a "Movant" until such time as he is granted permission to intervene. (See *ante,* § 244.) Counsel will thus be shown as "for Movant" if permission has not been given, and as "for Intervener" if permission has been granted. (See, e.g., *Continental Vinyl Products Corp.* v. *Mead Corp.* (1972) 27 Cal.App.3d 543, 547 [intervention denied]; *Drinnon* v. *Oliver* (1972) 24 Cal.App.3d 571, 574 [intervention granted].)

**§ 284. Law Corporations.**—Where a law corporation appears as counsel for a party in an appellate court proceeding the law corporation's name is listed when it is authorized to act as a law corporation pursuant to the Law Corporation Rules of the State Bar. (See particularly, rule IV (A)(5) and Bus. & Prof. Code, § 6164.) Participating attorneys are listed following the corporation's name in the style outlined *ante,* at section 269.

## C. Designation of Trial Judge

**§ 285. Trial Judges, Trial Judges Sitting Under Assignment, Temporary Judges Sitting Pursuant to Stipulation, Court Commissioners and Referees Sitting in Absence of Stipulation.**

**(a) Trial Judge.**—The trial judge's name should be given in the form in which it is printed on the judge's roster at the front of the latest volume of the California Reports. If the name does not appear on that roster, use the spelling from the order or judgment appealed from which is found in the clerk's transcript. A typical information statement would be: Superior Court of Lassen County, No. 12345, Sandra A. Dart, Judge. (See *ante,* § 261 where more than one judge has participated.)

**(b) Trial Judge Sitting Under Assignment.**—When the case is heard by a judge or justice sitting under assignment, that information, while published in the Official Reports in a footnote, should appear parenthetically following the judge's or justice's name, e.g., "Superior Court of Lassen County, No. 12345, Mary Green, Judge. (Retired judge of the superior court sitting under assignment by the Chairperson of the Judicial Council.)"

If the assigned trial judge is not retired, regardless of the court he regularly sits on, use: "(Assigned by the Chairperson of the Judicial Council.)"

Other parenthetical designations to be used with ". . . sitting under assignment by the Chairperson of the Judicial Council" to indicate fact variations for retired judges are: "Retired judge of the superior court . . ."; "Retired judge of the municipal court . . ."; "Retired judge of the justice court . . ."; and accordingly for appellate justices, "Retired Associate Justice of the Court of Appeal . . ."; "Retired Associate Justice of the Supreme Court . . ."; "Retired Chief Justice of the Supreme Court . . . ."

**(c) Court Commissioners, Referees and Other Attorneys Sitting as Judge Pursuant to Stipulation of the Parties Litigant.**—Where a court commissioner, referee, or other attorney is sitting as a temporary judge pursuant to the stipulation of the parties, call him "Temporary Judge" with a parenthetical notation as illustrated:

> Superior Court of Butte County, No. 12345, Ann Forrest, Temporary Judge. (Pursuant to Cal. Const., art VI, § 21.)

(See *People* v. *Tijerina* (1969) 1 Cal.3d 41; *In re Mark L.* (1983) 34 Cal.3d 171; *Sarracino* v. *Superior Court* (1974) 13 Cal.3d 1; *In re Frye* (1983) 150 Cal.App.3d 407; Cal. Const., art VI, § 21; Cal. Rules of Court, rules 244, 532.)

**(d) Court Commissioners or Referees Sitting in Absence of Stipulation.**—Where a court commissioner or referee who has not been qualified by stipulation to serve as a temporary judge is nevertheless empowered to perform "subordinate judicial duties" or to decide "uncontested actions and proceedings" and his determination in such situations is challenged, use "Court Commissioner," "Traffic Referee," "Juvenile Court Referee," etc., without notation, e.g., Keith Stone, Court Commissioner; Betty Bell, Traffic Referee; Marsha Monarch, Juvenile Court Referee. (See *Rooney* v. *Vermont Investment Corp.* (1973) 10 Cal.3d 351, 359–360; Cal. Const., art. VI, § 22; Code Civ. Proc., §§ 259, 638–645; Cal. Rules of Court, rule 532(b).)

**§ 286. Noting Trial Judge—Original Proceedings.**—Where there is an *appeal* from an order or judgment granting or denying an application for a writ, designate the trial judge and trial court number as in other appeals. (See *ante,* § 285.)

However, where an application for a writ seeking trial court relief is filed as an original proceeding in a reviewing court it is not necessary for editorial information purposes to note either the trial court judge or the trial court number for the underlying trial court proceeding. When the Supreme Court writes an opinion reviewing a decision of a Court of Appeal which determined a petition for a writ in an original proceeding filed in an appellate court, both the Supreme Court and the Court of Appeal numbers are provided. (See also *ante,* § 261.)

## D.  Names of Justices on Opinions

**§ 287.  In General.**—The names of participating justices are not printed in the Official Reports in exactly the same manner as shown on the original or typed copies of opinions. In the typewritten opinion, the name of the author is placed at the end, followed by the names of those who concurred and dissented in seniority sequence. As printed in the Official Reports, the name of the author is placed at the start of the body of the opinion in full capitals, with a dash, while the concurring justices are listed at the end, in capitals and lower case, followed by the word "concurred," e.g., Jones, P. J., and Smith, J., concurred. Where a justice dissents, without opinion, that justice is listed in a separate paragraph after the concurring justices in capitals and lower case, followed by the word "dissented," e.g., Black, J., dissented.

If a concurring or dissenting justice authors an opinion, participating justices are noted in the same fashion as in the majority opinion. (See also *post,* §§ 288, 289.)

**§ 288.  Single or Majority Opinion.**—Use only the last name, in full capitals, followed by C. J., P. J., or J., as the case may be. If a justice is acting as Chief Justice or as presiding justice, use the form "JONES, Acting C. J." or "JONES, Acting P. J."

If there are two justices currently sitting on the same appellate court or at the same appellate level who have the same last name, insert the first name or initials in parentheses between the surname and the title, as "JONES (G. L.), J." This form is used only when the omission of the name or initials may cause confusion. The name of a trial court judge assigned to assist an appellate court should be distinguished in like fashion where another judge sitting at the appellate *or* trial court level bears the same surname.

If the opinion is "By the Court," use merely "THE COURT," for the Official Reports, not "Per Curiam" or "By the Court."

**§ 289.  Concurring and Dissenting Opinions—Official Reports.**—If a justice files a concurring or dissenting opinion, that name is placed in full capitals at the beginning of the opinion in the Official Reports, followed by the word, "Concurring" or "Dissenting," e.g., "JONES, J., Dissenting." When a justice writes a concurring *and* dissenting opinion, use: "JONES, J., Concurring and Dissenting."

*Exception.* If the opinion commences with the words "I concur" or "I dissent" it is unnecessary to insert the words "Concurring" or "Dissenting" unless the opinion is both a concurring and a dissenting opinion and that fact does not appear from the first few words or first sentence of the opinion.

The name of any justice who concurs in a concurring or dissenting opinion is placed at the end of that opinion in the same style as for concurrences in the main opinion.

(See *ante,* § 287 and *post,* § 290.)

When several justices join as authors of one dissenting or concurring opinion, all the names are in full capitals in the order of seniority. (See *Treu* v. *Kirkwood* (1954) 42 Cal.2d 602, 621; *Estate of Dow* (1957) 48 Cal.2d 649, 654.)

**§ 290. Concurring and Dissenting Justices—Official Reports.**—As indicated *ante* in section 287 names of concurring justices are noted in a separate paragraph at the end of the opinion, in capitals and lower case:

Smith, J., White, J., and Robinson, J., concurred.

If a justice states that he or she concurs "in the judgment" or "in the decision" or "in the conclusions reached," that fact is noted by a separate sentence but in the same paragraph as the other concurring justices' names.

Jones, J., and White, J., concurred. Robinson, J., concurred in the judgment.

If a justice dissents without opinion, that fact is noted in the same style in a separate paragraph:

Black, J., dissented.

**§ 291. Order of Opinions.**—When a case has two or more opinions, the order, unless otherwise directed by the court, is: Main opinion, concurring opinion, concurring and dissenting opinion, and dissenting opinion. If there are two opinions in the same category, as for example two separate concurrences, they are placed in the order of filing.

**§ 292. Assigned Justices.**—If the author of the opinion or one of the concurring or dissenting justices has been assigned from another division or from a Court of Appeal of another district, or from a trial court, follow the style for noting the assignment of superior court judges, i.e., "JONES, J.*" (Footnote: "*Assigned by the Chairperson of the Judicial Council.") (See also *ante,* § 285(b).) A presiding justice of a Court of Appeal who is assigned to the Supreme Court sits there as a justice rather than as a presiding justice and is designated as "GREEN, J.*" and not "GREEN, P. J.*" (Footnote: "*Assigned by the Chairperson of the Judicial Council.")

Where the assigned justice is retired follow the style for noting the assignment of superior court judges (*ante,* § 285 (b)), i.e., "BLACK, J.*" (Footnote: "*Retired Associate Justice [or Chief Justice] of the Supreme

Court sitting under assignment by the Chairperson of the Judicial Council." [or] "Associate Justice [or Presiding Justice] of the Court of Appeal sitting under assignment by the Chairperson of the Judicial Council.")

Where the assignment is made by the Acting Chief Justice, as where the Chief Justice is absent or deems herself or himself disqualified, the footnote should read: "*Assigned by the Acting Chairperson of the Judicial Council." or, for an assigned retired justice, "*Retired . . . Justice of the . . . sitting under assignment by the Acting Chairperson of the Judicial Council."

### § 293. Supreme Court—Order of Names.—The names of the justices of the Supreme Court, when listed as concurring or dissenting, etc., should be given in the order of seniority, with the exception that the Chief Justice always heads the list when included therein.

If an assigned justice participates, that name is to be shown at the end of the list with an appropriate footnote. (See *ante,* §§ 292, 285(b).)

When a justice is "Acting C. J." list that name first regardless of the justice's normal position on the order of seniority.

### § 294. Disqualification or Nonparticipation.—If a justice is disqualified, or deems himself or herself disqualified, that fact is noted in a separate paragraph following the names of the concurring justices and preceding any dissenting opinion. The form will be governed by the notation at the end of the original opinion (usually copied in the minutes). The following forms have been used:

Jones, J., being disqualified, did not participate therein.
or
Jones, J., deeming himself disqualified, did not participate.
or
Jones, J.,* sat in place of the Chief Justice, who deemed herself disqualified.
(A footnote then notes the assignment of the justice. See *ante,* § 292.)

If a justice does not declare himself disqualified, but for some reason wishes it to be indicated that he did not participate, the notation will be similar in form to the foregoing, but will omit any reference to disqualification:

Jones, J., did not participate therein.
or
Jones, J., did not participate in the hearing or determination of this matter.

If the record does not show the reason for appointment of an assigned justice, it is sufficient to note the fact of assignment. (See *ante,* § 292.)

The presiding justice of a Court of Appeal, when sitting in the Supreme Court, is noted as Smith, J., not Smith, P. J.

## E.  Discontinuance of Use of "Pro Tem." and "Pro Tempore"

**§ 295.  Elimination of "Pro Tem." and "Pro Tempore" in Editorial References.**—The terms "pro tem." and "pro tempore" once used editorially in the Official Reports to describe attorneys, court commissioners, judges and justices sitting temporarily in a particular judicial capacity have been eliminated. The deletion of these Latin expressions resulted from the change in nomenclature in article VI of the California Constitution, adopted November 8, 1966, and the desirability of the use of more precise descriptions. (See *ante,* §§ 285, 292; Cal. Const., art. VI, § 21; *People* v. *Tijerina* (1969) 1 Cal.3d 41, 44, fn. 1; *Sarracino* v. *Superior Court* (1974) 13 Cal.3d 1, 6; Cal. Const. Revision Com., Proposed Revision (1966) com., p.98.)

## F.  Modification of Opinions

**§ 296.  Time Limitation—Formal Order.**—All modifications whether by way of addition, deletion or substitution must by court rule be made before the decision becomes final as to the modifying court. (See Cal. Rules of Court, rules 24(a), 107 and also *ante,* § 103.) Modifications of majority or lead opinions must be made by formal court order with the concurrence of a qualified majority of the court, and entered in the court's minutes. A minority opinion is modified by a filed order signed by its participants after circulation of the modification to the entire panel to permit response. Frequently modifications are made in connection with an order denying a petition for rehearing. The Reporter of Decisions is not authorized to make any modifications in the absence of such an order. The modification order upon filing is distributed in the same fashion as the filed opinion it modifies. It is not the function of this manual to specify what is contemplated under the Rules of Court by the word "modification." Parenthetically, however, it is noted that a formal modification order has traditionally been deemed required if the change will alter the written opinion as to substance, argument or authority cited, or where the change would add to or omit any consequential portion of the opinion as filed. If there is a doubt the better policy is to put through a formal order of modification. (See also *post,* § 301 re correction of clerical errors, and *ante,* § 102 re withdrawal of citation to a superseded opinion, § 264 re proofreading of opinion galleys, and §§ 88.1, 88.5(g)(2) & (h)(2), and 97 re citation of opinion modification.)

**§ 297.  Modification Order—Form.**—When adding, deleting or substituting material, note the following guidelines:

**(a)** When the opinion is published in the advance sheets refer to the published version rather than the typed opinion for page and line references.

**(b)** Quotation marks should not be used to enclose the author's instructions. However, quotation marks may be used to identify words or phrases that are to be changed. If the words changed are to be in quote marks in the opinion it is better to repeat the passage as adjusted following the instructions to avoid any ambiguity. It is preferable to indicate the new language by indenting or otherwise setting it off on the page.

**(c)** Note the paragraph, line, word, footnote, etc., affected with as much precision as possible.

**(d)** Prominently indicate the publication status of the opinion modified.

**(e)** A sample order and instructions follow:

(CERTIFIED FOR PUBLICATION)

IN THE COURT OF APPEAL OF THE STATE OF CALIFORNIA
SECOND APPELLATE DISTRICT
DIVISION ONE

| | | |
|---|---|---|
| JOHN BROWN, | ) | B012345 |
| Plaintiff and Respondent, | ) | (Super. Ct. No. 54321) |
| v. | ) | ORDER MODIFYING OPINION |
| | ) | AND DENYING REHEARING; |
| AJAX INSURANCE COMPANY, | ) | CERTIFICATION FOR |
| Defendant and Appellant. | ) | PUBLICATION |

THE COURT:

It is ordered that the opinion filed herein on November 1, 1988, be modified in the following particulars:

1. On page 1, line 9 of the first full paragraph, the word "limited" is changed to "absolute" so the sentence reads:

> The absolute liability issue is moot.

2. On page 2, the second full paragraph is deleted and the following paragragh is inserted in its place:

> Without concluding that the questioned instructions are
> a paragon of clarity, we do deduce that, taken together, they
> correctly state the law.

3. On page 3, line 3 of footnote 10, the word "material" is to be inserted between the words "only" and "evidence" so that the sentence reads:

> The only material evidence on that issue was the
> engineer's report.

4. At the end of the last paragraph on page 4, add as footnote 12 the following:

> [12] Statements filed on July 1, 1984, disclosed this.

This footnote will require renumbering of all subsequent footnotes.

5. The paragraph commencing at the bottom of page 5 and ending at the top of page 6 is modified to read as follows:

> The jury had the policy before it as an exhibit and could refer to it if necessary. However, the interpretation of the policy was entirely a matter for the court.

6. On page 8 at the end of footnote 16, after the word "mind." add the following:

> (See *Cozens* v. *Superior Court* (1973) 31 Cal.App.3d 441.)

Respondent's petition for rehearing is denied.

The opinion in the above entitled matter filed on November 1, 1988, was not certified for publication in the Official Reports. For good cause it now appears that the opinion should be published in the Official Reports and it is so ordered.

———————

(f) In the preceding mock modification instructions, if the opinion had been published in the advance sheets at the time the modification order was filed the initial paragraph should be altered as noted below and the references should be to the Official Reports pagination rather than to the typed opinion paging, e.g.,

It is ordered that the opinion filed herein on November 1, 1988, and reported in the Official Reports (200 Cal.App.3d 100) be modified in the following particulars:

1. On page 123, line 14 of the first full paragraph, . . .

Where the modification order refers to the filed opinion and the modification is to be published on an "a" page (see *post,* § 299) the publisher will automatically adjust the references to fit the Official Reports pagination.

(See also *ante,* § 102.)

**§ 298.   Modification—Preadvance Sheets.**—Where a modification is received in time to be incorporated prior to the advance sheet publication of the opinion, a legend in bold print is placed between the date-case number line and the title to notify the reader that the opinion is printed as modified, e.g., **[As modified Nov. 1, 1980.]**. This type of notation is of course unnecessary where the change merely consists of the correction of typographical errors such as misspellings, transposed figures, etc.

Whether the bound volume publication will editorially note that an opinion is printed as modified will depend upon the substantiality of the modification. (See *post,* § 299.) (See also *ante,* §§ 88.1, 88.5 (g)(2) & (h)(2), 97, 102, 296, 297 and *post,* § 300.)

**§ 299.   Modification—Postadvance Sheets.**—Where a modification is received after an opinion's publication and is not so lengthy as to require a reprinting of the opinion (see *ante,* § 97) it is published on an "a" page in the advance sheets. The reader is apprised of the modification by a notation on the Cumulative Subsequent History Table of the latest pamphlet. In the ordinary case of an order directing that a few words or a short passage be added, deleted or modified, whether made separately or in connection with an order denying a petition for rehearing, the change is made without any notation or footnote to show that it was done. However, when the modification is more substantial, as for example, where the order discusses contentions of counsel or deletes or adds material portions to the opinion, a notation is appropriate and will be made immediately following the publication of the opinion in the bound volume. Substantial modifications frequently require syllabi adjustments.

(See also *ante,* §§ 97, 102, 297.)

**§ 300. Modification—Uniform Pagination—Avoidance of Republication—Procedure.**—Under the uniform pagination system used in reporting decisions for the Official Reports, if an opinion is published in the advance sheets and a lengthy modification is thereafter filed it is usually necessary to reprint the opinion as modified at another place. Then for the bound volume the opinion as first published is deleted. Subscribers to the advance pamphlets are advised of such reprintings by a notation on the Cumulative Subsequent History Table. (See *ante,* § 97 and Cum. Sub. Hist. Table Preface.)

In order to minimize the number of such reprintings it is suggested that when appellate court staffs recognize that a lengthy modification is required they immediately call the Reporter of Decisions office. The reporter will notify the publisher that such a modification will be filed, and upon receipt of the order the opinion will be printed in the first instance as modified, thus obviating the need for a second publication.

**§ 301. Clerical Errors—Correction—Procedure.**—While an opinion must be modified on formal order before it becomes final (see *ante,* § 296) a clerical error may be corrected whenever it is discovered.

If the error is discovered before the advance sheet publication cut-off date, normally the first 12 days following filing, a phone call to the Reporter of Decisions office will often permit a correct publication in the first instance. Regardless of when the error is discovered, a letter clearly identifying the authorized change as a "clerical error" should be forwarded to the Reporter of Decisions office with copies to all publishers. Without such a descriptive identification it is often not ascertainable whether the change is a modification or the correction of a clerical error. While not required, some courts have adopted the preferable practice of making clerical error corrections by formal minute order.

An illustration of an appropriate letter of notification is:

November 1, 1985

_____, Reporter of Decisions
Supreme Court of California
4206 State Building
San Francisco, California 94102

Re: *Brown* v. *Brown*
A012345, Div. One
[159 Cal.App.3d 123 (where published)]*

CORRECTION OF CLERICAL ERROR

Dear Mr. _____:

The above entitled opinion was filed in this court on October 28, 1985, and certified for publication.

In typing the opinion from the final draft clerical errors were made in the following particulars:

1. On page 6, the second sentence of the first full paragraph reads:
Barbara and Jane sought leave to intervene on behalf of their children.

It should obviously read:
Barbara and Jane sought leave to intervene on behalf of their unborn children.

2. On page 3, the second line of the last paragraph reads:
defendant's second amended complaint.

It should read:
plaintiff's second amended complaint.

3. On page 10, line 6 from the bottom:
*Smith* v. *Hanson*

should read:
*Smith* v. *Handfield*

Please make these corrections.

Very truly yours,

Fred Able
Presiding Justice
by_____
Freda Good

cc:   Bancroft-Whitney Company
Editorial Department
3250 Van Ness Ave.
P.O. Box 7005
San Francisco, CA 94120–7005

West Publishing Company
Editorial Department
50 W. Kellogg Blvd.
P.O. Box 64526
St. Paul, MN 55164–0526

---

* Where the opinion is published, page and line references should be to the published opinion rather than to the filed copy since the typewritten copy is not always available to the Reporter of Decisions.

Where there are a number of minor errors to be corrected, time can be saved, while maintaining accuracy, by making the corrections on a copy of the filed opinion and then noting by cover letter (in addition to the fact that the errors are clerical): "Please make the adjustments noted on the attached pages of the filed copy of the above opinion prior to publication" or, where the opinion has been published in the advance sheet, ". . . prior to bound volume publication." Only the title and affected pages need be attached.

## G. Partial Publication

§ 302. **Partial Publication, Generally.**—Upon obtaining the concurrence of the majority of the court rendering an opinion, the authoring justice of a Court of Appeal or an appellate department of the superior court identifies it as one to be partially published by noting at the top of the opinion "CERTIFIED FOR PARTIAL PUBLICATION.*" The asterisk refers to the author's explanatory footnote which advises the reader that only portions of the opinion meet the standards prescribed for publication by California Rules of Court, rule 976(b) and that, accordingly, only those portions are published and therefore citable. (See Cal. Rules of Ct., rules 976.1, 977(a).) A typical footnote might instruct: "*Pursuant to California Rules of Court, rules 976(b) and 976.1, this opinion is certified for publication with the exception of parts III and V."; or "*Parts III and V of this opinion are not certified for publication. (See Cal. Rules of Court, rules 976(b) and 976.1.)"; or "*Parts 4 and 6 through 8 are not ordered published, as they do not meet the standards for publication contained in rule 976(b) of the California Rules of Court." More descriptive directions are of course appropriate and sometimes essential to advise of complex deletions. (See *post*, §§ 303 & 304.)

Where partial publication is ordered after the opinion's filing but before its finality (see Cal. Rules of Court, rule 976(c)(1)), essential information is provided by the court's order, and the Reporter of Decisions and publisher will make appropriate adjustments for the Official Report of the opinion. If the opinion has already been published in an advance pamphlet, the Cumulative Subsequent History Table will advise of the publication changes dictated by the court's order, and those changes will be reflected in the opinion's bound volume report. (See also, for guidance in structuring an opinion for partial publication, Partial Publication—Some Practical Considerations, paper by Robert Formichi (App. Cts. Institute, Carmel, Cal., Apr. 1984).)

**§ 303.   Deletion of Major Segments of Opinion.**—The Reporter of Decisions will carry out the author's instructions by printing the number or letter used to identify the material to be deleted and the author's heading if one appears. The printer inserts an asterisk footnote at that point referring the reader to the earlier footnote explaining the omission. The deletion of the material that follows would be signaled by a single line of dots. The reporter then proceeds with the publication of the following material until the next portion of the opinion scheduled for omission is specified. Where, however, consecutive sections are to be deleted, only one line of dots is noted following the inclusive numbers specifying the omitted portions, and headings are not specified unless the author advises the reporter to include them:

III.   DELAY AND DUE PROCESS OF LAW*

. . . . . . . . . . . . . . . . . . . . . . . . . . . . . . . . . . . . . . . . . . . . . . . . . . . . . . . . . . . . . . . . . . . . . . . . . . . . . . . . . . . . .

IV. DELAY AND SPEEDY TRIAL

It is equally clear that where there is a postindictment delay, prejudice to the defendant is presumed.

V.–VII.*

. . . . . . . . . . . . . . . . . . . . . . . . . . . . . . . . . . . . . . . . . . . . . . . . . . . . . . . . . . . . . . . . . . . . . . . . . . . . . . . . . . . . .

---

* See footnote *ante,* page 1. [The footnote on page 1 is the author's initial notice to the reader telegraphing the deletions to come (see, e.g., § 302 *ante*).]

(For additional examples see *People* v. *Guilford* (1984) 151 Cal.App.3d 406; *People* v. *Delgado* (1983) 149 Cal.App.3d 208; *People* v. *O'Connell* (1984) 152 Cal.App.3d 548.)

Where practical, some authors may wish to note the deletion where it begins in the text of the opinion and the point where it ends by bracketed statements, e.g., "[The portions of this opinion that follow (V–VIII) are deleted from publication. See *post,* at page 7 where publication is to resume.]" Then at page 7, a bracketed sentence might note: "[The balance of this opinion is to be published.]."

For the advance pamphlet the Reporter of Decisions, at the appropriate places, will employ the deletion styles previously indicated.

**§ 304.   Deletions of Less Than Entire Sections.**—Where the portions to be deleted are not entire parts or sections of the opinion (see *ante,* § 303) but rather a combination of scattered bits and pieces, two footnotes are required: one to note to the Official Reports reader that the opinion has been ordered published in part only, and a second to advise the reporter and the publisher which parts are to be omitted.

**(a)** Where deletions are easily described, and are few in number, a footnote to the Reporter of Decisions in the style of an opinion modification would be appropriate, e.g.:

CERTIFIED FOR PARTIAL PUBLICATION*

---

\* Pursuant to California Rules of Court, rules 976(b) and 976.1, this opinion is certified for partial publication. The portions directed to be published follow.†

---

† Note to the Reporter of Decisions: This opinion is to be published in full with the following exceptions:

(1) Delete the last full paragraph commencing at the bottom of page 7 and all subsequent paragraphs and related footnotes through the first full paragraph at the top of page 11 ending with the words: ". . . was adversely affected."

(2) At the end of the first full paragraph on page 14, delete the sentence beginning with the words "He was later detained . . . ."

The opinion is then published with or without notation to the reader of the specific locations of the parts omitted dependent upon whether, in the judgment of the Reporter of Decisions, such notation is appropriate in the particular context. The note to the reporter, being instructional only, is not published.

**(b)** Where the portions to be deleted are extensive, scattered or difficult to describe, and the effort to advise the reporter becomes a significant undertaking in itself, the better and mechanically safer method is to physically "mark the opinion" and instruct the reporter to take out the marked portions. If this technique is adopted, the filed opinion, as well as all filed copies, should note the markings, which become the court's deletion instructions. Then, following the footnote advising the reader that the opinion is to be partially published (see *ante,* subd. (a)) and describing the technique to be used, a second footnote to the reporter should be provided, e.g.:

---

\* Pursuant to California Rules of Court, rules 976(b) and 976.1, this opinion is certified for partial publication. Portions deleted are noted by the insertion of the following symbol at the points of omission [[ ]].†

† Note to Reporter of Decisions: The portions of this opinion to be deleted from publication are identified as those portions between double brackets, [[ ]].

[Or, where the deletions are short but frequent]:

† Note to Reporter of Decisions: The portions of this opinion and accompanying footnotes to be deleted from publication are identified in the text by strike-out type. [E.g., . . . ~~the defendant²~~ ~~was identified by gun powder burns on his index finger.~~

---

~~² Johnathan Tree, a codefendant, has not appealed~~].

The reporter will then use the symbol [[ ]] at the appropriate places in publishing the opinion. The instructional note to the reporter is not published.

**§ 305. Retention of Footnote Numbering.**—Where portions of a partially published opinion which contain footnotes are deleted, do not renumber the subsequent footnotes. Not only is this task a time loss but also it can result in confusion when footnote references are made by minority opinion authors or by counsel in their petitions for rehearing and review. Additionally, the accuracy of the author's internal cross-references is at risk when original sequences are changed. Readers of the reports will recognize that the broken footnote numbering is the result of the deletion of parts of the opinion.

**§ 306. Retention of Numbering and Lettering for Topic Headings.**—Do not renumber or reletter to give the partial opinion the appearance of sequential continuity. (See *ante,* § 305.)

**§ 307. Reading of Opinion Following Notation of Deletions.**—Following the preparation of the deletion notification instructions, the portion of the opinion to be published should be read to see that such matters as internal cross-references are appropriate and to confirm that citations are complete. For example, if a case is first cited in a portion to be deleted, a later citation to it in the published portion using a "*supra*" form should be adjusted to show a complete citation. (See *ante,* § 138.)

**§ 308. Minority Opinions.**—Where the minority opinion is directed to portions of the majority or lead opinion not published, it also should contain its own publication instructions deleting those portions relating to the unpublished material if the author desires to make that opinion consistent with the majority's publication instructions. Where the minority opinion speaks only to the portions of the main opinion that have been omitted, it too should normally be deleted from publication. (See *People* v. *Delgado* (1983) 149 Cal.App.3d 208.)

**§ 309. Partial Publication Ordered by Supreme Court.**—"After granting review, after decision, or after dismissal of review and remand as improvidently granted, the Supreme Court may order the opinion of the Court of Appeal published in whole or in part." (Cal. Rules of Court, rule 976 (d).) The Reporter of Decisions and the publisher will carry out the partial publication instructions of the Supreme Court by applying the publication techniques illustrated in the foregoing sections except that the opinion's heading statement will read ORDERED PARTIALLY PUBLISHED* rather than CERTIFIED FOR PARTIAL PUBLICATION*, and the accompanying asterisk footnote will describe the Supreme Court's partial publication directive, e.g.:

* Pursuant to California Rules of Court, rule 976 (d) the Supreme Court by order dated January 10, 1989, [or, by opinion filed January 10, 1989 (if that is the case)] directed this Court of Appeal opinion to be published with the exceptions of parts III and V.

(See *ante,* §§ 302–308 and, for the citation of opinions ordered published in whole or in part, §§ 88.4–88.6, 103.)

# CHAPTER VI.
## —Notes—

# INDEX

[References are to section numbers]

# INDEX

# CALIFORNIA STYLE MANUAL

CAPITALIZATION—Continued
Last clear chance, 32
Law and motion department, 14
Legislative bodies, 7–10
  Committees, 10
  Local, 7
  National, Congress, 9
  State, Legislature, 8
Legislative officers, 11
  Local, 11
Legislature, 8
Letter compounds, 36
Lieutenant Governor, 21
Local administrative bodies, 18
Local administrative officers, 11, 21 (e)
Local bodies, 7, 18
Local executive officers, 11, 21 (e)
Local ordinances, codes and charters, 53
Marshal, 16
Mayor, 21
Members of political parties, 27
Military courts, 12
Miscellaneous rules, 22–36
Municipal court, 13, 14
Names, geographical, 1, 22
Names in titles, 196
National bodies, 9, 10
National officers, 11, 21
Nouns, common
  As part of proper names, 2–5, 22
  Followed by numbers, 23
O'clock, 34
Officers
  Executive, 20, 21
  Legislative, 11
  Local, 11
  National, 11, 21
Opinion headings, 28
Opinion subheadings, 28
Order, 23
Ordinances, 53
Organizations, 27
Original source, correspondence with
  capitalization in, 131
Page, 23
Paragraph, 23
Part, 23, 35
Parties
  Names of, 25, 196
  Substitute designation, 6, 25
"People," 24
Plaintiff, 25
Plurals with proper names, 22
"p.m.," 34
police station, name of, 18
Political parties, 27
Popular titles of statutes, 30
President, 21
Presiding judge, 15
Presiding justice, 15
Prison, 22
Proper names, 22, 23 26, 27, 196
Public defender, 16

CAPITALIZATION—Continued
Quotation in middle of author's sentence,
  capitalization of first letter of, 133 (a), 139
Race, 32
Referees, 15
Religious bodies, 27
Reporters, 16
Res ipsa loquitur, 32
Respondent, 25
Rules, regulations, standards, etc., 19, 33, 64–67
Schedule, 25
Schools, 27
Secretary of State, 21
Section, 23, 35
Senate
  State, 8
  United States, 9
Senator, 11
Sheriff, 16
Small claims court, 13
Societies, 27
State Bar, 19
  Rules, 19, 33, 66
State boards, 4, 6, 7, 17
State bodies, 8
State courts, 13, 14
State departments, 17
State officers, 11, 20, 21
State Public Defender, 16
State Senate, 8
States, 4, 6
Statute of frauds, 30, 32
Statute of limitations, 30, 32
Statute titles, 30, 35, 46, 49
Street, 22
Subheadings of opinions, 28, 49
Substitute designation for parties, 6, 25, 180
Superintendent of Public Instruction, 21
Superior court, 13, 14
Supervisor, 11
Supreme Court of California, 13
Supreme Court of the United States, 12
Surname, with intermediate capitals, 196
Tax court, 12
Temporary judge, 15
"The" with proper name, 26, 27, 212, 219, 259
Time, 34
Time symbols, 34
Titles of officers
  Executive, 20, 21
  Judicial, 16
  Legislative, 7, 11
Titles of statutes, 30, 32, 35
Towns, 2, 6
Treasurer, 21
Uniform laws, 30, 46
United States Claims Court, 12
United States Court of Appeals, 12
United States Court of Claims, 12
United State Court of Custom and Patent
  Appeals, 12
United States Custom Court, 12
United States District Court, 12
United States Senate, 9

206     [References are to section numbers]

# INDEX

---

# CALIFORNIA STYLE MANUAL

# INDEX

[References are to section numbers]

# INDEX

[References are to section numbers]

# INDEX

# INDEX

EDITORIAL INFORMATION—Continued
Listing of Counsel—Continued
  Substitution of attorneys, 274, 281, 282
  Use of names of clients, 279
  Withdrawal of attorney's name, 269, 281, 282
Manuscript, indicating italics, 154
Memorials, publication procedure, 267
Modification of opinion
  Advance sheets, see Advance Sheets
  Avoidance of republication, procedure, 300
  Clerical errors, correction of, 296, 301
  Formal order required, 296
  Mock modification instructions, 297 (d)
  Modification order, form, 297
  Necessity of formal order, 296, 297
  "Paragraph, line, word," precise notation of, 297 (c)
  Postadvance sheet, 299
  Preadvance sheet, 298
  Time limitation, 296
  When order required, 296, 297
  Withdrawing citation of superseded opinion, 102
Names of justices
  Generally, 287–289
  For trial judges, see *ante,* Designation of trial judge
  Acting Chief Justice, 288
  Acting presiding justice, 288
  Another court, style of listing presiding justice assigned to, 292
  Assigned justices, 285 (b), 292, 294
    Trial judge, 288
  Author of opinion, 287–294
  "By the Court" opinions, 288
  Chief Justice, capitalization, 15
  Concurring justices, 287, 289, 290
  Disqualification, 294
  Dissenting justices, 287, 289, 290
  Dissenting without opinion, 287
  In general, 287–289
  Nonparticipation, 294
  Notation of assignment at appellate level, 288, 292
  Notation of assignment from trial level, 288, 292
  Official Reports, concurring and dissenting opinions, 287, 289, 290
  Opinion by the Court, 288
  Placement of, in Official Reports, 287–294
  Retired justice, style of listing, 285 (b), 292
  Same surname, justices with, 288
  Single or majority opinion, 288
  Supreme Court, order of names, 293
  Typewritten opinion, placement on, 287
Notation of denial of review or rehearing, Official Reports, 88.4, 88.5, 262
Official Reports
  Contract for publication, 260
  Editorial format of, 260
Opinion galleys
  Date for return, 265
  Editorial notations on, 264

EDITORIAL INFORMATION—Continued
Opinion galleys—Continued
  Proof reading, 264, 265, prefatory page xviii
  Queries, 264
  Return of corrected galleys, time, 265
  Substantive changes prohibited, 264
Opinion on denial of rehearing
  Entry on Cumulative Subsequent History Table, 97, 263
  Postal card notice, 262
  Uniform pagination, 263
Order of opinions, 291
Partial publication, see main index
Photocopies, legibility, 183
"Pro tem."and "pro tempore," discontinuance of use, 295
Real party in interest, designation, 237, 258
Rehearing
  Notation on denial, 262
  Opinion on denial, 97, 263
Reporter of Decisions
  Adjustment of titles, 198, 223
  Editing of opinions, 264
  Editorial notations, opinion galleys, 264
  Substitution of parties, note of, 223
  Superseded opinions, note of, 68, 102, 103
Reporter's notes, 103, 198, 223, 262, 264
Superseded opinions, 103
Subsequent history table, 88.4, 88.5 fn. 6, 97, 263
Supplement to style manual, see page vii
Title page format of opinion, 197
Trial court
  Designation of, 261
  Indicating number of, 261
Trial judges
  Designation, 261, 286
  See also, *ante,* Designation of trial judge
  Typical information pages, 261, 285
  Uniform pagination, reprinting opinion to preserve, 263
EMANCIPATION FROM PARENTAL CONTROL
See Main Title
EMPHASIS
Italics, see Italics
Quotations, see Quotations
ENCYCLOPEDIAS
Citations, 113
ENGLISH CASE REPORTS
Citation, 82
"ER" AND "OR"
Endings, 184
ERRORS
Correction of opinions, 296–301
Quotations, see Quotations
ESCHEAT ACTIONS
Main title designation, 242 (a)
ESSAYS
Citation, 117
ESTATES
Main title designation, 236, 242, 249–251
ET AL.
Use of, 200, 201, 203–205, 219, 220, 223, 258

---

[References are to section numbers]

# INDEX

[References are to section numbers]

# INDEX

# CALIFORNIA STYLE MANUAL

[References are to section numbers]

# INDEX

# CALIFORNIA STYLE MANUAL

# INDEX

MANDAMUS PROCEEDINGS
Main title designation, 226, 227, 237, 253
See Main Title, Original writ proceedings, and main index Extraordinary Writs
Substitution of parties in, 223

MANUALS
Citation, 118

MARRIAGE
Dissolution proceedings, 238
Nullification proceedings, 221

MAYOR
Capitalization, 21

M.D.
Punctuation used, 167

MEASUREMENT
Hyphenating units of, 161
Numbers and figures, 189, 190 (e)
Spelling out, 189, 190 (d)

MEMORIAL FOR JUSTICES
Publication of, 267

MILITARY COURTS
Capitalization, 12

MINORS
See main index under Child Custody Cases, Child Support Actions, Children, and Main Title

MODEL CODES
Citation, 67, 112

MODERN ENGLISH
Preferred over Latin phrases, 188

MODIFICATION OF OPINIONS
Generally, 296–301 and see Editorial Information, Modification of opinions
Advance Sheets, see Advance Sheets
Bound volume, grounds for editorial notation in, 298, 299
Citation, 97, 102
Errors, clerical, correction procedure, 296, 301
Formal court order required, 296, 297
Lengthy, reprinting opinion, 300
Order, 296, 297
"Paragraph, line, word," precise notation of, 297 (c)
Preadvance sheet, 298
Quotation marks enclosing author's instructions, 297 (b)
Subsequent to advance sheet publication, 299
Time limitations on, 296
Withdrawing citation of superseded opinion, 102

MONEY
Numbers and figures, 189, 190 (f)

MONTH, DAY, AND YEAR
Commas between, use of, 170, 190 (b)

MOTIONS
Substitution of counsel, 282

MOVANT
Main title, 244

MULTIDISTRICT LITIGATION
Citation of judicial panel on, 81 (b)(3)
Coordinated cases, 207

MULTIPLE CASES
Main title designations for, 207

MUNICIPAL CHARTERS, CODES AND ORDINANCES
Citation, 53

MUNICIPAL COURTS
Capitalization, 13, 14

NAMES
Attorneys, see Names of Attorneys
California names, capitalization, 1, 22
Cases, see Citations, Main Title and Title of Case
Citations, running heads, 91, 93
Commas with names, 167, 181
Companies, capitalization, 27
Geographical names, capitalization, 1, 22
Judges and justices, see Editorial Information
Proper names, capitalization, 22, 26, 27, 196

NAMES OF ATTORNEYS
Amici curiae, 270–272
Ampersand, listing firms using sign, 269
Appeals, sequence of names on, 270
Appearance for party, notation as to failure to make, 271
Appearance requiring listing, sufficiency of, 269, 274
Attorney General, 272–275
Attorneys "of counsel," 269
Brief, listing attorneys filing, signing, or adopting, 269
Change in name, listing showing, 269
Change of attorneys, 274, 281, 282
Clients, use of names of, 269, 279
Consolidated cases, 280
Court-appointed counsel, 276
Criminal cases, 275, 276
Deputy public attorneys, 273
District attorneys, 273, 275
Firms, listing of, 269
Individuals, listing of, 269
Information relating to, collection of, 268
Intervention, counsel on, 270, 283
Law corporations, 284
Law student trainees, 278
Listing, generally, 268–284
Motion for substitution of counsel, attorneys participating in hearing on, 282
Multiple cases, opinion covering, listing, 280
Nonattorneys, 269, 277, 278
Number of case, listing by, 280
Official attorneys, 272–275
Change during pendency of proceeding, 274
Opposing or unrelated theories, listing of parties, presenting, 279
Oral argument, listing participants, 269
Order of names, 270, 271
Original proceedings commenced in appellate courts, attorneys appearing in, 271
Parties litigant, use of names of, 269, 279
Party in pro. per., 269, 277, 278
Professional corporations, 284
Public attorneys, 272–274
Record as source of information, 268
Self, style of persons representing, 269, 277, 278
Sequence of names, 270, 271
Spelling, effect of divergences in, 269

# CALIFORNIA STYLE MANUAL

[References are to section numbers]

# INDEX

OPINIONS
"By the Court," 288
Capitalization of opinion headings, 28
Citation, see Citations
Clerical errors in, correction, 296, 301
Companion, 85, 88–88.6
Concurring, 86, 101, 288–293
Conformity of designation between title and
   body, 210, 211
Dating, 84
Dissenting, 86, 101, 288–293
Division of words, determining, 165
Errors in, see Modification of Opinion
Galleys, see Opinion Galleys
Headings, subheadings, capitalization, 28
Hearing and review notations, 88.5, 262
Majority, 85, 86, 98
Minority, 86, 101
Modification, see Modification of Opinions
Opinions ordered not to be published, citation,
   68, 88, 102–104, 302
Order of names, Supreme Court justices, 293
Partial publication, see main index
Placement and style of names of justices on,
   287–294
Plurality or lead, 86, 111, 288–293
Prior and subsequent history, 88–88.6
Quotations from adopted opinions, form of, 140
Rehearing, opinion on denial, 263
Rehearing notations, 262
Sequence of, 291
Subsequent history table, 88.4 fns 1, 2, 95, 97, 263
Superseded opinions, 68, 88 et seq., 102, 103
   Modification withdrawing citation of, 102
Title, see Main Title
Titles for citation purposes, see Citations
Two or more opinions, order of, 291
Unpublished opinions, citation, 68, 88.3,
   88.5(h), 88.6, 102–104, 302
ORDINALS
Numbers and figures, 189, 190 (i)
ORDINANCES
Citation, 53
ORGANIZATIONS
Capitalization, 27
ORIGINAL PROCEEDINGS
See Extraordinary Writs
OTHER NATIONS CASE REPORTS
Citation, 83
OTHER STATES CASE REPORTS
Citation, 76, 78, 90
PAGE
Capitalization, 23
PAGE REFERENCES
Citations, 69, 71, 78, 80, 85, 86, 90, 99
PAMPHLETS
Citation, 63, 88.4, 117, 120
Ballot pamphlets, 63
PARALLEL CITATIONS
Generally, 76, 80, 90, 151
Punctuation, 151
PARENTAL CUSTODY
Main title designation, see Main Title

PARENTHESES
Generally, 150
Brackets
   Second parenthetical statement within, 150
Explanatory matter, 150
In general, 150
Interpolated matter, 150
Multiple parenthetical expressions, alternate
   parentheses and brackets for, 150
Periods with, 44 (b), 151
Purpose of, 150
Unquoted matter, use with, 150
With citations, 40, 41, 44, 45, 76, 78, 83, 84, 87,
   88 et seq., 91, 95, 99, 105, 151 (a)
   Abbreviation within, 40, 41, 44, 45
   As part of sentence, 151 (b)
   Headnote rubric, 87, 99
   Page and section within, 105
   Parallel citations, 151
PARTIAL PUBLICATION OF OPINIONS
Certification for, by court on appeal, 197, 266,
   302
Citation, 88.3, 88.5(h), 103, 302
Consecutive portions of opinion deleted,
   303, 305, 306
Editorial adjustments
   Generally, 302
   Explanatory footnotes, 302–304
   Footnote numbering, 305
   Line of dots or symbol signaling
      deletions, 303
   Opinion heading statement, 302, 309
   Topic headings enumeration, 306
Footnote numbering, 305
Major part deleted, 303
Minority opinions, 308
Scattered deletions, 304
Supreme Court directive for, 88.3, 309
Topic heading enumeration, 306
Verification of deletions, 307
PARTIES
Alias, use of, 218, 232
Capitalization, 6, 25
Designation of parties, see also Main Title
   Consistency of reference, 210, 211
   Nondisclosure, 213, 214, 226, 241, 246
Dismissal of first-named party, 205 (d)
Distinguished between parties, main title, 206
Dropping name on appeal, 198, 200, 204, 205,
   223
In pro. per., 269, 277, 278
Main title
   Conformity throughout proceedings, 198, 211
   Joinder of parties, complex combination of
      party litigants, 208
   Sequence of names, 199
   Substitution, 223
Substitute designation, 6, 25, 180
PARTNERSHIP
Main title designation, 219, 259
PEOPLE
Actions brought by, main title designation, 225,
   231, 247, 252
Capitalization, 24

---

[References are to section numbers]

[References are to section numbers]

# INDEX

---

# INDEX

UNREPORTED CALIFORNIA CASES
  Citation, 70
"V."
  As part of citation, 91
VERBS
  Split infinitives, 193
  Verb and subject
    Rule as to agreement, 182
    Singular subjects followed by parenthetical
      expressions as taking singular verbs, 182 (c)
VIDEOTAPES OF CALIFORNIA PRACTICE
  Citation, 108
VOLUME
  Capitalization, 23
  Indicated by arabic numerals, 105, 190 (a)
WHICH
  Singular or plural verb, antecedent as determin-
    ing, 182 (f)
WHO
  Singular or plural verb, antecedent as determin-
    ing, 182 (f)

WORDS AND PHRASES
  Agreement of subject and verb, 182
  Apostrophe, 175–178
  Collective nouns, 182 (g)
  Compound forms, 191
  Division of words, 165
  "Er" and "or" endings, 184
  "Guarantee" and "guaranty," 187
  Hyphens with, 159–165
  Italics with, 153–158
  Plural forms, 191
  Preferred forms, 188, 192
WORKERS' COMPENSATION DECISIONS
  Citation, 74
  Main title, 257, 258
WRIT PROCEEDINGS
  See Main Title, Extraordinary Writ Proceedings,
    Original Proceedings and Habeas
    Corpus Proceedings

---

# —Notes—

—Notes—

# —Notes—

—Notes—

# —Notes—